PRAI

"A tour de force true story of surviving and surmounting the unthinkable. *Victim* is literary nonfiction at its best that plunges the reader into the during, the before, and the after of a horrific abduction and rapes. Moe's non-linear narrative interweaves the realistic spiral-like journey of healing with the covert and the overt ways society grooms many of us to be victims and others to be victimizers. Moe demonstrates how survivors can transform their pain and internalized victim-blaming shame into an unstoppable passion to ensure these crimes are never forgotten and that justice be served. This raw triumph over tragedy proves that a victim can also be a *victor*."
> —Sally Clark, author of *The Way of The Warrior Mama: The Guide To Raising and Protecting Strong Daughters.*

"*Victim* is a powerful, intensely personal and disturbing book, cutting deep into the soul about a topic that must be exposed. It is Karen Moe's impassioned manifesto ... an intensely chilling account of abduction, sexual assault and prostitution. But it is also the tragic and heart-rending story of untold millions of women and children worldwide who have been abducted, raped and forced into the brutal world of prostitution. *Victim* is visceral. It is a difficult book to read. It is a difficult book to put down. And it is a compelling must-read!"
> —Victor Malarek, author of *The Natashas: Inside the Global Sex Trade* and *The Johns: Sex for Sale and the Men who Buy It.*

"Karen Moe has penned a powerful manifesto. This book touched my soul deeply. Some areas were difficult to read, but from one strong survivor to another – WELL DONE. Victim no more. Through her trauma she found her calling, one far bigger than herself. Fighting alongside others for justice. She digresses from her story several times to ask and seek answers about how to make the world safer, especially for women and children. This book is a call to action for all of us—women and men. You will want to put it down, but you can't, because it's so compelling."
> —Marie McKenzie, author of *Things That Keep Me Up At Night.*

"Victim is an act of re-feminization (versus repatriation) of a trammeled word in a lexicon of blame and shame. In this epic of survival and triumph the term victim assumes the same resonance as victor, a position to which Moe ascends not only with her overcoming of horror but of her utter and fierce honesty. Victim will sound in your blood and psyche forever as you learn to see the world through unveiled and awakened eyes."
> —Catherine Owen, author of *Riven* and *Locations of Grief: An Emotional Geography.*

"Moe writes her personal experiences in the violent, misogynist world of men that women know all too well. This book embodies and forces us to look at the truth of the reality of male violence that women negotiate every day in patriarchy; and yet, it is also a story of triumph for women individually and collectively because we face that fear daily, and we are still here."
—Trisha Baptie Journalist and Founder of EVE
(Exploited Voices Now Educating).

"A beautifully written, forensically researched story of resistance and revolution. An important tool in the feminist fight against male violence."
—Julie Bindel, author of *The Pimping of Prostitution: Abolishing the Sex Work Myth* and *Feminism for Women: The Real Route to Liberation.*

"*Victim* is a brutally honest account of a brutal crime. But the most brutal thing Karen Moe asks us to face is the way in which her story is not unusual. Not every woman will be abducted and raped like she was, but the way men's violence constrains women is an everyday brutal reality for women. Moe's courage doesn't stop with telling a story of sexual assault. Her book confronts other kinds of pain—both the pain she has endured and the pain swirling all around us in a broken world. And all the time, Moe moves in and out of her story to the larger question: How do we make this broken world safe for women and children? How do we create a world worth living in? Without false optimism, she writes of how we can find authentic hope. *Victim* charts the complexity of her life, and our lives, and reminds us of a simple truth: To embrace life we must resist patriarchy."
—Robert Jensen, author of *The End of Patriarchy: Radical Feminism for Men.*

"A heartfelt chronicle of personal growth through mortal danger; Karen Moe has woven the elements of her life into a cautionary tale that unfolds like fiction but, as Truman Capote said, non-fiction makes the best fiction. This is a rigorously researched history of violence against women, and a treatise on how societal behaviour can be improved. Read this book and be informed."
—Dennis Bolen, *Stupid Crimes* and *Anticipated Results.*

"*Victim: A Feminist Manifesto from a Fierce Survivor* is a powerful, immersive memoir about patriarchal hierarchy and how it allows a climate for abuse to occur and go under-addressed. Moe writes with painful honesty that needs to be heard by men and women alike. She took what would break most people and turned it into a clarion call. This memoir serves as a powerful tool for awareness and advocacy—a voice for the voiceless. No doubt this book will go a long way in fixing our broken system, or at least bring attention to it. If you like books that could change the world, you will love this book."
— Readers' Favorite, Five Stars.

VICTIM

a feminist manifesto from a fierce survivor

KAREN MOE

Author Photo by Stasia Garraway
Edited by Jay Christoper Gowen & Catherine Owen
Cover Design by Bobbi Sue Smith

Distribution by Bublish, Inc.
Published by Vigilance Press

www.vigilancemagazine.com
@vigilancemagazine

ISBN: 978-1-64704-470-1 (paperback)
ISBN: ISBN: 978-1-64704-471-8 (eBook)

For my Dad

"Keep to Beauty. Have no fear. Learn to bear the unbearable. The raw of all things."
Nicole Brossard.

PART ONE

I got into the vehicle. He had offered me a lift back to my motel. I knew it was wrong, but I got in anyway. Some of you might think that I was stupid and that I had it coming. It was all my fault. But does that mean I deserved what is going to happen next?

December 19th, 1994. Around 5 p.m. Flagstaff, Arizona.

I have lost the mustard yellow suede jacket from that time. Maybe I gave it away and then asked for it back. Maybe I still have it packed in a box in storage. Maybe it's lost.

It had a Dino pin on the lapel. Platinum. About an inch and a half tall. I have always loved the Flintstones. Barney and Dino in particular.

The jacket was used. Vintage before vintage was vintage. I don't remember where I bought it. Did I buy it long before it happened? Just before? On the brink of during?

I remember that it barely covered my bum. It had slouching pockets from past hands. It was a bit tight across the chest and shoulders when I did the buttons up. Even when I was very slim, I was still well endowed, both a blessing and a curse. I used to wear it unbuttoned most of the time so as not to appear frumpy. It was ridiculous that I would even have considered that.

Has anyone seen my mustard yellow suede jacket?

I had checkered leggings. They were second-hand, too. Black and white. Some retro petroleum fabric that Gen-Xers like myself made Retro. I wore them so regularly that the knees were baggy, and there was a little hole on one knee with a small vertical run. I wore them almost all the time anyway.

I always wore very colourful socks. Maybe stitched with another Flintstones character or one from Peanuts. Probably Snoopy or Woodstock. I would tuck the checkered leggings into my very colourful socks and then pull on my electric blue Doc Martens. Yes, I think I wore my Docs then, but I have no pictures from that time to prove it.

Every part of my ensemble was light-hearted except for my shirt. I have always had challenges with shirts. The boobs blessing/curse again. It was a plain black T-shirt. Not fitted. A crew neck that is always a no-no when you have breasts larger than a B-Cup. The shirt hung like a block.

Like the jacket, the T-shirt just covered my bum. I don't think it hung lower than the jacket. Although I remember wishing it did. I remember wishing a lot of things about that T-shirt as I fussed with it daily in front of the mirror. Sometimes it would take me quite a while to get outside and do the sight-seeing I had come there to do and have the adventures that awaited my curious mind. I was chained to the mirror, scolding myself for not packing a skirt, pulling the T-shirt tight around my waist from behind, and wishing I had a clip to keep it there. Maybe the unsexy shirt was a way of concealing my sexuality, the always-violatable young womanhood. And yet, even though the T-shirt was far from fetching, I still felt exposed. Whatever the pathology, it didn't matter. I was in danger despite any inadvertent attempt to be invisible.

The motel was a very scary place. So much so that the memory of the motel cancels out the fact that I may have gone to some prehistoric cave houses along the way. Red cliffs. A bus tour. But I'm not sure. If I did, the experience is like a fading dream, a blur caught in mid-maybe. Lying on the well-used bed, looking up at the cracked ceiling, I could feel the thousands of sordid things that had happened there. The springs squeaked when I got up to prove it. My body knew there was danger twenty-four hours before it began. Flagstaff, Arizona. Route 66.

I was born in 1966, and I remember trying to console myself with this connection even though Route 66 kind of scared me too. "Get your kicks on Route 66." I always wondered what the kicks were. I knew they were supposed to be fun, but the whole idea seemed ominous to me. Like all the women Jim Morrison had had sex with or something. Or the first time I read Henry Miller. Or even *A Catcher in the Rye.* I hadn't read *On the Road* yet, but I bet Dean Moriarty got some of his kicks on Route 66 too.

Knowing what I know now, it was absolute madness that I was there alone. I was immersing myself in handgun central USA, in a hotbed of gender violence, in the birthplace of slasher B-movies. But I didn't know any of this. Despite this pang of awareness in the scary motel room, I was entirely oblivious. I prided myself in being an adventurer, living life to the fullest, learning, experiencing, writing, thinking, being a free spirit.

3

Like men could. I had no idea that women are not allowed to do this. I was perfect prey.

Sometime in 1997. Late Afternoon. Ventura County, California.

As soon as I got off the plane, they presented me with a teddy bear. "DA Bear," said the happy-go-lucky T-shirt Teddy wore. Pink, I think. With one of those cartoony fonts. When I was left alone in the hotel room, I immediately got rid of Teddy's T-shirt.

They took me for lunch. The District Attorney and the Chief of Police. I drank a beer. Maybe two. I don't think I ate much. We discussed what was going to happen in the morning, and they briefed me on what to expect.

"No problem," I replied, my voice intoned with the worldly nonchalance I had honed since my late teens.

"I got it all covered," I added, and my hand probably brushed away any concern. Even though I was there alone. Strangely, no one had offered to come with me. It was like everyone I knew wanted to forget, or maybe it was old news now, or they couldn't handle it. Even though I was the one who was still living it and always would be.

I had been waiting for three years to go down there and do the deed. The trial kept being continued as the defense attorney was trying to dig up dirt on me. Of course. Discredit the key witness to put a rapist back out on the street. Standard procedure that too often works because everyone knows rape victims lie. There are so many women with nothing better to do than make up a rape.

When I first got back to Canada, I gave my testimony over the phone. I wish I had that tape. I called a few years ago to try and get it. It's lost. Apparently, evidence of abduction and rapes are no longer important after a certain amount of time. The artifacts of our experiences, the talismans of our stories, are neglected, fall behind filing cabinets to be destined for the landfill as victims of spring cleaning. Perhaps it will be found in the far-distant future when our descendants dig into the archeology sites of twentieth-century garbage dumps, and my voice will add to the anthropological study of our current cultural plight. But, even though formal documentation has been lost, we can keep telling our stories. Maintain our own memories. Our proof.

I wish I could hear that voice, though: its texture, tone, the exact words I said. I know I sounded a bit cocky. Overly confident. I am sure I laughed a lot. Made jokes about the whole thing. I know I was also shaking and that I felt like I was made of vapor. I had to go to the police station and identify the mug shot after. I did it in seconds. I knew his eyes so well. The terrible droopy mustache. An assault in itself.

And now I was finally there. Three years after. Armed with a teddy bear. Ready to do my duty as a superhero. Again. Yes, a victim can also be a hero.

December 21st, 1994. Between 1:25 a.m. and 4 a.m. Various Locations in the Arizona Desert.

He called me his Little Girl on a String. That's because I was literally on one. But not a string. More like a rope. Now that I think about it, it was the kind of rope they always use. The slim kind used on TV or in movies. The kind that's easy to tie.

He had it tied around my neck. Not too tight. And there was a long end, so he could hold onto it whenever I needed to go outside and pee. This was the reason for the rope: so that I couldn't roll away into the darkness of the ditch, scrabble up a bank, or slide down a cliff on the side of the road, or run into the middle of the road and flag down a car. The expression on my face would have been terrifying. My naked white body emerging from the pitch-black would have definitely gotten drivers' attention. Arms waving wildly. Bruised. Desperate. Only the beginning. I would have made them stop even if they didn't want to. I would have jumped onto the hood. I would have lain on my stomach and gripped the edges of their car with my hands and feet. They would have had to pry me off. He must have read my mind the first time I asked if I could go pee.

When we were driving, he had me tied up and gagged in the back of the makeshift camper/van. He tied my ankles together and my arms behind my back and made me lie down, staring at the ceiling made of moldy insulation. He gagged me with silver duct tape. He seemed to like to talk to me when we were parked in one of our three locations, so he would take the duct tape off when it was safe to, when my yells for help would never be heard. I don't recall him being rough when he pulled off the tape. He was actually a bit tender. I don't recall having any abrasions around my mouth from the on and off of the sticky tape, each time a fresh piece. He said to me once,

"Sorry, I have to do this. We just can't have anyone hearing you when there are people around. I am sure you understand." Yes, I understood his abductor's logic, and now, in retrospect, I am struck by the fact that there is always a human in every monster, and there is always the potential for a monster in every man.[1] I am not going to apologize for such an essentializing statement because very few women behave this way. Karla Homolka was a sadistic accomplice to her husband's crimes, but this is a rare case.

I researched 'Women Murderers and Rapists.' The lists aren't very long. One digs back to Elisabeth Bathory from the sixteenth century (sensationally known as 'the Blood Countess'), who was accused of all sorts of acts of torture like chaining her servants so tight that their hands spurted blood, using her teeth to lacerate their genitals and one incident even broaching the freaky realm of hocus-pocus where she was caught "casting a magic spell to summon a cloud filled with ninety cats to torment her enemies." It has, ironically, been argued that the Blood Countess was innocent and that all of the legendary accusations of slaughter were a result of political slander and, very possibly, a bit of backlash against a powerful, take-no-shit kind of woman.[2]

Homolka is the only woman connected to rape when she gave her little sister to her boyfriend as a gift. Very grisly stuff!

Her actions can definitely be cited as an extreme instance of a woman being conditioned to please her man, that's for sure. To the point of sacrificing her own sister.

One of the most notorious female serial killers is Aileen Wuornos, the hitch-hiking prostitute who shot seven men in one year. She was certainly enacting her own version of the 1978 cult female revenge film *I Spit on your Grave*. In this film, as in the life of Wuornos, what started the revenge and murder is rape. For Wuornos, a lifetime of it, for the fictional character Jennifer Hills, a gang rape in a scene that lasts thirty minutes—quite a realistic duration when four men have their turn sexually assaulting and beating one woman. When you think about it, thirty minutes could very well be a conservative estimate.

The 2010 Hollywood blockbuster, *Monster,* tells the story of the life of Aileen Wuornos and her eventual execution. I don't know if I can speak for all of us but, as a rape victim and a survivor, I empathize with these revenge-getting victims (*all* of the revenge killings of the fictional Jennifer Hills and especially Wuornos' first killing of the man who had her tied up, repeatedly beat her, raped her himself and then with a metal pipe, until she got her hands free, got the gun and killed him). Either in the real-life version of Wuornos or the fantasy represented by Jennifer Hills, even though it's an of-course-no-one-should-ever-murder-anyone, for me, this is not 'just' anger, self-defence, and revenge: there is justice to these acts—a justifiable revenge.

How does a misogynist culture frame these women? Are they participating in the same male violence when it is men who pushed them to kill in the first place? Can such cases be used as evidence to prove that women are just as violent as men (even though neither of the women—one non-fiction, the other fiction—rape)? Certainly not. In *Monster*, Wuornos expresses the foundation of rape culture and how she, as a life-long victim, is onto it:

"You don't know what's goin' on. I do. So if you wanna' keep your eyes shut to the whole world, then at least hear me out."

Up to her death, eyes remained firmly shut.[3] No one heard her out. Society called her crazy. No wonder she went too far.

Yes, in the end, with her final murder of a good man who was trying to help her, Wuornos crossed a line.[4] Real life is always far more complex than the straight-ahead revenge of the fantasy film, not to mention less just. And yet, after confessing to all, when sentenced to death, Wuornos again nails it when she says to the judge: "Thanks, judge. May you rot in hell for sentencing a raped woman to death." And, again in an interview the day before her execution, she stated, "Thanks a lot society for railroading my ass."

It is a society based in power abuse that psychologically killed Wuornos and drove her to kill; the acts that had led her to murder were never taken seriously or even addressed. The white male judge, the traditional symbol and dispenser of justice in Western patriarchy, had no interest in considering the context of the murders, the justifiable whys they were committed in the first place. The system that rapes and (rarely) pushes a female victim to the point of re-enacting the violence that was inflicted upon her must definitely be denied; the unruly woman must always be disciplined for masculine supremacy to be maintained.

Go-to movie critic Roger Ebert condemned *I Spit on Your Grave* as a 'vile piece of garbage,' and *Monster* was celebrated with numerous awards. Regardless of the discrepancy in budget, could this have anything to do with the fact that in the former, pure revenge is achieved, and in the latter, the real-life Wuornos is sentenced to death, silenced, and proclaimed insane? Wuornos, a woman who endured a lifetime of sexual abuse, assaults, and poverty, had no choice but to be a part of what Robert Jensen calls "the sexual exploitation industry."[5] At the end of *Monster*, as at the end of the subject's life, an exploited woman is disciplined, discredited, and erased. Everything is back as it should be. In the final scene of *I Spit on Your Grave*, though, after having wreaked revenge on the rapists, the rape-victim-cum-revenge-killer is smiling. Unfortunately, justice is usually only achieved in fantasy.

People often point to Karla Homolka and Aileen Wuornos (and even to the Blood Countess) as proof that women abduct, rape, and murder, that we are just like men, that we have the same capacity for violence, and that, somehow, this makes male violence okay. These few women killers are held up as evidence that we are all like that, so violence is but a part of being human. A levelling. An equalization. An excuse. It's very dangerous when people claim that a smattering of examples is proof that undermines the validity of the majority. Yes, there are no absolutes, but generalizations exist for a reason. They speak of the general, of the majority, of truths that so often happen.

In 1405, French feminist Christine de Pizan wrote *The Book of the City of Ladies*. Christine was a member of the upper class and, as such, was as highly educated as women were allowed to be in those days. Idle in her privileged status, she had plenty of time to read, and she read every book in her father's library. In the introduction to her book, she relates how most of the women in mythology are represented as evil. She finds this very curious because none of the women she knows are like that. In *The Book of the City of Ladies*, Christine built a city inhabited by the women she knew. With a revolutionary snub at patriarchy, she just left all the misogynist female stereotypes out.

In unison with Christine six centuries later, I ask, once again: Are you like that? I know I am not. I know all of my women friends are not. I know my mother and sister are not. Would you abduct and rape someone? Would you take away a fellow creature's power for the satisfaction of your ego and alleviation of your fear? Would this turn you on sexually? I doubt it. Especially if you are a woman.[6]

⸻◆⸻

While I was gagged and tied up in the back of the camper/van, I didn't last long on my back; I spent most of the time on my side, feeling the crack of the back door with my fingertips. I had to shift incrementally onto my side so that he wouldn't notice;

he was always watching me through the rear-view mirror. His eyes were those of a frightened animal, darting sporadically from left to right but never straying from this moment of my taking. It was as though time had stopped. Perhaps for both of us. I know those eyes better than any part of him.

I kept my gaze locked onto his as I shifted my body into this futile attempt at escape. I worked to pry the door open. If I could get the door to release, a crack even, I could use the weight of my body and roll out—a fantasy that added to my tweaked adrenalin. I caressed the separation between the bottom of the door and the floor like an ineffable lover: searching, obsessed, ridiculous. The guarantee of severe injury and possible death when one rolls out of a moving vehicle onto a highway didn't matter to me. As far as I was concerned, I was already dead. And, even though I didn't know it then, thinking I was dead was starting to give me power—I had nothing to lose.

———⊰⊱———

In 1994, Courtney Love raged, "You gotta learn how to say 'NO'!!!" Unfortunately, I hadn't heard that song yet.

Despite the fact that I went to university and had read all kinds of theory, philosophy and literature, when I finally did hear Courtney's ferocious warning, it was one of the most profound things I had ever heard. It seems so obvious, but for women, saying no to men is not as easy as that. Like Courtney says, we have to *learn* and, to do that, we have to *un*-learn what we have been taught since girlhood. Why hadn't I heard Courtney's fierce advice somewhere else? It should be so 'Duh' and 'Of course!'

Roman poet Lucius Accius said in 170 B.C. "Let them hate, so long as they fear." If people stop fearing, they can stop hating! Like Courtney's big blunt, "No," this seems pretty obvious, but unfortunately, it's not. How do we stop fear? How do we end hate?

I wonder if rapists and pedophiles even think about whether or not they hate the person they are using for their sick pleasure and for the assuaging of their fear. I wonder whether the woman or child matters even enough to feel hatred towards. And what exactly is this fear anyway? Life? Death? The continuum we are all part of? Do they think their inherent vulnerability can be alleviated by taking everything away from someone else?

Fear, ego, and self-preservation at all costs seem to be key ingredients in testosterone. Yes, like it or not, anti-feminist backlashers, patriarchy is a rape culture; patriarchy is a culture built on hatred and fear; patriarchy is founded in aggression and conquest. To continue the containment of woman as the weaker sex, "women the feared," backlash is always geared up to rage primordial fury against all the gains of women because, maybe, when it gets right down to it, she can embrace her inherent vulnerability as a living/dying creature, and deep down, in her core, she is not afraid. And that's really scary.

December 20th, 1994. Prescott, Arizona.

After Flagstaff, I travelled to Prescott, Arizona. It was a kind of Wild West town that pleased my curiosity for authentic Americana. I found a motel on the edge of town by following a neon sign that flashed an arrow pointing to a string of buildings with picnic tables in between. If you had a car, you could park right out front of your room. Very convenient. Just like home. It was all ground level. I can't remember its name. The buildings were green with white trim. They had porches. Quaint. The middle-aged woman in the front office was relatively friendly, although I did sense some suspicion, something ominous behind her smiley welcome. She reminded me of a character from a 1950s TV show. This is where the Cleaver family would have stayed if they had happened through Prescott on the way to the Grand Canyon. I think the proprietor even had horn-rimmed glasses. I know this all sounds so scripted. Such a cliché. But scripts play by the rules—they are preordained.

I got my key and carried my green duffle bag up a little hill to my suite. The room smelt musty. It felt damp even though I was in a desert. I left my bag in the room, locked up, and went out to explore the town. That was the only time I would be in that room.

I think it was about five. I came upon a bar on the main drag. It had swinging saloon doors and, inside, all kinds of Western paraphernalia decorated the walls: rows of old bullets that pointed heavenwards as mini-missiles, mounted antlers—a few pairs still attached to their heads with eyes that gaped through glass—antique pistols delicately inlaid with ivory, and a set of crisscrossed rifles above the bar, the Prescott version of a skull & crossbones. I was pleased by such cowboy kitsch. It was called: The Bird Cage Saloon.

I pushed through the swinging doors and sat on a stool at the long, polished, wooden bar. It was one of those stools that swivel. Brown vinyl with a backrest. Some of the stools were torn and taped from so much sitting, adding to the charming ambience of rough-around-the-edges. There was a mirror behind the rows of hard liquor. The room had high ceilings lined with ornate molding, and I imagined when the main drag was a dirt road, horses' reins would have been looped over the hitching post out front, and one could have watched a stage coach occasionally roll through town, dressed in the dust of where it had been.

I glanced at the reflection of my face framed by leathery men and hardened women, all of us illuminated by bright sun streaming yellow through the high windows. Sunbeams filled with dancing dust. I looked very small. Like I was beginning to be eaten away at by something I had walked right into.

I probably ordered a beer. Most likely a Miller Lite. I didn't have a very sophisticated palate in those days, and I was usually on a diet. I pulled my journal out of my backpack in preparation to write. I had recently left my husband. The main reason for this trip to Arizona was to write a letter to him, my ex-husband, whose name I won't even bother making up to protect his privacy because it was so long ago he readily spills over into fiction.

He is not really of consequence to this story. Except as one of many examples of how I always chose the wrong men. I haven't seen him since I left him. Or thought about him much since I wrote the letter that was never sent. It's like his presence in my life was immediately overridden by what is about to happen next.

I have no memory of what I was going to say in the letter. But I do know I was going to climb a mountain, burn it as closure, let the ashes and the sadness blow away in the wind as a ceremonial goodbye. This is why I had stopped in Prescott: there is a little mountain there just outside of town. I was going to perform the ritual in the morning. This part of the story never happened.

Now that I think about it, now that I think about him for the first time in decades, my only-ever husband is the crux of this plot: the plot that put me in Prescott that particular day.

December 21st, 1994. Between 4 p.m. and 7 p.m. Prescott, Arizona.

Being young and pretty and not from around there, I quickly attracted attention, and the men sitting at the bar next to me wanted to chat. I abided. The bartender was a woman. A brash, saucy type with bleached blond hair piled on top of her head. She carried on a lively banter that bottomed out into an unruly smoker's laugh. I marveled at the extent of her small-town American drawl, so colourful compared with the clipped and often flat Canadian accents of where I come from. She was friendly, although a bit intimidating, with her ability to not take shit from any of the men. I would have liked to have been like her, so sure of herself, getting what she wanted but not taking crap from them, shooting down sexist commentators like hunters had shot down the deer that stared into the bar through glass eyes. The jukebox was delightfully eclectic, as is usual in American taverns. Everything from The New York Dolls to Johnny Cash to Guns & Roses to Patsy Cline to The

Sex Pistols to Elvis to Blondie. I was having a wonderful time. These were the kinds of adventures I lived for! This was the kind of life experience I needed to be a great artist, a great writer! I was soaking it all up, taking a few notes here and there between occasionally contributing to the conversations. Until he walked in.

I didn't actually see him walk in, but I was instantly aware when he sat down. Heaviness descended upon the levity, and the bar may have become quiet for a moment, a barely perceptible act of mourning or protest. The bartender's body stiffened. She moved reluctantly towards him. She knew him; she didn't like him.

"Whadda *you* want?" her eyes rolled, and her lips popped a stream of peevish disapproval. He ordered a whiskey.

"Bourbon. Double. Straight up." Matter of fact. Without expression. Something rough enough to cut away sin. To soften self-loathing. Conversations started up again, but darkness had descended upon the bright afternoon at The Bird Cage Saloon and, even though I didn't look in his direction, I could feel him staring at me.

Somewhere in the Fraser Valley, BC. Canada. 2010.

In 2010, a young woman was at a party. Fifteen years old. Still a child, really. She was there with her girlfriends. It was a huge party. Someone at the high school had a big house, and it was the typical parents-are-away-and-half-the-school-shows-up adolescent booze fest.

I heard this on the news eight years ago. I just made up that setting. I don't remember the details of exactly where and the specific occasion, and that doesn't matter. I will never forget what happened though, the core, the crime. The absence of heart. I am sure my setting is close enough. I know it was a party. Maybe a rave. High school kids. In the Fraser Valley. BC.

Canada. A wholesome place. Lots of churches. Great hiking out there. Picnics. Sports.

Danger lurks behind the guise of normalcy.

And so the story goes. The young pretty female was drugged. "Cursed are women who are young and pretty." I think I heard that in a movie, or maybe I read it somewhere. It's one of those contradictions that stir up densities of truth. Young women strive to be attractive to men, but then there is the brutal irony that this socialized need to attract the opposite sex ends up attracting danger. It is dangerous to draw attention, especially during wartime. By merely being female, mere existence is a risk.

Camille Paglia instructs us that if we don't want to risk being raped, we should stay home with mommy.[7] She says rape is an inevitable danger. She is right, unfortunately, but this reality also equates to the normalization of the male inability to control himself. (That kind of lets men off the hook, doesn't it?) Gee. Nice life. Either way. Indoors or out. And, in Paglia's system, men don't have to take any responsibility for developing self-awareness and learning compassion and empathy. They can continue to roam about revved up on unbridled testosterone. And men who claim to 'not be like that' have no incentive to analyze their urges, behaviors, and thoughts—both in the past and in the present—and their potential for being 'like that.' Paglia's unfortunate truth is downright damning.

On opposite sides of the feminist debate as to whether rape culture is something worth taking seriously or not, Roxane Gay ostensibly agrees with Paglia's damnation of the female sex when she asks the question, "[w]hat is it like to live in a culture where it often seems like it is a question of when, not if, a woman will encounter some kind of sexual violence?" However, unlike Paglia, who places no responsibility whatsoever onto the men who rape and opts for the cliché of 'boys will be boys,' Gay's invitation for discussion about 'what's it like for women' is extended to men as well: "What is it like for men to navigate this culture whether they are indifferent to rape culture or working to end it or contributing to it in ways significant or small?"[8] If we truly want to work towards a culture where girls and women can be free to live their lives without having to look over their shoulders, carry keys in their fist, or cross the street when a man is approaching, then men need to be included even if they have never followed through on a temptation, even if they are already on board to end violence against women and are not direct perpetrators of the fear and the violence, they need to still be accountable for their role in a male supremacist society. Like there being no prostitutes without johns, there would be no rape victims without rapists. And, even though the majority of men aren't rapists, there would be very few rapists without men.

She was unconscious. Five or six or maybe eight teenage boys raped her. One after another, they undid their pants and pulled out their hard cocks. Cocks that had gotten excited by their friend who had pumped her last, by the audience, as they performed their power, their manhood, at the expense of another. As one was done, the other jumped onto the prone fleshy thing to fuck. Were they looking around at the audience and laughing while they assaulted her? Did one of them support himself momentarily on one arm and sport a grinning thumbs up? I have no idea. I wasn't there. Even though I can see it all in Technicolor.[9]

"Go, Dude! Give it to her! She deserves it! The way she flaunts herself. The little slut. Leads us all on. Tortures us. It's all her fault. She's had this coming since fifth grade!"

Was her head flopping around on her rubbery neck? Were her eyes rolled back, lids occasionally fluttering with the electricity of still being alive, bound to the oh-so-sexy edge of consciousness, the ideal state of objectification. Just another instance of gang rape, some good ole' boys-will-be-boys Friday night fun.

Gang rape is an act of war. In Bosnia-Herzegovina, between 1992 and 1995, an estimated 20,000-50,000 women and girls were gang-raped by Serbian soldiers. Half a million women were raped, sexually mutilated, or murdered over a period of one hundred days during the Rwandan genocide of 1994. 173 incidents of rape and other forms of sexual violence, involving 625 girls and women (some of the children under the age of four), were committed by the Burmese army troops in Shan State between 1997 and 2002. 83% of the rapes were committed by officers, in most cases in front of their troops. The rapes involved extreme brutality and often torture—beating, mutilation, and suffocation. 25% of the rapes resulted in death. 61% were gang-rapes, and in some cases, women were detained and raped repeatedly for periods of up to four months.[10] And, more recently, there was methodical gang-raping of Rohingya women by Myanmar's armed forces in 2016 and 2017. From the enclaves of the First World,[11] we can detach ourselves by watching such atrocities on TV and proclaiming to one another: "That's always happening *over there*! What else is new?" In our detachment and demonization of the other, we brush off these gendercides as something from 'over there.' But it would be better understood if we remembered that it happens here too—there doesn't have to be an all-out war for war crimes to be committed.

Back at the suburban party in Canada: the event was photographed and videotaped, and shared on social media. The boys were careful to keep themselves out of the shots. Perhaps they had discussed this detail beforehand. The victim's girlfriends watched. Later, they said "she liked it" and that "she had asked for it."[12] No one tried to help her. No one. Not even the other young women—even though it could have so easily been one of them.

As I listened to the radio that day and heard this story, I felt like my insides were going to spew out of my mouth in a mighty viscous mass. I held my head; I moaned; I started to scream with rage. I still cry now writing this. How is this possible? How can a fellow-creature do this to another? How disgusting it is that men will rape an unconscious woman and then cheer on their buddies doing the same thing. I will never understand. I feel like I am a different species. And, worse still, how can other women support and watch another woman's assault and even go so far as to disavow the devastating effects of the act, allying themselves with the enemy and actually testifying that an unconscious creature was not only asking for it but also enjoyed a parade of cocks pummelling her young vagina, probably making her bleed, definitely causing massive bruising, inflicting severe emotional trauma that will plague her for the rest of her life? Yes, this all makes perfect sense.

December 21st–22nd, 1994. Various Locations in the Arizona Desert.

I managed to take a lot of sleeping pills. I remember still being tied up in the back of the vehicle at this time, so I must have asked him to get them for me from my bag, and he had complied. A contradictory act of kindness considering the context. As our hours together accumulated, it was as though he was trying to make me feel comfortable, like he wanted me to like him, maybe even feel at home.

I must have swallowed them without water because I don't think he ever gave me any. And I know I took a lot. I was pretty sure I was going to die, be tortured and sliced up, maybe hacked to pieces and my body strewn around the desert. I had no intention of being conscious for it.

The reason I had prescription sleeping pills is because I had left my husband. I had been having trouble sleeping. One would typically knock me out for a solid eight hours. Tied up in the back of his makeshift camper/van, I took about five. Under regular circumstances, I probably would have OD'd. But I was wide-awake. Eyes widened almost to unblinking, adrenalin pumping, heart pounding, spinning webs of get-away strategies.

He was sitting three or four stools down from me. There were people in between. I sensed a crowd had gathered. I looked in his direction to see what was going on. He had a case full of jewelry, and he was trying to sell it. This was his job, I later found out, besides abducting and raping women. But perhaps that was more of a hobby.

"Hot!" the bartender sneered. "All hot, the lot of it!" I don't know if he sold any, but I had looked in his direction, and that was all he needed as encouragement to strike up a conversation. Move in. He had his plans. The minute he walked in and saw me sitting there. I was the next one. Young. Alone. Female. All he needed now was information. He started to set his trap.

If I perch myself as a fly on top of one of those racks of antlers and watch myself from the distant future, I think about what a blatant example I was of how women are conditioned to be nice—especially young women—until we know better. It makes no sense. Especially in terms of the self-preservation men are so good at. It's madness. Even if we sense danger, even if another woman has warned us against him, even if bells have gone off and our gut is roiling, we are still polite. We answer questions, even offer others, like young ladies displaying their accomplishments at finishing school: "No matter what the consequence, I vow to keep my pinky raised, answer 'yes' and 'no' in an always endearing tone and put my fork down after each mouth-full even when I am about to be dragged into the antithesis of etiquette. So help me, God." We enact what has been imposed upon us. I had a bad feeling; I had been warned. But I was obliged to be nice. To not just say, "Fuck off, creep, leave me alone." (As I am pretty sure I would say now, but maybe I am exaggerating the 'Fuck off' part as he really hadn't *done* anything yet except exist. And I can still be too nice, a long-perfected quality I continue to struggle with). I could tell that nobody liked him, but who was I to judge? The old adages: it takes all kinds, innocent until proven guilty, let anyone among you who is without sin ....

People often tell me that 'everyone makes their choices.' This is one of my biggest pet peeves. Such people impose a levelling that assumes all creatures are born with the same positioning in the hierarchy of privilege. They often say this while they are throwing their arms up in the far too common 'why should we really care' about drug-addicted people. Apparently, the drug-addicted people make their own choices; they did it all to themselves and have never had any relationships with anything or anyone else in the world. "They chose to start using drugs," the self-righteous, smug folks say, "if they don't choose to stop, that's their problem." Read: not mine.

I had a boyfriend once who said that a serial killer was 'cleaning the streets' when he murdered drug-addicted, prostituted women. Of course, this relationship did not last long. I would say to him: "Were you sexually abused as a child? Have you been raped? Were you born into poverty with addicts and abusers as parents?" He would say: "No," but, strangely enough, he never got my point.

There is no such thing as absolute free will. We are not wholly responsible for all our choices. We are affected by the world we live in. We do not scoot about deflecting any misfortune and abuse that comes our way with our superhero deflection jackets. Such levelling claims are a reductionist crock and serve as self-righteous tools of blame. Ideally, as women who are trained from girlhood to be nice no matter what, we will eventually be liberated from this madness. Hopefully. But, unfortunately, as in my case, having to learn the hard way. And survive to tell the tale and maybe save another young woman from having to live (or not) through it.

He got my attention from down the bar. I think I was warned about him again by one of the men I had been talking to. A guy with a wife. Two kids. A boy and a girl. A ranch. Some kind of collie for herding. He was in town for the afternoon. Had to buy some supplies. Came to the Bird Cage for a couple of brews on the way home.

"That guy's bad news," he stated, firmly, quietly, emphasising a reality I should have long been aware of. But denial overshadowed my awareness: I doubted the dread.

Despite the warnings, the usual niceties were exchanged. Someone between us left, and he moved a stool closer. Like a game of chess. Was I a pawn or the queen? Definitely the former at this point. I don't remember if he got right next to me. Perhaps the other person in the middle was part of the conversation too. I hope so. That would make me feel better in this part of the recollection: that I had been telling too much to another person as well. Not only him. The one I had been warned against.

I have always made excuses for this transgression. This is one of the pieces of the shame that niggles at every woman who has lived through a similar experience. Such details always lead to:

"You asked for it. It was all your fault. What were you doing in that bar anyway? What did you expect?" The shame and the accusations are preordained, scripted; one feeds the other. I have always tried to cover my tracks with:

"Well ... my street smarts were down. I had just broken up with my husband .... I was used to having a man around. If I gave out too much information by being so obliging and nice, it didn't matter then. I had a man to protect me .... I had gotten used to that. My guard was down ...."

"Yes," I tell the younger me now, "it most certainly was. But that's only the surface of the story. You didn't know it then, but you had been made that way. A perfectly accommodating victim. You made it so easy for him. Just like you were trained to do. Good girl."

December 22nd, 1994. The Arizona Desert.

Whenever people talk about women falsely accusing men of rape,[13] I say:

"Ask them the details of their story." True stories cannot be made up. They are too unbelievable to not be true.

As I mentioned, my brain was tirelessly spinning possible escape plans. We were in a middle-of-nowhere desert. It wasn't a flat desert. It wasn't one of those beautiful white sand ones where the wind sculpts scoops and peaks like the marshmallow icing on an angel food cake. No, this was a pretty homely desert. The guy didn't have much taste. It was a yellowy colour, a bit hilly with lots of scrub and big Wile E. Coyote cactuses poking up all over the place with their hands up like creatures under perpetual arrest. I sat or paced freely outside the vehicle now. There was no longer much point, or so he must have thought, of having me on the string anymore.

"Where could she get to from here?" he may have thought.

"Anywhere and any way I can," I would have thought back.

He let me put my clothes on sometimes now. Maybe that was because he liked ordering me to take them off again. I was standing outside of the camper/van, drinking the last of his Miller, not having eaten anything for a good twelve hours by this point, packed full of sleeping pills, initiating another plot.

I looked at the ridge in the distance, spied a big cactus waving its dumbfounded arms on the top. He was a few feet away from me. Maybe he was sitting on the steps. Watching me. Always watching me. He got out his camera and took a picture of me. It was a Polaroid. I was leaning against the camper/van. He showed me the picture right after. A kind of celebration. Let's mark this special moment, never forget! I was wearing the mustard yellow suede jacket, Dino pin still intact. I know I had to conceal my shock when I looked at this barely recognizable me pasted onto this unbelievable reality. This horror staring back: a dissolving me. Wearing a face that didn't look like it had any blood in it. I wish I could see that picture now. Study it. It has gone the same discarded way of the cassette tape of my first testimony. What extensions to this narrative would it conjure? What other ghosts would it resurrect?

I gave the snapshot an indifferent glance. "Hey," I asked as though initiating a harmless game on a sunny day. "Do you think you could shoot that big cactus up there on the ridge?" He was pleased by my question, its possibility of a playful

challenge. Maybe I was interested in guns, and we had something in common after all, I saw his hopeful face say. He jumped
up and got his handgun from under the front seat.

"Sure!" he said. And yes, "Pow!" Sure, he did. My heart fell.
He hit it. The sorry thing hadn't fallen over or anything; I guess
those large cacti are pretty sturdy, but through the desert haze,
I saw it wobble. Enough proof for me.

You see, I had become so desperate at this point to get
away that I was resorting to a survival strategy from a 1970s
action-comedy. If you have ever seen it, you will know the one I
was thinking about. The men in the movie are all rich buffoon
criminals who somehow don't get shot because they have a
not-get-shot technique. It's called "Serpentine." When a bunch
of bad guys are shooting at them, one of the good guys calls out,
"Serpentine! Serpentine!" and they all start running in squig-
gles and sometimes overdo it for comedic effect with loops, so
no one can get a good shot at them. That was my plan. I asked
my gun-slinging captor if he could shoot that far-away cactus
so I would know how long I would have to serpentine for. And,
even though he was fat and could never catch me on his own
steam, he was one of those American men who are good shots
with good guns, so I decided it wasn't worth it. Foiled again.

No one could ever have made that up unless it really
happened.

December 21st, 1994. 7 p.m. to 12 a.m. Prescott, Arizona.

I am putting off writing about when it actually happened. I
think it's going to be difficult to write because I don't think
about the details anymore, even though they are always there,
embodied. So I will tell you about just before it happened.

He got up and left The Bird Cage Saloon. Abruptly.
Motivated by something. Didn't even say goodbye. I was relieved. I think the whole bar was.

The place had thinned out. It was closing. I got back to my writing for a bit and then decided to find another place to finish my letter.

I remember there was still a bit of daylight. Deep dusk. It was mid-December, so that's kind of weird because I thought more time had passed at the Bird Cage. But that's the problem when you are remembering from twenty-five years in the future. Details like: what time was it? When did the sun go down? How does the latitude of Arizona affect the amount of daylight when compared with my 49th parallel perspective? But they were never really important in the first place, although a defense lawyer would clog up the trial with:

"She can't remember exactly what time it was. She doesn't remember if the sun was down yet. She must be lying about everything." In the long run, what is important is what happened. The plot. And a victim never forgets that.

I don't remember the name of the place. It didn't have as much local colour as the Bird Cage. It was built of concrete. Kind of like a bunker. There were pool tables in the back, or was it the front, or did I come in through the back door, thinking it was the front door? I know I went out the back door. There were booths along the side. The bar was across from the row of booths. I think there were regular tables too and that the booths were on a low platform. It was dim inside. Couples were cozied up. People still smoked in bars then, so the cigarette haze added to the lack of visibility, the sordid intimacy. There were hanging lamps above the booths with dangling chains that you could turn on and off yourself. I needed light to write. I wanted privacy. I chose a booth.

The waiter was friendly, oddly effervescent in contrast with his workplace. He gave me the right amount of distance and the right amount of attention. Having been a waitress for many years, I appreciated his tact. I wrote for a long time. I have no idea what I wrote. It was so long ago. I know it was a letter of peace and forgiveness. Did I finish it? Did I have that satisfaction of closing the journal with a flourish, triumphantly tucking away my pen, and smiling with satisfaction at the thought of dramatically tearing the pages out in the morning to fulfill my humble epic? I can't remember. I have no idea what happened to that letter. I would love to read it now. I would love to remember what I know was softness. But I do remember him coming in through the back door.

"Oh no," my body felt.

But I didn't do anything about it. I didn't listen. Good girl.

December 23rd, 1994. Early Evening. The Rose & Thorne Pub. Vancouver BC.

I had just gotten home. Vancouver, Canada. It was the day after. I was sitting at the bar of the busy downtown pub where I worked. I made lots of tips there, one of the benefits of being young and pretty to counteract the corresponding dangers.

I didn't have to work that night. One would think that I would have had to return to work right away after being gone for weeks. But I was sitting at the far end of the bar reserved for staff and the regulars who had achieved the inner circle. I must have called in sick, but I had the special kind of sickness where one can still sit at the bar: the illness of the glamorous victim.

No one could believe it. This was a couple of decades before ambulance-chasing reality shows. The reality where people salivate over others' misfortunes, filling their faces with snacks while gobbling up another's trauma. People looked at me with horrified awe. They lapped it up. No one had ever heard such a story before, not to mention known someone who had lived it, who'd had the starring role. Surviving had made me into a kind of celebrity. The bruises around my neck were like a black and purple choker, lurid and titillating proof. I was pale, thin, my eyes most likely dusted with dark shadows, shining with a tinge of mania. Men often told me how pretty I was when I was messed up.

I remember that evening I was wearing my favorite pistachio green dress with the double-breasted buttons and half belt in the back that slightly cinched the waist with three-quarter sleeves circa late 1960s. Green Fluevog suede slip-ons with a chunky heel to match. Maybe I had dressed up for the debut of this trauma. In my recently victimized state, I had become a movie star.

December 20th, 1994. Approximately 11 p.m. Prescott, Arizona.

I could have ducked under the table. I know I thought of it. Did I want it to look like he wasn't getting to me? Even though he was? I saw him see me even though he pretended not to. He started up a game of pool with some of the guys clumped in the back. Acted as though he hadn't come looking for me. It was a fast game. Doubles, I think. I could hear the clacking of the balls, the thud as they were sunk into the pockets. I watched furtively from my permeable fortress, from my private booth that had already been invaded. The speed of the game caused me to panic. I didn't want it to end. I knew that as soon as the game ended, I would be next.

The light above the pool table set it off from the rest of the bar like a stage. It cast a fuzzy yellow glow onto the players when they bent over to take their shot. After shooting, each player flattened into a silhouette as they returned to the semi-darkness. Features flashed as they moved in and out of the light: cheekbones, teeth, knuckles, fists. I was happy when I almost couldn't see him anymore. When he faded into the possibility of non-existence. But he kept re-entering the scene, re-entering reality. At one point, I saw the whites of his eyes rise and look my way. I gulped. Blushed. Turned away. I wanted nothing more than for him to go. The game ended. He started to walk towards me.

I try to remember now exactly how I felt at that moment. I know it was many things. Emotions are never only one. I know I was pissed off that he was interrupting me. I know I felt sick. I know I was nervous. I know my face was hot. I know I wanted to stand up to him, act like everything was fine. Normal. Pretend that he wasn't getting to me. But I don't think I truly felt the danger. The encroaching density of it. The way I would now. Otherwise, I would have acted on it. I had no idea that this meeting was far from a coincidence.

Niceties. Again. He asked me to play pool. I'm terrible at pool. I've never enjoyed it because I rarely sink a ball. But, hey, why not? I thought. Feigning happy-go-lucky. Maybe it will be another adventure. Maybe there is nothing really wrong here. Maybe I'm making up this gut feeling.

"Yah, sure, okay. I'm pretty much done here," I lied. I walked towards the pool table like I was programmed to do. The game lasted until the bar closed. Neither of us sank a ball.

Lantzville, BC, Canada. 2018.

The present. 2018. My dad is dying. I love him. He is a good man as good men go. He did his best as a human being doing their best goes. He had his shit and unresolved traumas and lots of beauty. I believe more in the beauty now. He never hurt me. Physically, that is. I know my dad never meant to hurt me the same way I never meant to get hurt.

I have been taking care of him for the last two years. I sometimes wonder why I have such a deep desire to alleviate his suffering when he was the source of so much of mine. Why do I care so much? All I know is that it has made me so happy when I have been able to lessen a bit of his boredom, his suffering, the dissolution of his power as a man. A once so active man, who had climbed mountains and kayaked in the open ocean, was forced to sit on the couch all day watching the tube and now can only lie in a hospital bed and stare at the ceiling when his eyes happen to be open and, finally, at the end of his life, when he has no choice but to confront his own vulnerability, tells me he loves me. Over and over. As though he is making up for lost time. He tells me what I have always hungered to hear with a sweetness that dissolves into too much too late.

I was terrified of men.

In my earliest years, the world was my sister, my mother, and I, and a sigh of relief whenever you were not there, Dad. Mom was both goddess and savior to me; I constantly sought and clung to her hand and felt a sickening loss whenever she let go. I was always looking for men. I knew they were out there and that one would eventually pass by, going to and coming from places unimaginable, as phantoms that sporadically surfaced within the gaps between frames in the progression of a life that sputters insecurity. Immediately, as one entered my little girl's pensive gaze, I recoiled, hurled my arm forward, and pointed with disbelief, fascination, and horror to exclaim, "Guy! Guy!" I knew they would come, but it was always unthinkable when they did.

Sometimes, one of these men would enter the house. My mom would greet him warmly, an acute betrayal. Daring to spy around the corner at the top of the stairs, I would witness his foot, then his leg, then his other foot, then the other leg entering. Alarm! Terror! "He is going to come up the stairs! Bolt behind the biggest chair! Close your eyes! Mash your face into the upholstery!" I could smell the danger; the air bore down, electric, prickling, jarring everything opposite. When the man was in such close proximity, I no longer dared to look. I waited, aching to be invisible until I could resume breath.

You worked out of town in those days, and I dreaded your inevitable return—a dominating specter that would periodically bash its way back in and reclaim title over our vulnerable softness, an injured and brutal animal. You would drink your sadness into anger and your anger into sadness as you vacillated between silent tears and loaded guns, your internal struggles exploding and imploding in spasms, your reality, and ours, trapped within the sharp inscriptions of your un-exhumed demons. My small body was clenched, holding its breath until you would leave again and the thin flowers would re-appear. But doom always hung beneath the quivering surface, a black drape that would lift and then smother again with the opening of a door.

I painted swaths across dis-coloured sheets of paper. Paper that had sat discarded, not quite thrown out, originating in some corner of domestic anxiety. It is what I was given. "Use this for your sparkling eyes and fugitive hope," my mother didn't say. The paint was watery and formed unabsorbed pools that rolled off the edges. I didn't like the paintings; I was ashamed of them but thought they had to be good and that they had to bring brightness. I crept out to the edge of the street to try to sell them, my posture a hollow of feigned confidence. The sun blared; the trees were too green. Did anyone ever come by? Did anyone ever look, pick them up and feel the hard desperation of the paper, the unresolved paint? I can't remember. But I remember standing there. With an inexplicable feeling of doom, desperate to climb out of the low self-esteem that I was inheriting. And, when the perfect summer day began to mock, I would drag my feet back into the house of yellow air.

December 20ᵗʰ, 1994. Approximately 1 a.m. Prescott, Arizona.

I got into the vehicle. He had offered me a lift back to my motel. I knew it was wrong, but I got in anyway. Some of you might think that I was stupid and that I had it coming. It was all my fault. But does that mean I deserved what is going to happen next? That I am guilty when I didn't commit a crime? When I didn't hurt anyone? This is the worst part of the story. This is both the beginning of the violence and the core of my shame. The beginning of the violence I have worked the rest of my life to not inflict on myself. The violence of blame. The violence of self-blame. This is the part of the story that I never fully tell. Not even to myself—this is the first time I have told all of it.

I got into the vehicle. I knew it was wrong, but I got in anyway. Sure, I was tired; sure, it was late. I remember there weren't any cabs, but I could have walked. And yet, now that

I think about it, now that I am immersed in writing this, he would have gotten me anyway. Yes, he would have gotten me anyway. I have never thought of this before.

New Year's Eve 2017. Qualicum Beach, BC, Canada.

New Year's Eve 2017. I went to a party with a few friends in a sleepy seaside town. Qualicum Beach, BC, Canada. To me, the place has always had an aura of purity with its pristine beaches, vital forests, smells of soil and salt. But, as in all places, I am sure it has its secrets. The violence happening under bridges, in dark crannies of beaches, in nighttime forests full of phantoms and stumps.

The party ended at about 2 a.m. My ride had left hours ago, so I decided to walk. There are no cabs in this town anyway, and it only takes about half an hour.

"I will walk along the beach and suck in the pure air under the moonlight," I thought.

I don't think about what I might do if something were to happen to me anymore. I know it could. I have a lived surety that it can. As a victim and a survivor, I am always aware. Always ready.

I walked down the cliff to the beach. The tide was part way out. In the winter, the tides are never as low as during the luxurious stretches of summer, where the shore's edge reaches out and touches the horizon. Winter tides are humble. Less showy. But on this beach that starts off with good-natured round stones and then descends gracefully into bands of sand, even during a high winter tide, there is always a welcoming swath wide enough to use as a road to walk back on.

It was a full moon. I was surrounded by an inky blackness punctuated by the bright moonbeam that connected the beach to the universe. I sniffed around. All the lights were out. The pub was locked up with its dangling vestiges of the celebrations that would have ended an hour or so before. Yes, in Qualicum Beach at 2 a.m, everyone appears to be asleep.

There could have been some stragglers, though, some drunken, angry men up to no good. Looking for prey without even knowing that's what they were doing. Driven by instinct and their unquestioned, primordial rights. But I didn't care. I felt the crisp salt air on my cheeks, breathed it in like water. This was the best part of my New Year's last year. And I carried a barnacle-covered stone in each hand.

December 20th, 1994. Approximately between 1:10 a.m. and 1:15 a.m. Prescott, Arizona.

"Hey, you have the same bag as me!" I exclaimed. What a jovial princess I was, fulfilling her well-bred responsibility to make small talk to break his brooding silence. I was incredibly naïve. I still can be. Someone actually got me a few years ago with the joke:

"Do you know that the word gullible isn't in the dictionary?" I became six again, stared, bewildered, and eventually responded, eyes wide, in a voice as sweet as Dr. Suess's Cindy-Loo-Who without her Santy Claus:

"It isn't? Why?"

It was a man who pulled this joke on me. Most likely a bully back in his schoolyard days. He had the right amount of insecurity and its corresponding aggression. He laughed and pointed and laughed and pointed and wouldn't shut up about it all day. I don't think I would have fallen for it if a woman had told it to me, but I may be wrong. Perhaps, if the woman had had power over me, I would have still been duped. This has never happened, so I have no way of knowing.

He turned left. Started to go up a hill. The wrong direction.

"Why are we going this way? My motel is that way!" I asked, incredulous at this change of what I had thought was going on, even though my gut had been lined with apprehension since I had gotten into the vehicle. I turned around and looked at the green duffle bag again that was exactly the same as mine, and I understood what had happened. It was the same as mine because it *was* mine!! He had gone to my motel. I had told too much at The Bird Cage Saloon!

"Why did I tell him the name of the motel!" I scolded myself seconds before the crime.

"I didn't tell him the room number," I consoled myself. "So it should have been okay. But it wasn't. Somehow, he had figured it out. Rapists are very resourceful. He'd found my room, taken my stuff, and come to get me."

I reached for the handle of the door. There wasn't one! I fumbled around, groping for a non-existent handle. There was no way to open the door! There was no inside handle on the passenger side. He had done this before. The vehicle was designed for this. I dug in my pocket for my pepper spray. The pepper spray that I had shifted to my right-hand pocket just before getting into the vehicle. You see, I had sensed danger. I had taken *a* precaution. Yay! I was not so careless and stupid after all. Impotent as it ended up being. He stopped the vehicle. Lunged.

His large hands were around my neck. Tightening. Tightening.

"Oh my God!" I remember thinking, "I am actually being strangled! How can this be real?" In that moment, I felt as though I had been torn from the narrative of my own life.

I pulled out my pepper spray. Madly pushed the button. Unfortunately, I had bought a stream, not a spray (make sure to always buy a SPRAY!). His hands were so strong that he could restrain my hand that was holding the spray with one and continue strangling me with the other, my head pinned against the back of the seat. As the stream ineffectually grazed his neck, throat, and ear, all my attempt at self-protection did was make him angrier.

"You have pepper spray? How dare you! You little bitch!!" he shouted and squeezed my neck tighter as if to punish a betrayal.

"Oh my god!" I remember myself thinking again. "I am being strangled. How did this happen? This can't be happening! I am going to die! Oh my god … I can't breathe…."

Just as I could feel myself start to slip into unconsciousness, just as I couldn't take it anymore, just as I had no choice but to tell him this, I managed to squeak out: "Please stop. I'll do whatever you want."

Within less than five minutes, my life had changed forever.

As I lay in the back of the camper/van, gagged, tied up, freshly strangled, staring at the ceiling and singed by the onset of trauma, I said to myself in a Dorothy Parker droll,

"Gee, Karen. How are you going to get yourself out of this one?"

PART TWO

Lantzville BC, Canada. 2018.

I want you to know that this story has a happy ending. I am still alive. I have experienced great joy and triumph, especially connected to writing and art. Once, during one of my photography exhibitions, a young woman came up to me and said, "I have always known there is something wrong, but I didn't know what it was until now." What an honour to have been the person responsible for that awakening.

Expressing ourselves beyond ourselves can make a difference, rage against what we know is wrong by embracing what we know is true, do our best to participate in the fight for justice, especially when having survived an epicenter of violence, and become aware of an urgency that cannot be denied. And we don't have to be abducted and raped to know this: we just have to look around and care for others beyond ourselves.

———◈———

On September 26, 2014, forty-three student teachers from Ayotzinapa, Guerrero, Mexico, disappeared. They were young Indigenous men and were training to teach rural, disenfranchised youth like themselves. Like most incidents in Mexico, with the ins and outs of overt corruption composed of a sticky web of the military, the police, the government, and the cartels, the story is a complicated one and, to this day, over five years later, no one really knows exactly what happened. Except for the fact that the forty-three young men are dead. And disappeared. Even their deaths have vanished.

I moved to Mexico in 2015. I moved there to witness, make art and write about a society that endures violence on a level unimaginable in Canada and the US. I moved here to experience art with guts. Blood. Truth. In 2016, there were nearly 23,000 intentional homicides—the second-highest murder rate in the world, next to war-torn Syria. In 2017, there were 29,168. In 2018, it climbed again to 33,341.[1]

These murders are rarely of foreigners; they are Mexican people being murdered at such a rate, predominantly because of the war on drugs and the competition to get those drugs to the drug-addicted people in the US and Canada. Ironically, Mexico is blamed for the violence. In one of his 'Mexico will pay for the wall' tweets, Donald Trump proclaimed that Mexico could "stop all of this illegal trade if they wanted to immediately." He continued on in his usual reductionist fashion: "we get the drugs, and they get the cash."[2] He left out the massacre of Mexicans in the process of getting the drugs to Americans.

Canada and the US are involved in the drug trade as the demand side of the equation. We are complicit in the subsequent murders of the Mexican people. As with there not being a whore if there were no johns, like there not being a rape victim if there were not a rapist, the drug trade and the slaughter of Mexicans would not exist if there were not a narcotic-hungry market to the north.

———<(•)>———

During my first year in Mexico, I had the honour of interviewing and writing an article about the late activist artist Francisco Toledo. However, it is ironic because, even though Toledo is lauded as an activist throughout Mexico and internationally, the first thing he told me is that he has no hope. He didn't see any connection between art and social change.

Despite his disbelief in art's ability to transform society for the better, for over a year following the disappearance of the student teachers, Toledo created one hundred and fifty ceramic sculptures dedicated to the 43 Disappeared of Ayotzinapa. One hundred of these sculptures were exhibited at Mexico City's *Museo de Arte Moderno* from October 2015 to March 2016 as *Duelo*, a word that means grief, suffering, and pain.

The moment I walked into *Duelo*, I stopped dead in my tracks. But I was far from frozen as this idiom implies: I was fully alive. My stomach wrenched; I felt like I was going to be sick; my eyes filled with tears, and I immediately began to grieve an atrocity that I knew next to nothing about. This art is so strong that it has the power to pull an outsider into its heart immediately.

I knew I had to write about it. I had to learn. And yet, even though the exhibit had such an impact upon me as grief, I also felt joy, relief, exhilaration. Look: this is real! Look: an artist has the courage to bombard us with the unspeakable! Look: an artist is forcing us to never forget! I ask Toledo now—and he would undoubtedly disagree with me—how can this not have some sort of effect, tearing open a heart, and of a foreigner, nonetheless, a person who had no direct connection to the pain?

Toledo explained that *Duelo* is not an act of resistance as that would imply a fight and the possibility of change. Rather, he stated, "*Duelo* is an accusation, a statement to the government, declaring it internationally, telling the whole world about this injustice and that Ayotzinapa is going to remain like a stain on the history of Mexico, like the 1968 Tlatelolco student massacre:[3] year after year, it gets memorialized—and so will this."[4]

Accusations, especially when memorialized, hang in our consciousness and keep pointing the finger at the guilty, at the perpetrator; they serve to pillage the surface by continuously excavating the lies and undermining the complacency of a lethal lack of heart.

At the end of our interview, I asked Francisco Toledo: "Why do you do it if in your heart there is no hope and when you believe art affects nothing in terms of achieving social justice?" He said he was aware of this possible contradiction. He paused, then responded: "Necedad, solo necedad." The English translation of the Spanish 'necedad' is not only necessity; it is also a combination of both stubbornness and folly. Of: no choice. Of: no matter what.

Due to my own micro-realms of violence, I have lived through decades of internalized shame, depression, and PTSD. I still fight it every day. But even though we are fighters, be we artists or rape survivors or both, it doesn't mean the after-effects of trauma will ever fully go away. And is it even possible? How could we forget what changed our lives forever? Why should the Mexican people forget Ayotzinapa like the authorities wish they would? Why should they? Why should they stop marching? How can we forget the violation of our bodies, the disappearances of our children?

Violence touches everyone beyond our personal stories, and this is the reason to remember. Like art that memorializes a human tragedy, assault victims are individual parts of the same human tragedy. Violence. Power abuse. As Toledo's *Duelo* memorializes the bodies of the 43 Disappeared of Ayotzinapa, the bodies of rape victims stand as accusations. As sites for vigilance. Our scarred, vibrant beings are memorials.

December 21st, 1994. Approximately from 1:15 a.m. to 5 p.m. Somewhere in the Arizona Desert.

In the beginning, I thought very seriously about getting the gun. I knew where it was because I had seen him tuck it there, under the driver's seat. I knew it had a long snout that, from watching American TV shows, I suspected was a silencer. But I could have been mistaken because I am from Canada, where it's even complicated for hunters to get a hunting rifle. I really don't know much about guns except that they are used to kill with.

This was back in the time of the string. These were the first sexual assaults. We were parked on the side of the highway above the town of Prescott. Sometimes I would hear a car race by and feel strangely detached from the world I had so recently been a part of. I have put off writing this part, even though I have been thinking about when to write it since the beginning. This particular trauma is still very much alive in me. Even twenty-five years later, it still affects all of my relationships, especially the ones with men. Just thinking about it now makes me nauseous. But as a psychological analysis of the survival instinct, this part cannot be left out; the time has come to perform an autopsy on my twenty-eight-year-old psyche.

He had a small penis. Maybe that was part of his problem with women. Maybe some had left him because of it. Maybe he had been laughed at, humiliated. Maybe that is one of the reasons why he felt that he had to abduct us. Women can shame men for not being big enough in a similar way that women can be shamed for just being women. Despite the asymmetry in terms of abuse of power, men, too, are victims of the gender binary, the crevasse between the tippy-toed female and the lumbering Neanderthal male. We all know the types: she with her blond locks and porcelain cheeks setting off an exquisitely turned-up nose, blue eyes, immaculately curved boobs, and butt to match and somehow, despite such voluptuous feats, still having a waist reminiscent of Scarlett O'Hara. He is dark, swarthy, tall, far too virile to remain clean-shaven for long, the returning shadow of his manhood darkening in time with day moving into night. Having a small cock is a disadvantage in the masculine-centric world of bigger is better. I imagine the teasing in the high school locker room, the shame of ducking into a stall to urinate rather than peeing with the big boys against the wall. The hurt of inferiority a man feels for not measuring up is often taken out on women—the inferior of the inferior because we don't have one at all.

Yes, his penis was small. I don't know if that was a good thing or a bad thing under these circumstances. He definitely couldn't physically hurt me with it, but he made me suck it all the time. It was my responsibility to make it big.

"Make me cum, Bitch," he would command, pants around his ankles, lying back on the bed, a white trash king, me on my knees, naked, in front of him on the floor. I imagine what we must have looked like, the ghoulish distortions of our shadows on the walls. I still feel ashamed as I remember and write this,[5] even though I had never signed up for the female lead in such a loathsome duet.

"Make me cum, Bitch!"

"Make me cum Bitch!"

"Make me cum Bitch!"

And he would slap my face, keeping time with each Bitch, Bitch, Bitch, each hit a startling fortissimo in his composition. My face burned with pain and disgrace; I gagged, tears rolled down my cheeks, and yet, beneath the horror, I was involved in a serious negotiation with myself about how to get the gun. In counterpoint to the composition of the surface, I chanted internally:

"I could bite his cock off right now ... and lunge for the gun."

"I could bite his cock off right now ... and lunge for the gun."

"I could bite his cock off right now ... and lunge for the gun."

"But how much will it immobilize him?" I asked myself from Stage Right. "Will he be in a state of shock and lie there screaming or be instantly enraged? Will he get a burst of adrenaline from the pain and beat me to the gun? Will I have time to get the gun?"

"Take the chance," I instructed myself from Center Stage. "You could get away. Who knows what is going to happen!

"Do it. Now!"

Silence.

"This may be your only chance.

"You have very sharp teeth. You may not even have to tear. It may be a clean cut.

"Take the chance.

"Bite.

"Lunge for the gun."

"Make me cum, Bitch!

"Make me cum Bitch!

"Make me cum Bitch!"

Staccato slaps from the pit.

"Shoot him."

"Should I shoot to kill?"

"Aim for his leg. Don't kill him. You might be accused of murder.

(I have always been very good at thinking ahead).

"Immobilize him. Jump out of the vehicle. Run. Flag down a car or climb down the cliff back to the town.

"Do it.

"Bite.

"Now!!!"

From the Performance Area, my body was diligently suck-ing, squeezing, making sure he didn't suspect the drama play-ing out in my mind. At that moment, I learned what a powerful chemical adrenalin is; I had become a kind of wizard and could fully exist in multiple places at the same time.

I heard cars whoosh past and round the bend and then silence again except for his grunts and commands and my breaths of exertion, underscored by the tightening of my ab-domen to repress the gags. The negotiations in my mind had ceased, momentarily, as all possible scenarios settled. It was as though my flesh had become the shadows on the walls and the physical actions were on auto-pilot while the real action was the debate going on in my mind. As an ironic survival strategy, I had initiated my own mind/body split.

After a brief intermission, the rational, cautious Me took Center Stage:

"Look, let's be realistic here. Even if you got the gun, you wouldn't know how to use it. There is that big silencer that you aren't even sure is a silencer, and have you heard of something called 'a safety'?

"You have no idea how to turn the safety off and how to even turn the gun on."

"By the time you got it and figured out how to use it, he might have been able to get to you ... and then what would he do? He would probably really use it on you.

"Not worth the risk," it was determined.

"Not worth it."

It was at that moment that I began to wait. To watch. To listen. To say one thing and be another. To build an opposite reality. To embody the lie. I became a cat crouching in a bush off to the side of the action, as intent upon my prey as the rope pulled tight when I went out of the vehicle to pee. All senses tweaked. But at the same time, I was also the preyed-upon. I was like a mouse being tortured for the enjoyment of the preda-tor. I was my mind, and I was my body, playing both roles. The mind lived the truth while the body was forced to live the lie. I became two people fighting for my life.

-----◆-----

In the morning, he started to sigh. These sighs were deep, drawn-out, articulating the extent of his tortured existence. He was trapped by those sighs. They bound him more tightly than the ropes he had me tied up with. I realize now how I instinctively knew his sighs were a language I could use to take control. They happened in the gaps between raping me and confiding in me, in the silences when he was alone with his fear he could only momentarily dull by taking from me. These sighs called to me, and I answered; this dialogue was the beginning of my freedom, and my ears pricked as a predator who has just smelt blood.

"Are you okay? What's the matter?" I pounced with a velvet voice, steeped in the forgiveness of the Virgin Mary.

"It's okay," I would soothe. "Everyone makes mistakes." And my deception became his lullaby, full of the well-honed sweetness and compassion I had been taught since my girlhood, my face soft and gentle, with no hint of the iron beneath. He would look up at me with the moist eyes of a lost boy who was suddenly being invited inside, but then, as soon as he began to open to that hope, he would snap back into the fear that fueled his self-hatred and its corresponding misogyny. I would feel him about to lash out at me again, fill himself by taking from me, and, to make matters worse, my escape strategy now scripted me to pretend I liked it. I would continue, desperate to not be raped again, even for a few more minutes, seconds, keep him talking, keep bewitching him into believing my immaculate lies and I wouldn't have to do any of this anymore.

He wasn't falling for it. I had to go farther and make him believe I was just like him, or maybe even worse.

"You haven't done anything to me that hasn't been done before," I would toss off, like a woman who had lived unscathed by every possible sordid scenario, as exquisitely hardened as

Faye Dunaway in *Barfly*. The more elaborate my web became, the denser the untruth.

"I won't tell anyone. We all make mistakes. I am just like you. I have made a lot of mistakes in my life, too. Let me go, and I will forgive you. We can be friends. We can write. You can come and visit me in Canada."

This became my mantra for the rest of our time together; this was the reality I was bent upon imposing.

"I won't tell anyone. We all make mistakes. Let me go, and I will forgive you. We can keep in touch. I care about you. I know you have suffered, been treated unfairly. It's not your fault. I know you didn't mean to do this. That you want to change. You can change! I did! And the first step is letting me go."

He would cling to this as truth for a moment and then shudder and shake off the insidious shift of our positions in our micro-hierarchy, like a grazing animal that pauses to flick their tail in order to rid themselves of attacking flies, and take me to the back of the vehicle again to re-assert his dominance and I demonstrate my false forgiveness. But, gradually, the raping was what became the in-between; his sighs and my consolations were starting to dominate. Even as I lay there, taking it, floating above my body, my spirit was a hawk, my flesh a sacrifice for my undying fight for liberty. I had given myself real hope.

————⫷◉⫸————

The vehicle had an ominous squeak that I will never forget. As we drove from one remote location to another, the camper part jiggled back and forth in time with the bumps and potholes or push of the brakes. I am sure people could hear it coming, or going, this mutant camper/van whimpering its sad lament of the hell it was forced to contain.

And so, a power-play had fully begun within the walls of this ambivalent vehicle. Between a man and a woman, between a victim and a victimizer, between the vanquisher and the vanquished. And neither side was going to claim absolute victory. Damage would be taken on both sides, and roles would be switched as this real-life game progressed. But, in the end, one would lose more than the other, even though the winner definitely lost a lot and, paradoxically, gained a lot too.

"Are you okay? What's the matter?" I would call out from whatever station I was currently at in the world of the back of the vehicle. I know there was a progression as to where I was permitted to sit based on the increase of my power. I know there were in between phases, times when I was no longer tied up in the very back, times where I can see myself lounging on the couch playing the part of an insolent princess, times when I sat on the edge of the vehicle with the sliding door open, feet on the desert, eyes scanning for possible escape routes in the middle-of-nowhere while keeping up an amicable conversation to seem to be having a good time. But I most vividly remember the two extremes: lying down and being tied up in the very back and then, near the end of the story, when I sat next to him in the front seat, riding shotgun.

Vancouver, Canada. 1994–1997.

I had been waiting over three years to lock him up, so there would be no more victims perpetrated by this particular predator. When I think back on the time between the abduction and the trial, I see a swirl of circus where all the colors have become smeared together, and nothing ever stops. I suppose that's because it was a kind of circus.

The first thing I did upon my return to Canada was to drop out of university and start a Rock & Roll band. It was the 90s, the time of Grrrl Power, shredded stockings, teased hair, leopard print mini-skirts, vintage bustiers, and the clever, irreverent lyrics that only come from having experienced sources of rage, a justified anger born in the heady aftermath of victimization. It may sound strange, but this was one of the happiest times of my life: the birth of myself as an artist, the artist I had been born to be who, until then, I had been afraid to be. Triumphing over terror had made me no longer afraid. Even though this healing path I had dove head first into was riddled with angst, and I don't remember all of it, after the abduction and my escape and having stared death in the face, I became fully aware of my power. I had no fear. And, when it comes to fighting for justice and raging against exploitation, I still don't. A back-handed gift? Perhaps. But more likely, being a victim has given me the opportunity to turn trauma into victory.

Sometime in 1997. Ventura County, California.

The only things the defense attorney could get out of me further discredited his case. I exhibited my skills as the natural performer who had saved my own life, the difference being that this time I told the truth, the whole truth, and nothing but the truth, except when he took the typical tactic of trying to make the rape victim into a slut and, therefore, somehow deserving of brutalization. I certainly wasn't going to tell the truth about that lie.

I confess now that I actually *had* slept with my friend in Las Vegas the night of the day I got away. There you go, twenty-three years later, I told the truth about the lie.

I can make lots of excuses about this accusation that ended up being true, about the touch of shame that the ridiculous attempt to undermine my credibility had nevertheless managed to instill:

1. I didn't even want to have sex with him.
2. It just happened. We were sharing the same bed. He only had one.
3. The not knowing how to say 'No' psychosis again.
4. He had a crush on me and I just wanted to go home.
5. He was the only person I knew in Las Vegas and very kindly came and gathered up my fragmented being from the bus station after my escape.

6. He insisted that I go to the police station to report the crime.
7. He took me for the rape kit.
8. He let me stay with him that night.
9. He drove me to the airport the next day.
10. He gave me his bottle of Pert Two-in-One shampoo and conditioner because he liked my hair.
11. He was genuinely upset by what had happened to me and I am sure he was also genuinely upset when I didn't answer his letters.
12. I remember his kindness and that his breath smelled like fermented apples.

"You liked it. You wanted it," proclaimed the defense attorney, fully confident he had caught me with this one pathetic attempt to tarnish my credibility. "We *know* you had sex with another man right after. The same day even! You are a SLUT!!!" He turned towards the jury. Triumphant.

Wow. I still wonder. That's quite the leap. I have no idea how they found that out. About my sleeping with the man who was kind to me after I got away. Whose name I now forget. As the defense was working to undermine my credibility, that's all they could find to come to this grand conclusion of my not only deserving, but inviting, brutalization.

"Yes," I responded, deadpan, without flinching. Speaking directly to the jury. "You are right. You have me all figured out. I am nothing but a slut. I go looking for this kind of stuff. The more violent and despicable the better. It was my lucky night when the defendant stalked me and abducted me. I really enjoyed being held hostage for almost twenty-four hours, tied up, gagged, blindfolded, strangled, tossed in the back of a vehicle, driven who knows where, raped constantly, threatened with a gun, slapped in the face repeatedly while being forced to suck his stinky cock, degraded, tugged around on a string, certain I was dead. Yes, that really turned me on."

There was no exclamation mark at the end of this factious confession. I spoke calmly, drawing out each salacious syllable for ultimate effect. It was as though the defense had given me a gift with his stereotypical attempt to discredit my character and blame the victim. I conjured my Dorothy Parker droll once again and undermined the power of such a ridiculous accusation. I wasn't aware of exactly what I was doing at the time. Call it instinctive justice. Or logic.

December 21st, 1994. Approximately 4 a.m. A Gas Station off an Arizona Highway.

What was he thinking when he sat, legs opened wide, smacking his lips, licking his fingers, and sucking the bones clean as I lay gagged, wrists and ankles tied and naked on the cold metal floor at the back of the camper/van? I smelled the chicken as soon as he climbed into the back after filling the vehicle with gas, envisioned the grease-soaked, floppy cardboard box, and, as he hunched over his Kentucky Fried prey, I was instantly aware that none of it was for me.

He couldn't see me watching him. It was dark, and the vehicle had no windows in the back. My face was in the shadows, but some of the bright light from the parking lot came in through the windshield and passenger window, casting most of him in silhouette, while some wrapped around his ear, inked in the bridge of his nose, illuminated the flare of a nostril and placed a sinister catch-light in one eye.

I could hear voices outside. Cars pulling up. People getting out. Car doors slamming. The gas pumps turning on and off. I heard a mom ask her son what he wanted from the store. A dad called to his kids that they should use the bathroom while they could. Car doors opening again. Slamming shut. Engines starting. Cars driving back off into the darkness. I remember feeling incredibly alone. I wanted so much to join these normal people doing normal things.

I imagined the gas station as a beacon in the night, an island of light on the side of the highway, cars hurling themselves through the dark void to land, momentarily, amidst the warmth of this highway oasis. The freedom to peruse the aisles of a Mac's or a 7-11 became a miracle to me, something I would give anything for. Here they were, these invisible people I knew so well, coming and going, doing things people always do, and there I was, separated by a thin piece of metal that may as well have been a universe, yearning for the mundane that had become the exotic.

I thought about bashing my head against the wall. Routines would be disrupted, and people would wonder what the hell was going on in the suspicious vehicle parked over on the side, definitely up to no good. Bad things always happen in these kinds of vehicles, don't they? Surely they would hear the bangs I would make in the few seconds before he noticed, suspected trouble, and came over to have a look. After all, these kinds of things happen all the time. Every night on the news: reports of murders, mass shootings, abductions, rapes. Don't you remember?

But what good would it do? He was right here. Under the whirl of get gas, buy chips, go to the bathroom, someone might hear my few bangs in the split seconds before he was roused from his brooding feed, before he jumped up and forced me to stop, only to shrug their shoulders and carry on. No one ever suspects that the horrors on the nightly news could be happening right under their noses. Even though they are a part of our lives, they are simultaneously inconceivable. These are events that are only experienced through the separation of screens. People are horrified only to the extent that someone can be horrified by something they have never touched. They eat cherry pie while watching a report on a deadly car crash. Or mow down on a bucket of chicken tenders as a serial killer's crimes are pornographically described. And here he was: guarding me against any attempt at escape, me the rape victim, me the maybe soon-to-be-murdered, devouring chicken in such a way that had been previously unthinkable to me in real life, that I had only seen in horror movies. I had crossed the line of it-will-never-happen-to-me.

Spring 2019. Lantzville, BC.

Last night, I traumatized my eleven-year-old niece with my trauma. As soon as she was born, the first time I held her in my arms, I began to worry about her becoming a young woman, the Lolita-aged girl/woman who is, in a misogynist world that preys upon feminine flesh, made for violation. I began to worry about a baby's destiny as a sexualized surface, objectified even by herself with her desire for too-tight jeans, half-tops, enjoying the lascivious stares from predatory men long before she knows where they so easily lead. I have never had this fear with my nephews. In patriarchy, boys are allowed to be boys for much longer than girls. Boys have always had the good fortune of just being, of just growing up, and are not instantly transported into what I pray will never be my niece's future. My psyche is damaged goods. But there is wisdom in that damage because these concerns so often come true.

Social media started the whole thing; it opened my wound and started hers. Having been her age in the late 70s, I didn't have to negotiate the pressures of cyberbullying that adds to the in-real-life bullying, the imposed obsession with one's online representation, the careful maintenance of a surface, the enforced prioritization of sexuality, the duck lips, the porn star posturing, girls pressured to be women long before their time. She has a good mom who tries to monitor her daughter's online presence. As we sat between dessert and another game of Hide and Seek, 'the cool girl' filled the screen of my niece's first phone in all her premature, self-sexualized glory,

"Show your Auntie Karen this!!" the mother commanded, undoubtedly thinking my feminist self would say something helpful. Far from it. My ire was instant; I told her the whole truth in brutal chunks, and it ended up that my words were more about me than her. I was on the stand again, fiercely telling the truth, but this time my audience was a girl I love.

"I know you admire her. I know everyone thinks she's cool. I know you feel you should be like her. This all must be so confusing for you. But dressing and representing yourself like her is very dangerous. People will think of you as only a surface. Not valuable. Not the substantial and special creature you are. You will be stereotyped as only good for one thing because you 'choose' to represent yourself that way, like a slut. And then boys and men will rape you." There you go. That is what I said to an eleven-year-old girl last night.

She cried. I cried too. I knew I had hurt her in my clumsy attempt to save her. And I didn't stop there. As we cried together, I added:

"If any man ever hurts you, I'll kill him." What a ridiculously Shakespearean thing to say to a creature who is just starting her life. Of course, she will be hurt by men and, of course, she will hurt some too. But that isn't what I meant. Not only hurt. I meant deep hurt. Violation. Rape. Like I have experienced on more than one occasion and that I have imagined will happen to her since her birth.

I have never felt so guilty about any act in my life, and I think this is because even an attempt at apology would only make things worse. How can I possibly explain to someone so young and so far so sheltered where such anger comes from without doing even more damage? Ironically, it ends up that I am most likely the one who inflicted the first dent in her innocence.

December 21ˢᵗ, 1994. Approximately 1 p.m. Somewhere in the Arizona Desert.

He had an airstream trailer that I never saw. It was plunked in the middle of the desert, and he stated proudly that no one would ever find us. He wanted to take me to live with him in the trailer and keep me forever. My stomach plummeted. My strategy for getting him to care about me had become a serpent that was starting to nibble at its own tail.

I imagined the trailer sitting out there, a glaring curved thing blasting its reflection from the deadly desert sun, surrounded by miles and miles of miserable scrub. I imagined

vultures circling overhead like toxic butterflies keeping time
with me as a Betty Crocker cum lap-dancer, writhing in her
delicious delusion of Easy-Bake-Oven bliss as she performed
the age-old fantasy of the virgin/whore.

As this surreal plot of captivity kept thickening, I was living in more and more of a twisted cliché. I was in a Quentin
Tarantino film that had gotten even worse. I was being held hostage in a world that I had only previously experienced cinemat-
ically, and the script I was desperate to escape was closing in.

I had to conceal my devastation. What if he really did take
me to his trailer and lock me in? I would be stuck there in the
suffocating heat. Maybe there would be no windows like in
his customized abduction camper. My enforced home would be
a bunker in the shape of an easy-to-swallow pill. This scene
flashed, fully formed, when he stated,

"I have an airstream trailer in the middle of the desert, just
south of here. I want to take you there and keep you forever. We
can fix it up. It can be your new home."

I stared, stunned, but managed to maintain my poker face.
My mind clicked, a shrewd survival machine that I never knew
I had, programmed to keep fighting for my escape, calculating
how best to manage this recent escalation of events into such
a horrifying new possibility.

Click click click, my mind computed.

Click click click until:

"Gee. That sounds swell, but what would I do all day?" I
queried sweetly like I was actually considering the idea.

"You could clean, cook ... give it a woman's touch ...."

My God. He was a so-called regular guy who wanted the
traditional heterosexual life he had been denied! And I was
destined to be Mrs. Abductee baking chocolate chip cookies in
the middle of a scorching desert. Pot roast. Flowered wallpaper,
a garden, shriveled Forget-Me-Nots hanging from baskets on
either side of the front door. My mind spun with the madness of
it all. This man had abducted his domestic fantasy, and I was
about to become his beaming June Cleaver.

I shifted back into gear.

Click. Click. Click.

"That's not the kind of life I want," I velveted again, maybe even laid my hand lightly on his as though we were planning our future together.

"I wouldn't have any friends. I wouldn't be able to finish my degree. I wouldn't be able to fulfill my plans and dreams." Click. Click. Click.

"I know you care about me like I care about you," I said, nearly gagging on this lie. "Surely you want me to finish university, have friends, a career."

And then, my cold-blooded machine-mind ejected my trump card: I blackmailed him with my own life.

"Listen. If you take me there and keep me forever, I will die." I played the card, my voice as authoritative as a judge delivering a verdict.

"I am young and have the right to live out my dreams. I guarantee you: I won't eat, I won't drink, I will turn my face to the wall. You can kill me, but you can't force me to live. I will die. And then what good will I be to you?"

He looked at me for a long time, processing, considering the logic of this proclamation. I stared back, unflinching. He didn't say it, but I could tell by the way he was looking at me that he wasn't going to take me to the trailer and keep me forever. And I was right. It seemed that he had actually grown to care if I lived or died. For my sake, separate from his.

His name was John Linnihan and he had a broken heart. He told me the story of his life, as much as he seemed capable of articulating it, that is. As with many messed-up men, he was not one of many words. No way to express his emotions. Not even to himself.

I listened to the tale of his life with morbid fascination. The story wasn't as long as I would have liked. It was a most welcome respite from all the raping and a switch from my suffering to his.

I was amazed by the extent of his obsession with normalcy and his exclamations of fierce betrayal at not having been given what he deserved, what society had promised him: a wife, children, a regular life. Of course, I am sure that he had something to do with this injustice, and it wasn't all the women's faults as he claimed. But now, stuffed full of self-pity and betrayal, he prowled the edges of his just deserts, and I was struck by how societal conceptions of normalcy and the potency of their failure can create a monster.

As he told me his story, he moved back and forth between anger and sadness, with the two emotions often overlapping in irresolvable confusion, his face contorting into the volatility of well-wrought self-pity. He understood nothing, living in his constant state of poor me.

It was as though he was trying to get my sympathy so that I would care about him. He was confiding in me because he was starting to trust me. But was he stretching the truth? Was he lying? Was he not? Had he told this hard-done-by-story so many times that it had become true, ingrained through years of repetition whenever he found a comrade in misfortune, and they slumped over their whisky exchanging their why-me-woes?

All I know for certain is that I became his therapist. I became a fusion of the suffering victim and the one with the power to assuage her victimizer's suffering. Cut off from the rest of the world, life and death rubbed up against each other until they were one and the same thing. The world inside the camper/van was like a pressure cooker where everything was reduced to its edges and boiled down into a friction of ready irony. I offered advice, analysis, tried to bring up possibilities he hadn't thought of before (like every good shrink should). But, even though I got into the role so much that there were moments when I felt like I really did care, all of this was merely a ploy to deepen his trust and continue to gain the upper hand. Everything I did was about convincing him to let me go. My empathy was generated by my repulsion.

He had been married. Her name was Rose or something like that. I can't remember if there was a child. I think there was. Rose'd dun 'im wrong. He never got over it. Johnny Cash all over the place with "Please give my love to Rose" descending into "Cocaine Blues" where Billy Lee shot his woman down because "he thought he was her daddy, but she had five more." I don't think John Linnihan had shot his bad bitch down, though. Not yet anyway. I don't think he had killed yet. Or else he probably would have killed me. In the end. Once I had betrayed him too.

He took to life on the road. Decided he had every right to take whatever he wanted from a world that hadn't given him what it had promised.

"What's the point in trying to be good?" he exclaimed, almost blubbering, his voice lethal with resentment. "I tried. It's not worth it. You never get what you want. Better to be a man. Follow your instincts and take what you need, what you're entitled to."

He started to rob houses in wealthy suburbs, travelling back and forth across state lines stealing from the rich and selling his ill-gotten wares in small-town saloons—and abducting and raping young women along the way to fill his loneliness and "right as a man," or so he said, and most likely with a dash of revenge and maybe he would shoot one of us someday after he was done. We would deserve it, after all. They're all liars, he confided. Women: they are built to hurt you. He wouldn't put up with that anymore. What all the bitches had done to him.

"I was so patient. So loving ..." his face trembled like a neglected child's. "I gave everything. And she just took! That's all they ever do. Take! Take! Take!"

What is the psychology of rapists? Susan Brownmiller states that rape (and one could add all forms of sexual harassment) is "the ultimate test of his superior strength, the triumph of his manhood"[6]—the tempering of his fear.

Beverly A. McPhail explains how "rape occurs due to multiple motives rather than a single motivation. The multiple motivations include, but are not limited to, sexual gratification, revenge, recreation, power/control, and attempts to achieve or perform masculinity."[7] I would add, all are connected to power and control: male entitlement.

According to patriarchy, men deserve sexual gratification. They are the ones on top, after all. Hierarchy is built to take what is beneath you. This is what women are traditionally for (and millennia has a long memory): gratifying men. If the men don't get what they are entitled to, if the women won't willingly give it, if the poor fear-based darling is rejected, they will far too often just take it. The deprived men will buy the sex they deserve from prostituted women and children, rape their wives and children, or abduct to get what they deserve.[8]

To add to the pathology of male entitlement, women tempt men. Tease them. It's so painful! So humiliating! Why should men have to control themselves, be accountable for their actions, when women are asking to be abused by merely existing?

Patriarchy and male rights advocate Jordan Peterson talks about how scared the majority of young men are of women and how only a very small percentage get to legitimately 'have' women. Most young men have been so rejected, their hormones are raging; who knows what they might do![9]

Regardless of their insecurity, does this make raping one of those so-called intimidating young women if she is passed out at a party okay? Really? I was scared of men. Especially as a young woman. I am sure such an attitude as Peterson's is one of the reasons why. In male supremacist patriarchy, the stakes are obviously far higher for women.

No excuses. Regardless of hormones. And it's ridiculous, not to mention horrifying, that such a proclamation of male horny-helplessness is still being taken seriously.[10]

Returning to McPhail's argument of the multiple motivations for rape, let's see how many of those motivations were held by John Linnihan. Did he have a need for sexual gratification? Check. Apparently, most men cannot live without that, originating in the teenage plague of the blue balls.

"You have to have sex with me! I am in pain! I have blue balls! You have no idea what this feels like! Please help me!" If you have ever experienced the Lament of the Blue Balls, the sufferers can actually achieve a state of begging. When I stood watching as a young teenager, both the object of the desperation and the voyeur, I thought it all quite odd how a sixteen-year-old young man could transform from an authoritative being with a cocky swagger to a wincing mass bent over in cartoon agony or, sometimes, even going so far as to fall dramatically to his knees.

Are his blue balls really blue? I used to wonder. And I imagined these mysterious orbs clenched like baby's fists in mid-tantrum. I never acquiesced, so I never found out. I never met the Blue Balls.

Revenge? Check. John Linnihan definitely was out for revenge. He'd been betrayed by a whole slew of bad bitches. Check to recreation and entertainment as he drove back and forth between California and Arizona, burgling houses. Check to power and control; he was very set upon keeping me in my place even though I eventually overturned his hierarchy. And, undoubtedly, check to his attempts to perform masculinity as he had been emasculated by all of those heartless wenches. Poor pathological baby.

It can be argued that rape is a product of male disempowerment. This is certainly not meant to excuse disempowered men who rape, but it is meant to point out how every action is always bigger than one individual. Silvia Federici says: "The more the man serves and is bossed around, the more he bosses around."[11] For a man in patriarchy, where he has been trained to be big, servility guarantees emasculation and must be compensated for. When a man is not permitted to be the man he is supposed to be, when he does not have his necessary allotment of promised power from a male supremacist system, he takes it out on us, women, the ones directly beneath him in an attempt to reassert his status by re-masculating himself, most often through our bodies. From a Third World perspective—the patterns that Sayak Valencia describes as the even more brutal

B-side of the First World—men who are deprived of what they have been conditioned to perceive as their right are "damaged machos" and become absolutely enslaved by "the masculinist logic of defiance and the struggle for power."[12]

But what if women were not allowed to be women? (I must qualify here that, because of the contemporary confusion, or deletion, of the difference between sex and gender, I am talking about the 'woman' who is also female, the same way the man I am talking about is also male). Would women/females rape to perform the power they were deprived of the same way as men/males can and do? Would they become all balled up in what Valencia calls a "predatory logic"?[13] Would it be understandable that they exploit, often in a brutalizing physical and psychological fashion, to feel powerful? To Be?

Let's imagine (if we can) women/females being denied being "women." But first, we need to decide what kind of woman we are denying. Are we talking about the historically repressed woman who exists to fulfill a man's needs so that he can maintain his manhood; are we talking about the post-feminist, outwardly empowered woman whose so-called empowerment is fully grounded in her individual sexual freedom, the twenty-first-century woman who states that feminism isn't necessary anymore because she voluntarily devotes the majority of her time to attracting the male gaze to be able to enact her empowerment by fucking whomever she wants, read: fuck like a man (or try to anyway);[14] are we talking about the woman who fights for empowerment and equality both individually and for all women, but is often considered a bitch or too manly, stepping on men's toes, making the poor fragile darlings feel disempowered (again); or are we talking about the transwoman who has experienced gender dysphoria all of her life who is often denied being a woman at all in the patriarchal state of binaries[15] and now, in the current hot-bed of transgender denial of the reality of biological sex, natal born women have been reduced to front holes and non-men to the point where it is uncertain as to what a woman is at all anymore. Are we talking about the woman who is being erased, again?[16] In short, in patriarchy, do we know what it means to be a woman to the same extent as we know what it means to be a man? The answer is: No. As Hélène Cixous expresses in her essay "Sorties" (Exits), in a male supremacist culture, "[e]ither the woman is passive; or she doesn't exist." The idea of the woman is much more malleable than that of the man because, since the onset of a society based in his violence and domination,[17] she has been repressed to the point of non-existence. Cixous: "[w]hat is left of her is unthinkable, unthought."[18] After reading Cixous years ago, I have often thought it is a back-handed blessing to exist outside an oppressive and fear-based culture—the unthought-of have the power to be otherwise.

In a male supremacist culture, whether they know it or not, men are acutely aware of what they are supposed to be: supreme, dominant, and entitled. This is precisely because patriarchy is defined by the construct of 'man.' When a man perceives himself as having failed at or been deprived of achieving the gendered male ideal, patriarchy tells him he has the right to take what has been denied him, be it through all-out rape and/or femicide or sexual harassment or emotional abuse. The more oppressed the man, the more violently he re-asserts his mythical manhood and satisfies his necessary ego.

Anti-feminist, male rights activist Mike Cernovich comes from an oppressed background. In the introduction to his book *Gorilla Mindset*, he relates how he grew up on welfare, had holes in his clothes, was overweight, and was bullied. He tells the story of how he started to seriously body-build, take his life into his own hands, and begin to invest absolutely in himself. 'Self' being the main ingredient.

Don't get me wrong: obviously, believing in yourself is crucial to a fulfilling and productive life. But shouldn't we be thinking more, again, about the bigger picture? Why were his parents so hard-up? Why are bullying and the ideology of exploiting another for personal gain a fundamental part of Western culture?

The symbolically castrated and beaten-down male often results in a severe 'Me' response, a drive to focus 100% on his needs, which re-enforces an ideology of brute domination, and created Cernovich's childhood oppression in the first place. *Gorilla Mindset* is a book that promotes a re-perpetuation rather than any sort of transformation and, tragically, such a mindset goes so far as to result in denial of date rape and the sociological complexities that lead to a young woman wondering if her body and emotions have been exploited, whether the sex she didn't want to have is also a form of violence. Cernovich claims how "[l]ying about being in love to sleep with someone isn't rape .... Getting *played* isn't rape. Regret isn't rape. Thinking, 'I might have been date raped,' means you weren't raped"[19] (Italics mine).

Jordan Peterson's young man can't help it: his hormones are raging, he is not responsible for his actions, and his behaviour is inevitable and somehow okay. Such an extreme, not rigorously thought-through belief system results in the indolent repetition of the binary of the female victim and the male victimizer. And yet, ironically, in the end, both are victims: the male and his apparent need to brutalize, his drive to violence as something he cannot control, and the female in her position as the brutalized, a person who has been trained to not trust her instinct that she is being and was raped and that it is *not* okay that she had been coerced. Sure, maybe she hadn't literally said 'No,' clawed at his face, poked out his eyes, tried to or even succeeded in overpowering his most-often-bigger-body, but can't the male, instead of being excused for his selfishness, insensitive and violent behaviour, be encouraged to feel for another, learn empathy and how to get beyond himself to read another's body language and to not, in Cernovich's solipsistic words, 'play' a woman for his personal gratification? Paradoxically, Cernovich talks about transcending hate. Why is it not painfully obvious that 'playing' a person and lying to them in order to fuck them is a product of hate? It appears that Cernovich has played all his followers too.

Even though male rights activists like Cernovich and Peterson proclaim empowerment by embracing their apparently innate brutality, in the patriarchal system of domination and subordination that they fight to uphold, both male and female, both the exploiter and the exploited, are prisoners of this trap. And we will never evolve as a species until we are busted out. But for those who justify brutality, evolution is the last thing on their minds.

The rapist I had the misfortune of meeting also fell into this trap of the downtrodden and victimized male exercising his right to satisfy himself even if it meant playing the women to such an extent that he has to trick, tie them up, and threaten their lives to do it. Rapists, like all males who justify their entitlement, are products of a culture that subjugates others to maintain itself. When a man does not get what patriarchy has promised him, when he feels his power is being taken away, there is always the possibility that he will become threatened and resentful. Men are damaged by patriarchal hierarchy, too, but certainly not as much as women: the ones they oppress when they are not the man they have been conditioned to think they have to be.

However, does any of this failing within his own system justify him taking out his existential disappointment on others? In patriarchy, all of the 'objects' constructed for his exploitation and use are feminine or feminized: the woman, the helpless child, the prison 'bitch,' the earth.

In *Bad Feminist*, Roxane Gay confides that male anger makes her intensely uncomfortable, but also how, perhaps paradoxically, "male anger, the white heat of it, fascinates [her]."[20] I have seen so much male anger that very quickly accelerated into a blinding rage because the man's power was being threatened, his manhood, his natural position as the dominant one was being undermined, often by the smallest thing like being accused of making a water jug leak, mistakenly knocking down a curtain rod, then not putting it back on straight, like not knowing how to put on a motorcycle helmet and, perhaps worst of all: being right. Despite the panic I experience—especially when the anger is directed at me—the revolutionary-me has the power to detach herself, stand back and watch, and be amazed by the spectacle as the face reddens, neck tendons jut and eyes flare in a deadly combination of confusion and fear.

Yes, of course, women get angry, too, and we have the capacity to hurt. Especially emotionally. But our anger almost never results in rape or 'masculinicide'— the counterpart to femicide that doesn't exist.

Even if men who rape and sexually abuse are disempowered, we have the right to not put up with it anymore. If such acts didn't exploit and traumatize others, they would simply be pathetic. But as it stands, rape is not only pathetic; it's inexcusable.

The Love Letter. December 1994. Vancouver, BC.

A few weeks after my return to Canada, I received a letter. It came from prison. It was from him. Believe it or not, I must have given him my mailing address. I try to think back and retrieve this memory, the moment of my writing my address onto a piece of paper and handing it to him. I have blocked out this part. At this moment in writing, how he got my address is a mystery to me.

I must have done it. Otherwise, how could he have gotten the address to send me a letter? Was it at the Bird Cage? Did I give my real address to a creepy stranger? I must have. I existed in the traditional world of woman-the-dominated-one, so fully that I put myself in danger. I must have known it was wrong. My stomach must have sunk into unheeded anxiety as I wrote and embodied the defense attorney's damning accusations: "She asked for it. She led him on. It was all her fault."

Or, maybe he found it in my bag. Maybe I had addressed an envelope to my ex-husband and had written my return address on it. Yes, from remembering twenty-three years later, I certainly prefer this version. And I think this is what I may have told people. When they asked me how he got my address.

"He must have rummaged through my bag." But did he really? Has my blocking out this very possible shame made me believe my very necessary lie? Even though there was no safety shield of email back then, my having fucked up enough to actually give a strange man my literal address would have pushed me over the edge from empathy and awe to disdain and rebuke. I wonder what you are thinking now, as you read? As I confess all.

If I actually did give it to him, this is an extreme instance of socially conditioned carelessness. My ingrained need to sacrifice myself to please a man had escalated to the point of pathology. I was like a cyborg, hard-wired with patriarchy's ultimate weapon of internalizing misogyny to the point where I risked my own safety. Threatened my own life. All to appease a man. Even a rapist. I can, now, as I dig back into the young woman I once was, into the woman I still am, feel myself doing it. Feeling myself doing so many things that, deep down, I knew were putting myself in danger. And feeling imprisoned as I did what I knew, in my gut, I shouldn't do. But doing it anyway. And hating myself for it. Hating myself for not being strong enough to listen to myself.

Along with being socially conditioned as a woman comes the subsequent self-blame. For years, I have chastised myself for acts that justified the reductionist summations of "she asked for it" or "she had it coming to 'er!" This is another source of my shame, something I have never disclosed until the writing of this memoir that I have realized, along with being a manifesto, is also a testimony, a confession. I am trying to be as brutally honest as possible, even to the point of self-condemnation, to lay myself bare and begin to unearth the contradictions that exist inside me. Contradictions that, when exposed, can rupture the delusions of the surface so that we can dig into their foundation and begin to undermine the power they have over us.

But sometimes, I wonder if I will ever be absolutely free of this debilitating conditioning that infiltrates with its insidious toxins. Whether I am destined to live out my life as a mire of contradictions, a trap that goes so deep it feels impossible to fully plumb. If it is even possible to free myself of the bonds that I am made of.

When a woman has been abused by men, can she ever stop being re-traumatized when a man is angry at her? Will she ever cease craving the return of a man's affection that comes and goes and exists in a perpetual state of being taken away to the point that love and hate become one and the same thing?

All I know for sure is that I can become freer through these disclosures, through this witnessing of my own constructed behavior, through these attempts to write it, document it in art so that the evidence cannot be ignored. Look here! The document. This is true. It has been expressed. It exists.

I know that in being fully honest, I must also acknowledge that whatever I make, whatever the form these liberating disclosures take, it will always be built within the crap that made me. And, I must say, at this moment of writing, there is something beautiful about conjuring the biggest and most merciless shovel I can and finally digging into it. No longer allowing anything to lie buried. Show it all for what it was and is. Shed the shaming and the shame: "Hey, look, I am showing it to you. I have no shame because I am not ashamed." And I know that none of it was ever my fault. I am composed of history, what made me and what hurts me; I must look back and stare it down. It's never going to go away completely, but I can lessen its power over me. And men can do this too. Even if they have never literally assaulted or abused, in a system where one group of people has more power than others, the potential to abuse is always there. And it affects everyone. And must be looked at. Confronted. So that a culture built with power abuse may, eventually, be toppled from within.

⸺•◈•⸺

It was a love letter. Written from the prison cell I had put him in. I can't remember all the details. It is a part of all that was lost during the aftermath when I raged the raw beauty of Rock & Roll in combination with the heady romanticism of sensationalized angst, the roller coaster ride of delicious debauchery where I was comforted by the pain I had been weaned on. The familiar.

I remember the gist of the letter, the outrageous proclamations of love for me. He even forgave me. Said that he knew I didn't mean to do it. Ironically, he told me back my lies that he had converted into truths. He knew I didn't mean to turn him in, he wrote. I'd made a mistake. The one who had betrayed him so that he received a life sentence wasn't really me. He knew the real me, he said.

I also remember that it was pretty cool to have a love letter from the rapist you had put in prison. No one else had one, that was for sure. I know I was a bit proud of it. It added to my new-found celebrity status. I showed it to people, told the tale as a scrumptious morsel that I shared with a combination of trauma and swagger. People were both horrified and impressed by my story, a story that could never have been made up. I even had the sordid evidence in the handwriting of the rapist. Something everyone could touch.

At the same time, though, I was so desperate for acceptance from men that I used the letter as proof that I was desirable. I had the power to trick a man, and he still loved me after a be-trayal that landed him in jail. Even more clearly, this love letter from a prison cell showed how much I lived on the edge. I was a fighter you don't mess with; I had the real-life ammunition to be a rock star. And yet, beyond the bravado, the letter scared me. How could I have done such a thing? What if he ever got out? He would come looking for me. I was happy when we moved so that if he somehow escaped and came up to Canada, he wouldn't be able to find me. As he terrorized me, I had also terrorized myself.

When I was eight, I played house in the forest.

I built a stove and an oven out of stones and scraps of plywood I had found leaning against your shop, Dad. I imagined it had a chimney.

It was old-fashioned. Like the *Little House on the Prairie* TV show, of which I was a big fan. Where the two daughters, Laura and Mary, frolicked about innocently on the wide-open prairie during the day, and their Pa played fiddle for them at night. I don't know what the chairs were made of in my little house in the forest, or the table or any other furniture for that matter. Maybe they all floated in the realm of the imaginary. Child-made chimeras that could be believed in. Or maybe they didn't exist at all, and my house felt inadequate. It could never live up to the idealized relationship between the father and his daughters in my favourite TV show. My game of pretend was fueled by my pangs of anxiety.

But the stove existed. With its oven. And I would pretend to cook and bake. I must have gotten a pot from somewhere. Dirt and plants were my ingredients. I would fry my mud-pies as pancakes or hamburgers. I was a provider, a dutiful housewife at eight. It was a rehearsal. It was already a reality.

I made up a song. I didn't spend any time composing it. It just popped into my head like it had been there all along. The song begged for love. It all had to do with men. I know that. I knew that. But what I didn't know at the time is that it was about you, Dad. You were the first man who rejected me, who made me feel like I didn't have value, who humiliated me in front of your friends when I was so desperately trying to get your approval, who scoffed at my accomplishments, who implanted crippling low self-esteem that, to this day, has the power to assert itself when I need confidence most. I remember longing for what I didn't have. What you took away by not giving it. And I remember the hollow feeling in the pit of my stomach of how it all felt so hopeless. That it would never come true.

I moped about while I sang this desperate song, grasping at what I didn't understand and knew I needed. I knew it was a kind of sickness. But I couldn't stop singing it either, out loud and anguished when I was alone or furtively to myself when I was not. It was a secret I was ashamed of. And it went like this: "Please let me love you. Never go away. And now you love that Suzy Q, and she's always in my dreams with you." I wondered who Suzy Q was. I know now that she is the subject of a song by Dale Hawkins in 1957 that was covered by the Stones, Bobby Vee, Johnny Rivers, Creedence Clearwater Revival, The Everly

Brothers, José Feliciano, Bobby McFerrin... Suzy Q must have been spinning around in my little girl not-good-enough brain. It goes like this: "Oh, Suzie Q Baby, I love you, I like the way you walk, I like the way you talk, Suzie Q. Oh, say that you'll be mine Baby, all the time, Suzie Q Oh, Suzie Q Baby, I love you." Maybe you sang it, too. Or whistled it. Even if I didn't know where she came from or what she represented, I knew she wasn't me. I felt lesser-than when I sang or whispered her name. I dreaded getting to that part. I wanted to deny her, but she was everywhere. And she was better. More deserving. I was jealous of the more-desirable-than-me Suzie Q even though I had no idea who she was. Love and rejection were fully intact at the age of eight; I desired the love of a man who was inaccessible to me. Your Suzie Q was desirable, wanted. I was not. This was the first song I ever wrote.

This hole, this lack, the emotional absence and fear of men that began at the beginning of my life, had festered to the point that I even revelled in the long-distance attention of a rapist. My rapist, the one I got to know, the one who I had succeeded in making fall in love with me. I destroyed his life, and yet he still loved me. And I liked it.

Sometime in 1997. Ventura County, California.

The morning of the trial, I was very unhappy with my choice of shoes. I thought I had carefully packed before this trip; I mean, I'd had three years to get ready, three years to decide what to wear.

But when I pulled the shoes out of my suitcase and placed them onto the bed next to my dress of choice, I was completely bewildered as to why I had chosen bright green shoes, and not any kind of wholesome evergreen or sea foam: peppermint green, the colour of the stray mints that were clotted with lint at the bottom of my grandmother's purse and, sometimes, when she happened to come upon one while rummaging for something else, she would pull it out, peel off the skanky plastic wrapper and offer it to us, an act of grotesque generosity.

Not only were the shoes a shade of blasting green, they were not even leather. Cheap shiny bands crisscrossed over the top of my feet, with others bound around my ankles. The shoes were made of unforgiving plastic that cut into my flesh with the guarantee of blood after any significant walk. When I put them on and glared down at them disapprovingly, I prayed that they would not break the skin before I had ever so gracefully exited the courtroom.

Maybe it was because I was coming to California and I assumed I would need sandals. But something black and classic would have been so much more appropriate, not to mention empowering. Mary Janes, for innocence and good-girl femininity or chunky Lois Lane heels, not too high, solid, with their connection to secretaries and Superman, would have been the best choices. However, because I could never hold onto a job during the post-traumatic stress Rock & Roll mania years, I was probably strapped for cash. These very well could have been the only ones I had—some bargain-basement find that had ended up pushed to the back of the closet until the day I was digging around looking for what to wear to the rape trial.

And what does a woman wear to her rape trial? Does one ever have a rape trial outfit ready, like the since-girlhood-planned wedding day one? Perhaps, considering the fact that one woman every 17 minutes is raped in Canada, one woman every 2 minutes in the US, and one woman every 18 seconds in Mexico—and it's been estimated that a good 50% go unreported—we should.[21]

And when I found them, undoubtedly sweating and flustered from the stress of what-does-one-wear-to-their-rape-trial, I pulled the discards out from the depths of the closet. I must have turned one of them over in my hand, analyzed the sole, the height of the heel, so as not to trip and not to look like a slut, but still look feminine, attractive, and not only special but exceptional, so that I would embody the role of the star witness that I apparently was. I must have tried them on, walked in

front of the mirror, imagined myself striding through the courtroom towards the stand. The sound they would make on the
serious floor. A tap-tap-tap, a delicate ring through the room
as I entered and moved confidently down the aisle: my carefully
chosen version of "Here Comes a Victim."
But as I stared down at them in the hotel room, I despaired
at this choice. What had seemed like such a good idea in the
safety of my home had become a horrifying blunder in a pre-trial
hotel room. Did I actually think they were a strategic choice, emanating grace and savvy, I asked myself, representing a young
woman's desire to be admired and credible? Yes, I must have.
But, instead, here, now, this tawdry footwear risked corroborat-
ing with the defense attorney's inevitable tactic of making me
look as cheap as the flesh-cutting plastic of these merciless shoes.

However, when I stepped up onto the stand and turned to
face the courtroom, the shoes were no longer an issue. They had
done their job, gotten me to my destination, and no blood had
been let. Everyone in the courtroom had turned to look at me
as I made what apparently was some sort of grand entrance.
I wondered why they all looked at me, turned their heads in
unison when I entered. There were a lot of people there. More
of a packed house than I had ever had at a gig. This was a
sold-out show. Everyone must have known I was coming, and I
wondered how my testimony today had been presented during
the previous hearings. Whispers trembled beneath the heavy
hush that pressed down upon the brightly lit room.

I stood and scanned the crowd, intent upon finding that
one face, the one I had come here to confront. I looked over to
where I thought the defense attorney would be sitting with the
defendant, the opposite side to where the DA was. I scanned
across to the DA, the only face I recognized. I think he smiled
at me, but then I caught a glimpse of his concern as my eyes
scanned the crowd, landing briefly on each face that was frozen
in the same expression of expectation, a tautology of stares.
Everything in the courtroom had stopped except my looking.
Back and forth and then again and nothing. The DA stiffened
along with my anxiety. I couldn't see him.

My mouth started to open in a what-the-fuck-is-going-on-here, and just as I was about to say, "Where is John Linnihan?" I felt him. I will never forget those eyes. Those eyes that had been framed by the rear-view mirror, always watching me, monitoring my every move. Panic surged. I was abducted all over again as I felt those eyes on me, eyes that reached out, brutal in their desperation, and wouldn't let me go.

He must have been most interested in seeing me again, after three years, the one who had betrayed him so absolutely. I know he didn't stop looking at me during the length of my testimony. I could feel his eyes burning into me. The same way they had as he kept tabs on me at The Bird Cage Saloon. Making sure that his prey was staying put until he could begin to set his trap. But, as soon as I saw him and I knew John Linnihan was present, I had no intention of looking back.

At the time, after I knew he was there and my disdain had enabled me to shrug off the jolt of tweaked trauma, I couldn't care less about what he was thinking and feeling. What he thought about me. Whether he was twistedly happy to see me or wanted to kill me for putting him in jail. For outwitting him. For winning. Or maybe even for not answering his love letter. What must he say about me in prison to the other rapists and murderers? I had probably made him hate women more than he already did, and he would have done a lot more harm if he had gotten out. Now he had even more ammunition for his statement:

"Those bitches, you can never trust them. They are always out to get you. They use you. They take advantage of you. They lie and cheat. Snakes the lot of 'em. They deserve everything they get. Those bitches."

But now, I would definitely look back. As an artist, with decades between the raw edge of victimization and the onset of trauma, I would be fascinated by the fact that, except for his eyes, he was fully unrecognizable to me. I would probably look for at least a minute, take mental notes to fully absorb the now that was in such sharp contrast with the then, what incarceration can do to a person.

The last time I'd seen him, he had a big gut, jeans that would only stay up with the assistance of the flesh-buried belt, jowls that obliterated any possibility of a jaw line, and a red face that told the tale of his daily consumption of hard liquor. His shaggy brown mustache matched the overall downward heave of his unkempt appearance as it drooped over any sign of a top lip and smelled of fried chicken, cheap bourbon, and body odor. A mustache that violated even more than his cock as I was forced to pretend to like kissing it. Yes, the terrible mustache. As he mashed it into my face, I resorted to inventing an activity for our tongues where we swirled around the tips, a safe distance from the overhang of such traumatizing facial hair. Ironically, this was one of the details he cited in his love letter as proof of our connection—a far lesser of two evils strategy to keep myself from being suffocated by one of my versions of hell.

He had had an alcoholic's swollen nose mutated beyond any sign of its original shape. He had worn a big cowboy hat tilted to conceal the intentions of his gaze, the street thug hoodie of the Wild West with bad-ass boots to match so he could swagger into saloons and command authority by fitting in so absolutely, with his added edge of loathsomeness.

He had been triumphant in achieving that redneck rapist cliché. Or the cliché I had always believed in. But not anymore. His perfected stereotype had been stripped away by his three years in prison. In that one quick glance of recognition I had twenty years ago in the Ventura County courtroom, I saw a man who had aged twenty years in three. Emaciated. Fully grey. Gaunt, sunken cheeks. His pallor and hair were both so blanched out that I couldn't even tell if he had his defiling mustache anymore. He was a broken man. But none of this interested me then.

I was focused on the job I had to do, and I did it better than I ever would have imagined. I was a rock. I was a ramrod. I was a sword. I was a spear. After my testimony, the DA called me a bulldozer. I was showing him the power of who he had messed with. This was the real me. All of my pretending I cared was a way to put you there. Right there, right now. Asshole. What kind of moron are you to think I would care for you at all? You actually believed everything, or even anything, I said? A creature that did what you did to me and to others? Boo-hoo poor you with your weakness and your fear and your hatred. Everything I did was to put you here: in cuffs, going down, having aged so much in such a short period to the point where you were corroding into non-existence. This woman, this bitch that you thought you could take and use and toss away for the momentary assuagement of your own tragedies, was a warrior.

December 1994. Approximately from 7 a.m. to 5 p.m. Somewhere in the Arizona Desert.

"You haven't done anything to me that hasn't been done before. I won't tell anyone. We all make mistakes. Just let me go and I will forgive you. I understand. It's okay. You've had a tough life. I know you didn't mean to hurt me. You have a broken heart. You've been fucked over. But don't take it out on me. It's not my fault some women are assholes. I am different. I care about you. I would never hurt you. I know deep down you want to be a good person. I know you aren't a bad person. I know lots of people who have turned their lives around. I did. I used to get into all kinds of trouble. You can do it too. I can tell you have remorse. You don't mean to do this. You can get help. And you can begin by letting me go. Just let me go so I can have my life back. It's not fair that you are taking my life from me. You need to start thinking of others besides yourself. That's the first step towards a new life. Empathy. Letting me go. We can be friends. We can keep in touch. We can write."

I know I wove all of this web and more during our life in the camper/van. I was relentless as I shrewdly mashed hope into his psyche. But these were nothing but fighting words. And I won.

When he said he was going to let me go, I couldn't believe it, even though I had to pretend that I did. "Oh, really, John? You're the greatest!" And then purred, "I knew I was right. Deep down, you ARE a good person!" It was about five p.m. The sun was still brutal, and the scrubby desert was still ugly. He invited me to sit in the front seat with him. Bucket seats, thankfully, with a big stick shift in the middle so he could hardly reach me. I was already starting to achieve my freedom. But still, I wouldn't believe it until I was out of this vehicle. Back in the world of the public. Out of this prison. If I let myself believe it were really true, I would be devastated if it weren't. Even though things were definitely looking up, I couldn't let my guard down, not even for a second.

We started to drive out of the homely slump of desert. The world with the slight slope leading to the ridge topped by the gangly cactus that I had asked if he could shoot, and he did; the one where I became an actress who could pretend rapes were not rapes; the one where he took the polaroid photograph that I wish I had now so that I could see the expression on my face, the shape of my stance as I acted so cocky while I was crumbling inside; the one where he told me about his broken heart; the one that seemed like a lifetime all balled up into a few hours. The sad vehicle began to squeak its mournful song in time with the erratic bumps of the bedraggled terrain.

As we bumped along rocky desert non-roads, I still didn't dare to believe it. He was taking me to the airstream trailer. He was taking me somewhere worse. He was taking me somewhere to kill me. As the vehicle kept up its whimper in the background, I chattered about my next semester at university, my future plans.

How great it is he was letting me go to continue to study and fulfill my dreams, I gushed. Like he could, too, if he really wanted to turn his life around. My impeccably feminine voice deceived as it tinkled. I kept complimenting him, touching his arm, occasionally reaching over and squeezing his hand with gratitude and affection, deploying my sweet-tart-girly smile, my flawless-eyelash-flutter. He put some music on the radio.

Some southern US twang. I loved it, whatever it was. The sound of the DJ made me actually start to believe. A voice. From outside. The world of not-abducted people. Then we hit a real road. It wasn't a highway, but it was a road. It wasn't a road where other cars were driving by or anything, but I could tell that they had. The scraggly desert I had grown to hate began to shift into the frivolity of a carefree summer day. The windows were open. I stuck out my nose. Sucked in what was becoming a possibility. The suffocation cooled. Fresh. Clean. The dust was no longer made of desperation, but rather something quaint to be remarked upon by a tourist: "Look, it's like the Wild West when stage coaches would race across the plains pulled by frothing horses kicking dust!" And, as I looked out of the side window and watched the brightening world speed past, I think I may have sincerely smiled. But I didn't let him see that smile. It was not the smile I had led him to believe in. It was me: strong, bold, and maybe even getting away with it. But I remained fully on guard. Fear and dread still festered from my groin to my throat. There was only silly prettiness for you. The living was for me. And then, in operatic timing with the dissipation of the afternoon's sizzling haze, I saw cars racing across the horizon on a highway.

PART THREE

2017–2019. Lantzville BC.

I can only write this manuscript from the safety of home, within the innocence of where I grew up.

I am starting to get increasingly attached to ritual in art-making. I breathe Zen-like upon entry: in through my nose and out through my mouth, emitting a toxin-purging sound upon exhalation to slow down my metabolism and connect myself fully to gesture, a sung note, the precise placement of the pieces of a collage, the decisive snap of the trigger on a camera, the revelation of a first sentence.

The writing of this manuscript requires rigidity and repetition. Along with the opening of the mind that surfaces to the music of an opening sentence and orchestrates the energy and direction of text, *Victim* requires the same table in the same pub with the same view in the same town with the same order of drinks. Table 104. The Lantzville Pub. Lantzville, BC, Canada.

It's okay if the waitress varies (thank goodness. That would be tough if I had to arrange my writing sessions based on the staff schedule). But of course, I have my favorites and feel luckiest when they are there. I order a tea first with lots of additional hot water. I have brought more tea bags in my pocket (two to be exact) and add them surreptitiously as I drink tea for the first four hours. Then I switch to white wine and sip on that for another one and a half hours before heading back to my family home. I need to go for a walk on the beach beforehand to clear my head and open my mind with the sharp, salty ocean breezes of the north. I have two walks I can do, depending on the tide.

This is the most beautiful beach in the world to me. Even when it's raining, grey, and cold, it's beautiful. Small islands are to the north, each its own fairyland, and to the northeast the Coastal Mountains, where snow appears as magic on a rare, sunny day after weeks of November rain. All are set within an ocean that changes from turquoise to navy blue to robin's egg blue to slate, depending on whether the air is brisk or balmy or if the sun has reappeared from the brooding grey of winter.

Whatever the season and quality of light, the Lantzville beach, banded by the Salish Sea, is always alive with creeks, sand, stones, sandstone, boulders, cliffs, seaweed, crab grass, crabs, sand dollars, starfish, clams, mussels, seagulls, crows, oyster-catchers, eagles, hawks, robins, seals, sea lions, still quite a few fish including herring, cod, flat fish, rockfish and salmon, whales, dolphins, driftwood, logs, arbutus trees, fir trees, alder trees, cedar trees, salal, moss, grasses, maple trees, daisies, ducks, sandpipers, pine cones, buffleheads, barnacles, white caps, calm water, choppy water, big waves, wind, breeze, the cleanest air in the world and not too many people. Have I missed anyone?

So, yes, after the stimulating walk on my childhood beach, I go up the hill to the pub and cross my fingers that table 104 will be vacant. Usually, it is. Especially in the early afternoon after the lunch rush. My usual time of arrival.

Sometimes, though, I have to take a nearby table and move in closer as people leave. Sometimes it's only a one-table jump; others, it's two or three. I have no choice but to be patient, as I sit, tense, keeping track of the interlopers' meal progress, the level of their drinks, the signs of a tab about to be given so that I am ready to pounce as soon as they finally stand up and gather their things.

I can't begin to write until I am settled at the table in the front left corner, right against the window that looks directly at the sea I just walked with, the good-hearted rumble of conversation behind and to my right, the occasional clatter of a pool ball break to my back left, where I can stare out at the meditative sea when my mind must float to find what I need next, become immersed in the *there*, with the joy and release of living chains of ideas where nothing else exists except channeling the perfect words to paint with.

I try to imagine myself writing this anywhere else but here where I grew up and I can't. The fact that this place is giving me this manuscript makes me fall more and more in love with it. I will always be grateful to the land where I am from. It is what I am made of, and, strangely, this story of my abduction, when I was taken against my will to places where I had no idea where I was, is bringing me back to what I know best.

Striations of high clouds have just arrived. The ocean is blue-gray, and the occasional white cap rises as though a sea lion is breaking through, causing the water to split and crest. Looking up at this ocean between torrents of text is the most nurturing act in the world and spurs another flow from the raw of existence. I know the names of every island. I have been on most of them: Maude, Winchelsea, Texada, Lasqueti, Ballenas, Thormanby.

This is my second to last day here for a few months. If I am actually still able to write this when I am elsewhere, maybe you won't be reading this part of my story. Or, maybe I will leave it in as I trace the evolution of this victim.

I think a big reason why I played the part so well

is because I had been preparing for the role all my life. Thanks to patriarchy and with a special thanks to you, Dad, I was and am incredibly talented at being the accommodating female. Ironically, what had been used against me all of my life saved it.

My father is dead now. He just died a month ago. I have never grieved before and don't know what it is or means when experiencing it oneself. I get tired of thinking about you. I try to shut you out. Think about other things. Like John Linnihan. Like this manuscript. But since the beginning, you have been creeping in, Dad. This manuscript is being written during the incremental process of your death and its aftermath. And I have realized, since your death, you are very much a part of it. A part of *Victim*.

I insisted on going to your cremation. To enact some sort of ritual. In honour of your memory. And our relationship. This is not regularly done in North American culture, even though cremation is now the most common mode of corpse disposal. The usual route from the death bed to the urn is like the expediency of a direct flight with nothing in between. From dead body to inoffensive ashes. A lot of people told me I shouldn't go. They said that seeing your corpse would be the last thing I remember about you. That it would be too upsetting. Giving my father a ritual would be too upsetting.

So, I was the only one there. Besides your corpse, of course, and yet you weren't really there either. You didn't even look like you anymore as you detached further and further from your living self, as life was overtaken by the carcass. I thought of your wrists burning, your hands, your ears, and how it can't be so. How you would have hated that. It was a good thing you were no longer really there. I was painfully aware of the fact that you had wanted to be buried. You had always told us that. You had wanted to continue the burial tradition of your family. But you could never bring yourself to buy your plot, to fulfil your last wish. Why was that? You burned when you wanted to be buried. How you would have hated what you didn't do for yourself.

You were raped too.

You told me this sometime in the late 90s or early 2000s. When my trauma still instantly flared into ire.

I was the only person you ever told. I thought you may have told Mom but, after your death, when for some reason I brought it up, I found out she didn't know about it then and didn't want to know about it now. You must have wanted to tell your wife. But those were different times. People didn't talk about things like rape then. Or emotions. Or trauma. Especially raped men because it was a sign of weakness. And still is.

Only recently, men have started to speak out about being sexually abused or assaulted, most typically as boys. In 2010, it was estimated that 1 in 33 men in the US has experienced an attempted or completed rape in their lifetime, and the statistic increases to 1 in 6 when one factors in sexual abuse as children.[1] Like women, males who have been victims of sexual exploitation are prone to PTSD, depression, drug and alcohol abuse, and problems in intimate relationships. But for men, even in the twenty-first century, because of the necessity to maintain the construct of the supreme male in patriarchy, having been victimized is still something that is often kept hidden. And it certainly wasn't talked about in the 1940s.

According to you, you weren't affected at all by being raped as a boy. Maybe because culture forbade you to be, and the assault was buried like an overgrown splinter that continued to fester unseen. You couldn't tell anyone, so it became as though it didn't happen. And then, for some reason, you felt you had to tell me.

Why then? Finally. You told someone. Half a century later. Me. The daughter who you took your damage out on was the one you trusted to tell. Maybe it was because, besides so many other things, we had this in common. Or maybe you just wanted to win another argument with me and continue undermining my intelligence and integrity to assuage yours. Even though you loved me so.

You told me when we were sitting outside of my friend Lisa's house. It was a sunny spring day. There were pink cherry blossoms, the colour of renewal, birth, and innocence.

Lisa is mentally ill. She is mentally ill because she was sexually abused by three or four different men when she was a child. I can't remember the exact number. I know, when she told me, I was horrified by how many. And one is already far too many.

One was a cop. A friend of the family. He would take her and her twin brother camping. She told me that he would have them sometimes for as long as two weeks. He would force her onto her knees, shove his cock into her little-girl mouth and command her to do something she had no understanding of. Again and again and again. This was her purpose, her duty, her dreaded daily chore that she was obliged to be cheerful about. Maybe this was some kind of payment for the camping trips, she justified. After all, he was one of her mother's friends.

Surely it must be okay if her mother sent her there. She had no knowledge of whether it was right or wrong; she only felt an unnameable shame that kept her silent and compliant. She remained silent until her early twenties. Her throat was closed off. I remember how she used to comment on how some days she couldn't swallow. The liquid would sit in her mouth until, eventually, she would give up and spit it out. She often complained about how dry her throat was. This was the only vestige of memory. All else was lodged where the esophagus almost touches the heart.

At twenty-two, there was an explosion; her trauma had been buried for so long that it came out like Disneyland twitching on methamphetamines. Lisa started composing elaborate quests for Lenny Kravitz. He was coming in a heart-shaped helicopter. He was landing on the roof of the Holiday Inn on Tuesday at 2 p.m., she told me. She had to deliver a letter to him about love. He was expecting her. She strode across the bridge in sweet-tart pink pajamas, disheveled and radiant, the enigmatic palimpsest of the grotesque and the glamour of mania, with a plush purple snake around her neck, gripping a letter written in the hand of a child.

I told you this story. I told you others. I blamed men. My trauma-tweaked aggression was a war mask made of iron.

"You can't blame it all on men," you told me. "It happened to me too." I shook my head, jolted into disorientation, like a boxer who had just taken a straight blow to the temple.

"Yes," I said, after re-orienting myself. "But it was a man who raped you. Just like me. Just like Lisa. Just like pretty much every victim of sexual abuse and assault in the world."

Your long-withheld secret that you pulled out at that moment as ammunition worked against you. Your attempt to shut me down foiled again. I would add now that, no, we can't blame rape on *all* men, but we can blame it on those who maintain a culture of domination and subordination, men who, as Susan Brownmiller wrote, keep women in a state of fear through the threat and act of rape to enforce their superior strength and power[2]; and men who, in Thomas Page McBee's words, don't have the courage to look at the injustice within themselves to join the fight for something better.[3]

Such deep tenderness

I had for you when you would fall down on the trail. You had doubled back to where you had begun, where we all begin, and how we all end up if we live long enough. My father, my first authority figure, the first man who had taken from me what he never gave, had become a helpless child. And I, his protector.

You would always fall onto your same side and exclaim "Ow!" that was also an "Oh!"—a combination of surprise and the remembrance that you actually couldn't walk anymore. You would lie there as if rolled up in an invisible blanket. Heartbreak and confusion lined your brow as you never stopped struggling to get up. Like a fish that had suddenly found itself lying on the beach. Out of its element. Like when you could no longer climb the mountains. The world was no longer your element.

When I would call you in the hospital and then in the care facility, you were always trying to escape.

I would never ask, "How are you?" because that's a ridiculous thing to ask a prisoner.

"Hey, Dad, what are you doing?" A pathetic attempt at humor because I knew you were always trying to escape.

"Trying to check out of this joint" or

"I have to get out of here" or

"I am headed towards that door! I think it's the way out!" or

"Where is your mother? She is coming to pick me up. She's late" or

"I'm on top of a hotel, and I can't get off," or

"I'm in an airport, and I missed my flight."

"Where are *you*?" you asked me, one of the last times we spoke.

"I'm in Mexico, Dad."

"Well, that doesn't help!!!"

And I laughed. How ludicrous, how beautiful: your relentless belief in an impossible escape. Thinking until the end that someone would and could get you out. That you could suddenly stand up, shove the wheelchair aside, and stride through the locked door. Your determination verging on folly. I miss that so much. Your stubbornness. Your unwavering hope. Your never giving up. Your unintentional dark humour. Until you were forced to take the only exit available to you. As your mouth gaped in the shape of your final breath, you had finally escaped.

When I moved to Mexico in 2015, I didn't live there all the time. Pretty much half-and-half because I was always coming back to see you. I looked forward to climbing the stairs. Reaching the top where I knew you would be sitting on the couch waiting for me. Not consciously. Your dementia had splayed your memory into the immediate and the distant. What is it about dementia that muddies everything in between, the bulk of a person's life? Why is it that, as a mind corrodes, we only remember its beginning and become cruelly aware of the dilapidation of its end?

"Hi, Dad!" I would call out, my voice as bright as a birthday cake, just before my head popped up at the top of the landing, unable to wait a couple more seconds to announce my arrival. And you would turn. The TV was instantly turned off. And your voice, as equally bright,

"Karen! You've come to see me! How nice!"

The Great Escape (that almost happened)

Like most things, it runs in the family: your dad had dementia too, and he also ended up in 'a home.' But your dad slumped defeated in his chair; you fought to get out of it.

The last time you walked, you almost made it. You almost made it to the elevator, out the front door, into your dream of outside. Everyone said you couldn't do it. You would fall. It would be dangerous. Just like that time the swallowing specialist said you would never swallow again and you and mom went out for lunch after the appointment. I knew you could. Especially if I helped you.

And you did. You stood up. I held the safety belt from behind and spotted you with the wheelchair. And you walked. I helped you achieve what everyone said was impossible, a miracle that could have been the everyday, our teamwork fired on by the same irreverent blood and your enormous will that they had bashed out of you with their tepid attention until even you finally gave up. Compliance was your only escape in the end.

You are giving me strength now, Dad.

You got 'slappy' (as they put it). So no one wanted to help you. Punished for your determination. Your frustration that no one really *would* help you. So afraid of a lawsuit, their help was cautious. Like watery milk. The physiotherapists, with their training in safe mediocrity, striding around the hospital wearing their know-it-all labels that proclaim "Physio" which equals: 'I know, and you don't,' oblivious to the spirit that we both knew would get you up. Walking. And it did. When they all said you couldn't, so why bother.

We walked down the hall of the hospital ward together. A flagship of 'Fuck You! Told you so!' My head high; yours would have been if you hadn't been stuck in a foreign, bent-over body that had been forced on you by the trap of the chair, but I could feel the smile on your face. The beginning of your great escape.

"Where's the elevator? Let's go!" you kept telling me every four footsteps or so.

"Just up there, Dad. Almost there." I was always lying to you now. About your great escape anyway. It made you feel better. Even if only until your next impatient question-command combo. And that's all that mattered to me. Giving you even a minute of vitality.

We walked past the elevator. I couldn't let you see it, or we would have had to get in. You wouldn't have stopped until we did. And our symbolic triumph would have been flattened by a mash of grappling orderlies, restraining belts whipping around, and a humiliating sedative shot into your arm. I wanted our miracle walk to be tall, clean, pure, with Beethoven's 5th cheering us on.

And everyone clapped. The hallway erupted in applause. Even those physios with their know-it-all badges. Everyone. The nurses. The doctors. The orderlies. All the other patients sitting with their heads nodding despondently in the hallway looked up and clapped. People who didn't know you joined in. Visitors decided 'what the hell everyone else is.' Must be important. Everyone clapped. Didn't that mean anything? You all saw what he could do. There it was. Walking past you. Proof. Still living. "You see," I said before I left. "Everyone saw. Everyone clapped. He can do it. You just need to be patient. You just need to believe he can." But no one helped you again. No one believed in the strength I knew so well. Because I have it too. You gave it to me.

———— ◦◉◦ ————

"Don't worry, Dad," I said on the phone from Mexico. "I'll be there soon, and we'll escape!!"

"Really?" You asked. Increasingly incredulous.

"Yes. Soon. As soon as I can. Two weeks to be exact."

"Two weeks ... that's a long time ... " Your voice trailed off into the most heart-wrenching whisper from a place where a day is another lifetime. I heard you sigh. Resigned. Digging for some belief. And then, I felt you sit up straight with eager acceptance, and at least it was something. My coming fourteen torturous days from now. No one else was doing anything to help you achieve your obsessive dream.

"Ok. See you then," you stated, matter-of-factly, like we were secret agents conspiring to take down a government or little kids playing a game of pretend-we're-truckers speeding down the Interstate: "Copy that. Over and Out."

When I arrived, the sun couldn't have been more brilliant. It shone as triumphant wedges through the windows. The perfect day for our great escape!

You were ready. I had instructed you in Morse Code to have your street shoes. A jacket. Your sunglasses. And your favourite ball cap. You sat at attention in the wheelchair. Everything in a tidy little pile on your lap. If you were a dog, you would have been panting. Eyes bright. Tail wagging round and round and up and down and back and forth. You would have been jumping around if someone had actually taken you for a walk regularly, as I had asked. But, no matter, your spirit was hurling itself up into air-born circles, joyfully chasing your wild and crazy tail.

I put all of your escape supplies in my backpack.

"Okay, Dad," I whispered into your ear. "This is it. The great escape. But we have to keep it all on the QT." You nodded exuberantly.

"Por supuesto," you responded as your pant switched to a grin.

I pushed you out of the cell and towards reception.

"What are you two rascals up to?" the receptionist asked in a sunny voice. "Looks like you're up to no good!"

"Always," I responded, dead-pan. "That's what I'm here for." And I gave you a conspiratorial elbow on your shoulder along with a playful smirk. Your ear-to-ear had not abated.

"Just going for a walk in the sun. Back in an hour or so."

"Remember. Only around the grounds," she did her job.

'Por supuesto," I responded. "Oh, I mean, of course."

"Aren't *you* lucky, Richard, having a daughter to come and visit and have fun!" She beamed. You nodded, invisible pants increasing with every second closer to the epic elevator. You had spotted it. Your eyes became locked onto its longed-for possibility. Your iron-willed hope had started to falter lately. Even a chance was a guarantee.

I signed you out. We got into the elevator. You pushed the button to M. Main. M. Main. The door to the real world. The real world. The one that promised fresh air. A purifying breeze. Trees waving and calling. The birds. The mountains. The ocean. The life that you had lived so absolutely.

"Remember, Dad. We're not out of the woods yet," I played the game, knowing full well that you knew exactly what to do.

M arrives. The door opens. M arrives. The door opens. We move towards the main entrance, the final exit, once only a door, now a portal, as each step, each push, each breath elongates, and we start to dissolve and shimmer as phantoms into the light. Now mere outlines, like the bare bones of a plot: the sharp brim of your ball cap, your body leaning forward, your hands gripped with fierce anticipation around the arms of the chair; my head high, my smile serene, my eyes closed. Fading
Fading
Fading
...
I push you out into the wide-open sun
And let go.

You should have died ten years before you did.

That was your time. I half-joked with a doctor that, if you had been a moose, that is when you would have died. But you were kept alive by a death-avoidant culture. Keep the precious human alive no matter what. Even if she or he only has a broken beating heart. Human life is sacred! So sacred that we torture one another for its sake, force-feed the dying our own fear of death, our own denial of vulnerability.

Ironically, we treat our pets with more mercy when it is their time to go. One cat I knew was taken to a cabin on an island paradise and put down gently in front of a blazing fire, on a sheepskin blanket, with Leonard Cohen playing, by a vet who had made a cabin-call. My cat didn't have as elaborate a passing but, when it was her time, she was rushed to the cat emergency, an IV was put into her leg and she was given cat morphine, placed in an oxygen tent where she lay, legs crossed, with the dignity of the queen she always was. When it was time to put her down, she was transferred from her glamorous oxygen tent to a private room where I was able to be with her until I decided to give the signal to start the flow of the pento-barbital, the anti-seizure medication most commonly used to put our pets to sleep. She was always a big fan of my singing, so I sang to her as she gradually, ever so gracefully, was permitted to leave this world.

Your death was the exact opposite.

'Comfort Care' it's called. In Canada, for a person to pass away through this process, they are given no food or liquids. Only morphine. A diet of euphoria, a semi-conscious dream world dulled of pain or anxiety. And yet, now that I think about it a year later, you may have been enjoying the opioid bliss, and maybe your torture was worse for me than it was for you.

When I raced back from Mexico just in time to see you not being permitted death, too late to fulfill our fantasy of the Great Escape, you were being kept alive until your system eventually shut down. Or your heart stopped. The problem for you was that you had the heart of someone who never gave up. The endurance of a person who had climbed mountains. The physical strength you had built from a lifetime of determination stood against you in the end; your undying spirit kept fighting for beauty despite the darkness you had endured and inflicted.

I can't help but make a comparison between the prolonging of death with the prolonging of trauma through avoidance. In a pain and death-denying culture, suffering can become more about the witness than the victim. At the end of your life, a life that should have ended long before it was permitted, there is a parallel between a lifetime of unacknowledged trauma and the excruciating duration of your passing. Ironically, through these acts of avoiding and drawing out the inevitable, denial is the death of true empathy.

I didn't even have to go into the room. When I marched into the care facility as your fierce ally, I took one look through the door and freaked out.

"Why does my dad look like he is in Auschwitz?

"How long has he been like this?

"How long will you keep him like this?

"Let my Dad die!"

"We are keeping him comfortable." The response. Stepford wives all, subservient to the secular god of 'keep them alive at all costs.'

"Comfortable? How? As he lies here for days drying out? Let my dad die!"

From the gash of your profile in the middle of the room, did you agree? Or was I being presumptuous?

As I stood outside your door looking in, it was as though you were in a theatre one could only wish was all an act. As in a Francis Bacon painting where the artist's subjects writhe livid within linear confines, you were trapped in sharp edges that jilted your fury, your agony hushed, sanitized. The set of your final days was a quiet torture chamber where you were nailed down by morphine to the bed beneath the indifferent buzz of fluorescent lights. A specimen of sanitized hypocrisy on a padded gurney. Your mouth open but deprived of sound. They say this is mercy, to starve and dehydrate someone like a rat that's been tricked by some double-dealing poison. But you were never tricked. You knew this wasn't what you wanted. But they gave it to you anyway. The gift of an agonizing, compassionate death.

"How long has he been like this?

"How long will this go on?

"Why won't you let him go?"

You were lying on your back, your body etched in air. Everything about you was sharp. Except your senses. As I held your hand and felt your still-strong pulse, I leaned over your face. Yes, as you may have expected, tears fell.

"Dad! I came back. It's Karen." Your eyes were facing in my direction, but there was no staring up at me. Pupils pinned. Your bright blue irises clouded over with opioid depths. I kept calling you back:

"Dadadadadaddadaddadadadadaddadadadadadadadadadadd-adadadadadadadadadadadadadadadadadadadadadadadadadada-dadadadad."

I could see the focus of your retina tightening with each call. It took a good thirty seconds. And you were back. Almost.

As back as someone thoroughly tweaked on morphine could be, busy floating towards death. You said my name and your last word to me, your voice like an overgrown forest trail that had momentarily been found,
"Karen. Hi."

They gave you more morphine the next day. Your warrior-princess had given a stern talking to the care home doctor who came to check up on the languishing once a week.
"Are you aware that my dad has been like this for a week?"
"No."
"Can you please make it stop?
"I'll see what I can do."
A compassionate end was put to your comfort care. And I hope, as you finally floated up and away in an opium cloud, the stars were dancing heel to toe.[4]

With another dash of life's ironies that just came to me with this writing: if you had died your natural death, if you hadn't been forced to live through a decade of decline, the steady taking away of all you had lived for, you and I would never have lived forgiveness. And I would never have had the gift of your final smile, at me, solid. A smile that I believe in. That, if I could paint, would be of Francis Bacon's palette: bruised royalty.

"What do you mean 'It happened to you too'?"

I responded. My defenses clogged up like the lump in Lisa's throat.
"I have never told anyone this before. But I am telling you." You turned off the engine. The surrounding spring was

put on hold. I was only aware of our breathing. Mine was sped up; yours was unaffected, like what you were about to tell me was not that big of a deal, even though you had never told it to anyone before.

"It happened when I was a boy."

"How old?" I interrupted, my voice sharp, already imagining the worst, wanting to know the depth of violation right away. As if that would make it better. Knowing what was coming.

"Eleven or twelve," you responded.

"Where were you? What happened?!"

"I was walking home. Down the back lane. It was about 5:30. In the fall. I had rugby practice after school. In the winter. So it was dark." I couldn't breathe. "A man jumped me from behind."

You didn't have to say anymore. You didn't, and I didn't ask. What happened next is still as vivid as though I am watching from an indifferent backyard. Your pants were pale blue; your shirt was probably a soft plaid with matching blue, cream, and maybe a stripe of yellow; your hair was probably slicked back and waved as was the rage in the late 40s; maybe you had just started wearing it that way, still a boy, teetering on the edge of manhood. I can see him ripping down your pale blue pants. Pants the colour of your still-bright eyes. Maybe not even undoing your belt. Maybe the button flew off. All was silent. He forced his way into you. Grunting. Maybe verbally debasing. Maybe flattering your boyhood, your flesh still soft and pliant as a woman's. Maybe even the robins had ceased their good night calls as your reality was ruptured forever. Your face is slammed into the gravel. The sharp little rocks dig into your cheek.

Had you ever imagined such a thing could ever happen? Like I hadn't? Did anyone prepare you for this? Did you know what was happening? Did you know anything besides the immediate shame and the instant awareness that you could not call for help? The rapist probably covered your mouth while he mounted you. But you could have bitten. You could have yelled. Vancouver was a small town then. Surely someone would have come, dashing down the stairs of a back porch with their apron flying. Someone would have heard your call for help. Your voice transitioning from boy to man. But you didn't. You knew it was pointless. You would have been stigmatized. It would have ruined your life.

December 21st, 1994. Around 5 p.m. A Small Arizona Town.

Once Linnihan fell for my act that was far from fiction, he believed me until the end—even to the point of overlap. That is to say, he believed me past the betrayal, after I had announced most emphatically that the jig was up. His conditioned desire for the idealized woman was working against him as my feminine servility was coming in useful and giving me the upper hand. I was subverting submission.

Civilization came into sight in the form of a Burger King. He wanted to buy me some food for the bus.

"A Whopper and a milk," I replied as I was suddenly living my dream and stepping out of the vehicle into a public space. He didn't stop me. He didn't lock me in. He didn't gag me and tie me up again. He didn't even turn to check on me as I followed him in and floated upon the metamorphosis of it all.

In one of those sweeps of divine destiny, a bus full of senior citizens had pulled up just before us. There was a long line-up. He took his spot at the end and I went to the bathroom.

As soon as I walked in, I saw myself in the mirror for the first time in almost twenty-four hours. As I am sure you won't be surprised to read, I was a complete mess: blood-shot eyes that bottomed out into dark circles, pale skin verging on transparent with red blotches from being slapped and, the worst part, a thick rope of red, blue and black marks from his hands squeezing my neck. For the first time during this whole grim episode, I fell apart. All my weight dropped onto the bathroom counter and I started to bawl uncontrollably, spasms of shock, grief and horror shaking my body.

An elderly woman from the bus tour walked in. I can't remember what she said. I know she was as surprised as I had been at the sight of me and, for a moment, I think I saw her face stiffen as though repulsed. But she quickly reinstated the smoothness of her rose-petal skin, and I think she had the same soft scent as my Grandma. She said something like, "Oh, my dear, what happened to you?" Whatever she said made my sobs hurl from an even deeper place, and I think she may have given me a tentative white-person hug with a light finger-tip-tap on the back as my cheek brushed against hers.

I didn't ask her if she could help. I don't remember even considering the option of asking. Thinking back, though, this could have been a possibility. I could have not left the bathroom. I had made contact with another human, a human from the outside world that I had been so desperate to re-join. She could have left and alerted the staff, the bathroom could have been locked, and the police would have been called. I wouldn't have had to continue to risk my life.

I think I was also ashamed. I think I felt like a freak. Dirty. I think, behind her pretty, pink, well-moisturized skin, she may have been judging me, assuming I was to blame for my roughed-up state, like it must have been my fault in some way. I mean, this was the kind of stuff you see on TV, not when you are out on a sightseeing tour. And this may have been the first worm of self-blame entering my system. Coming from the world I was so relieved to be rejoining, the world that would most likely condemn me to the point of me judging myself. The evangelical power of the outside looking in. Claiming their all-knowing ignorance. But maybe she didn't mean any of that at all.

What would he have done if I had confided in her and asked her to get someone to call the police? Surely he would have noticed the kerfuffle. There would have probably been a twinge of panic amongst the seniors and the adolescent Burger King staff. He may have driven away. With my stuff, too.

No, I didn't think of any of this. I just went out to get my bag and get myself to the bus station as quickly as possible.

———◈———

I have discovered that I actually can write this manuscript in another place besides my madly romanticized hometown. I can write it on an airplane; I can write it either in the place where I am most intimately familiar or a place that is virtually nowhere. It's a start.

———◈———

When I got back to the vehicle, there was no way I was getting back in except to reach in and get my bag. He hadn't locked the doors, so I opened the sliding one and grabbed it and started to walk towards the bus station. I took about twenty steps, reconsidered, considered again, and turned back. I had to get the license plate number. Damn. I thought. After hours of this one wish of getting away, all I wanted to do was keep walking and walking and walking as far away as I could get from this place where what we never think will happen to us did. Damn, I thought. I had to go back and do the right thing.

Despite my determination, I was absolutely terrified. Maybe, finally, at this moment, I felt the way one would expect a person to feel when being abducted because I was so close to being free. I was so close to having saved myself. Realized my dream. And, maybe because I was breaking out of the web of lies I had been spinning, the lies that I was so committed to even I had started to believe them. The world of the lies had become the familiar.

I walked back just far enough to be able to read the numbers, dug into my bag, fumbled around, managed to find a pen and a scrap of paper, and wrote down his license plate number. Just as I was stuffing the paper and pen into the pocket of my mustard yellow suede jacket and about to spin around on my magic heels, he came running out, Burger King bag in hand.

"Where are you going? What's going on?"

"I am leaving. I will never get back into your vehicle!!!" I shouted, the edges of the upset from the bathroom serrating the heavy afternoon heat.

"But I have your Whopper and milk ... I'm driving you to the bus station," he managed.

"Are you *kidding* me?! As if I would get back into that vehicle!" I barked and spun around and began to march down the road. There was only the Burger King and the bus station in this barely-a-town, each oddly plunked a long way apart. I had spotted the bus station as we drove in, had panicked when we pulled into the Burger King and my eyes had been forced to release themselves from the Greyhound sign, my so-close-but-still-yet-so-far salvation. With nothing in between, it was about half a mile from the Burger King to the bus. I slung the green duffle bag over my shoulder, might as well have done a Dorothy and tapped the heels of my ruby red shoes together and set off, intoxicated by my re-found freedom.

I don't think he had killed yet. Or else he would have killed me. I had so obviously betrayed him. He should have known that I would keep betraying him and that he was now in danger. If he were a real monster, he would have shot me dead.

I mean, he had a gun. It had a silencer. There was no one around. It was a long way from the Burger King to the bus station with nothing in between except gravel and grass. It was starting to get dark. The only other people were adolescent Burger King employees and, I am assuming, unarmed senior citizen tourists. He could have driven up and popped me right then and there. No one would have known until someone happened to see me lying there as face-down or fetal-positioned roadkill the next day, when the blaring desert sun came out, started to cook me and alert the vultures and flies. He didn't. But if I were him, that's what I would have done. I would have killed me. Thanks, John, for not being me.

Nope, he didn't. I keep saying this because, to this day, I still can't quite believe it. Instead, he drove up alongside me as I stomped, head down, glowering a don't-fuck-with-me face, and he said, as he reached towards me offering the paper bag, "Here's your Whopper and milk...."

Did I give him the finger? I very well may have. That was definitely the mood I was in.

PART FOUR

There was a spider in the basement.

It was one of your pets. I assume it was a 'He' because you said
so. His name was Harry because, yes, he was very hairy.

Harry was a big spider. He often sat on the windowsill above
your workbench and enjoyed the direct sunlight that made it
to the low window in the high afternoon. The high afternoon:
12, 1, 2—the time when kids are supposed to be happy, outside
playing, especially on a sunny day. But I wasn't. The warm
yellow sun added to my inexplicable childhood depression as I
moped about, feeling guilty for being unhappy, not out playing
with the other kids who I could hear through the walls of the
basement, walls that, despite the cloying warmth from the few
hours of direct sunlight, were always cool to the touch.

The sunbeams were filled with dust. "Air dust," I thought,
as it was magically suspended in the yellow light, any movement as imperceptible as the darkness I kept locked beneath the
surface of my youth. When I dared to go downstairs, I liked the
basement to be dark—because that was how it was supposed to
be. But I always seemed to end up there in mid-afternoon when
the cruel sunbeams infiltrated my heavy secret.

I wasn't scared of spiders like little girls were presumed to
be. Maybe it was because you liked them, and I always strove
to get you to like me, to get your approval, to love me. I liked it
when I could see Harry slumbering in a sunbeam or crawling
about amidst your mysterious configurations of paint cans,
tools, jars of nails, occasionally emerging from his workbench
rambles as an inevitable surprise. You always greeted Harry,
pointed him out to me.

"There's Harry! He came out to see us! Hi Harry! What a
nice spider." The big, black spider was like a truce between us
even though I, like you, had never started the war we were in.

I was drawn to going down to the basement and sleuthing
about when you were away at work. Nothing made sense to me
in your workshop, and I was trying to understand. You. There
were drawers of tools, saws hung from the ceiling, and a sticky

oil can on the workbench. I think you had a lathe then where you made the coffee table that was in the living room for the rest of your life. You were very proud of that coffee table. During your final years, when your mind started to go, you would often say, "Did I make that coffee table? Yes, I think I did! Now that's a very good coffee table. Sturdy. *That's* not ever going to fall apart! Not like the crap thrown together nowadays. Mickey Mouse the lot of it! That coffee table is made of Maple. BC Maple," you would point out proudly. "That's very hard wood. Look at the detail I did with the lathe. We have had that coffee table for years! What a fine piece of work, don't you think?"

I went down to the basement as little as possible when you were there. But sometimes I had no choice but to go down when you were home because you had a job for me. A job with no purpose. Not a job at all. A pointless job. Rather, a test. An impossible test. A test I could never pass. A test that would prove I couldn't do it.

When you hollered up at me from below, "Karen! Get down here," I was stabbed by the fear that was part of my flesh. I would robotically detach myself from whatever I was doing and step onto the first step. An ominous chill hit my cheeks. I felt a cold wind channel up the stairwell, heavy with the pulpy scent of apples stored in cardboard boxes on the edges of the shadows. I walked slowly, each step measured by my dread. Like most little kids descending into a dark basement, I believed there was surely a monster under the stairs about to grab my legs and pull me under or jump out as soon as I arrived at the bottom. I believed it would drag me around the corner and do who-knows-what to me amidst the who-knows-what was stored under the stairs. But there were other monsters in the basement as well. Not only the imaginary ones.

I always think that if I tell people this, they will think I dreamt it. Or that I'm making it up. But I know I didn't. It's absurd, I admit. Cruel. Strange. And like most things that are both bizarre and true, I could never have made it up. It is as vivid as any memory from my early childhood, perhaps even more so because it has followed me around all my life.

I entered the workshop. Timid, horrified, dying for love and acceptance. There was a child-height table set up for me. On it was a hacksaw and a piece of plywood. It wasn't a new hacksaw, one that may have a hope of jagging its way through a sheet of wood: it was the old hacksaw, the one that hung from the side of the cupboard. I think it had been your father's, one that would warp and jump back when one attempted to claw through the wood with its dull teeth. And the plywood, to match the impossibility of this task, was not the thin, conventional sheet: it was a thicker one.

On this piece of plywood, you had traced a giraffe, or an elephant, or some other kind of exotic animal. You told me to cut the animal out of the wood with the hacksaw. This was not a game to be shared on a Saturday afternoon: it was an order. And the child-sized table was set up like a counter in a chemistry class, where the teacher had placed all the tools and chemicals in tidy rows for the students to perform their designated experiments. I don't think I even tried. I don't think I even gripped the hacksaw and held it with determination against the wood's rough edge. I remember just standing there, my eyes wide with confusion. And my being undoubtedly pleaded,

"Why? Why would you tell me to do something that even you couldn't do? Why would you intentionally set me up to fail?"

Some readers may think: What of it? Big deal. What are you complaining about? Maybe your dad wanted to share something with you, and it was only a harmless game on a Saturday afternoon. Maybe he thought you could do it. Maybe this impossible invitation was actually an example of his deep love for you, his faith in you, his encouragement. I mean, he could have sexually abused you. Then you would have something to complain about.

And yes. You are right. My dad didn't sexually abuse me. Like the rapes I have lived through as an adult, things could have been so much worse as a child. But, I ask, where did this memory that has been with me all of my life, that has contributed to my low self-esteem and debilitating fear of men, exactly in this form, come from? Even if there were a slight chance that he had good intentions, that this impossible task that even he couldn't have achieved was an act of his deep faith in me, a foundation had been laid. Nothing ever comes from nowhere. And I was not consoled after. "It's okay. I know it is really difficult." I was left. Standing. Eyes wide with shock and defeat. All I remember is feeling not good enough.

But, at the same time, I know my dad tried his best. In his own damaged way. As Dr. Gabor Maté writes: "[as a parent] our best is circumscribed by our own issues and limitations that originated in *our* childhoods—and so on down the generations .... [A] blaming attitude is an entirely useless commodity."[1] There is no blame here but rather, empathy and truth, getting to the bottom of what has damaged me to help me understand. Only with understanding comes wisdom, forgiveness, and transformation. And, in the end, that's exactly what my dad and I achieved.

I just realized that I've been writing a lot of this manuscript on the bus.

The bus that I took to the hospital to visit you. The time you didn't get out again. Even though you were miserable and thinking of nothing but escape, we had fun there together, and I looked forward to going. Other people said you were no longer yourself and how depressing it was visiting you as you wasted away there. Ironically, these were some of the best times between us. When you were no longer the man you used to be.

Your smile when I walked in was luminous. You never smiled at me like that when you were free. I anticipated these smiles as I sat on the bus, madly scribbling, this manifesto pouring out of me. I never thought that these two manuscripts were one: the stories about you and I and the story of my abduction. My writing the story of the abduction and of you losing your life were happening simultaneously. My losing my father, who in so many ways groomed me as a perfect victim. And, as the perfect survivor, too.

I would take you on adventure rides in the special wheel-chair they had you in. It was, in reality, a push-chair as there were no wheels you could use to move yourself around with. That was a definite No-No as you would most certainly have used them. I would get them to unlock the medieval restraining belt they had you in because you kept trying to stand up and make a run for it on your legs that didn't work anymore. They couldn't have you escape or hurt yourself trying. Their mandate was to keep you safe in their trap.

I would push you around the horrifying beige corridors of the hospital, horrifying because nothing could have been more boring, despite the dramatic announcements that blurted out semi-regularly about hemorrhaging or cardiac arrests in other parts of the hospital, parts of the hospital where the walls should have been painted blood red as an act of aesthetic jus-tice but were probably still the same shade of suffocating blah. But you were immersed in the trauma of a painstakingly slow death. So, I took you for rides and pretended it was fun. And, for me, it actually was. You were so sweet as you suffered.

We avoided the cafeteria: absolute dullsville with its Jell-O cubes in tiny plastic cups and Red Rose tea in those leaky metal teapots with the crooked lids. One could look through windows that stared back into the drudgery of the corridor, and then, through other windows, there was a sorry attempt at a green space. We tried out the green space a few times. But I'd quickly give up on it and turn you around. It was a lie. A few trees hemmed in by concrete do not a nurturing experience-in-nature make. Better to be in the honesty of the beyond-boring inside. We knew the truth about nature, having lived its bounty all our lives. Can't fool us.

Our rides would end up in the coffee shop. With lemon loaf and surprisingly good coffee. You ate very little in the hospital. But you ate the lemon loaf like a person who had never lost their appetite. It was a thick slice in a yellow reminiscent of a baby's crib, delightfully moist. And we would chat. Like a father and daughter who had been chatting that way for a lifetime. You were keenly interested in everything I had to say. As though I was the most interesting person, and you were just finding out now.

It was always so hard to leave you there in your prison. You kept saying,

"Anyhow, let's go. Let's go home. Which way to the elevator?"

"Sorry, Dad. You can't come. You can't walk, so you have to stay here."

"I can walk!!!" And you would try and stand. Fall back again. Defeated and horrified.

I would get the nurse to come and lock the restraining belt around you before I left because that was the only condition they had agreed to undo it in the first place. It was certain you would try and get up again. Your unrelenting fight to be free. Your unquenchable fire.

"I'll be back tomorrow, Dad! I promise!"

"Espero que si," you would respond. Your conversational Spanish always came out at the most poignant of moments.

But I couldn't always keep my promise.

I have no idea how you did it.

When I clung there. Years before. On a mountain face. Fingers wedged into flimsy grooves. Feet pressing onto bare ledges. Freshly released pebbles rattling hundreds of meters straight down. My stomach plummeting in sync.

"Dad, I am paralyzed with fear," I managed to squeak. "I can't move." The redundancy emphasized the urgency. You were above me. Had already mounted the top ledge.

I really have no recollection of what happened next: what you said, how you got me to move. How you helped me get to the top. All I know is that whatever you did was kind and patient and strong. I felt the protection of a father descend and hold me. The all-encompassing warmth contained in the sweet illusion of always being kept safe.

When you found out what happened to me in Arizona, it was never spoken of. You must have found out when the police phoned from the States. Because I know I didn't tell you. I never had the chance. It was just not spoken. No one ever asked, "How are you?" Or told me, "If I can do anything for you, if you need anything at all, please let me know. Call anytime." None of these openings were ever given.

I still don't understand why the American police would have called you and Mom. Maybe because they thought someone in my family would support me. I hate to say it, but no one in my family was there for me. Apparently, they couldn't handle it. It was too much for them, the sanctity of individual self-preservation and personal boundaries cutting up the family unit to the extent that we cannot openly care for each other. Beyond ourselves. No wonder so many people are on the street. Homeless, often drug-addicted, typically mentally ill, and alone.

I found out quite a few years later that you couldn't think about the abduction and the rapes, or you would have gone down to California and killed him. At least you couldn't handle it to avoid being incarcerated. Your inability to acknowledge was a result of too much love. I must admit: that does make me feel better. Ours is, after all, a happy ending.

Somehow, I moved. You must have climbed back down, steadied yourself on more substantial toeholds above, and extended your arm towards me, given me your strong, warm hand. I must have let go of the side of the mountain. There would have been a split second of release, a slice of just before falling as I reached up and grabbed your wrist, a perfect shot, and your hand encircled mine. Linked. You pulled me up.

Such levity. Such sweetness when you are released from the possibility of plummeting from a mountain face or any almost certain death, for that matter. As I write, I reach back to that moment of surety when I was finally free from John Linnihan. The moment that his sorry vehicle bounced and squeaked away and down the highway for the last time. My disbelief. He was leaving. Was this really happening? Was it really over? Yes, it was. I was free. I hadn't died. I remember I was floating on relief. But with you, there was no disbelief. In those few minutes clinging to the side of a mountain, I knew you would reach down and save me. Of that, I never had any doubt.

There was still a lot of snow on top. We strode around tall and proud like we owned the place. Admired our triumphant view. For this moment, it was our mountain top. The air was never crisper, made of particles of ice, and each breath was like the purest drink of water. It is all about superlatives when I remember climbing mountains with you.

One of us had brought a tripod. We took a picture. This was long before the days of selfies with their impossibility of nobility as the taker's arm fills up a quarter of the frame. This picture was taken with my old Nikon FE. My first camera. I know that because I printed the picture later. Black and white. The photo still sits on the dresser in my childhood bedroom.

Beep run beep beep run beep run beep beep beep run pose beep beep beep beep beep beep beep: click. We are on the summit of Mt. Cokely. Cliffs and peaks and snow are our backdrop. Your smile, perfect as always when on top of a mountain or in any posed photo for that matter, your imperative to be documented as fully happy, perhaps so that you would believe it too and perhaps because in these moments you truly were. But I know as I look at the photo now that my bright smile is not entirely what it was. A forced ideal. I knew it then, too. I can tell you what was beneath that cutie pie-little-girl cock of the head exuberant I'm with Daddy smile: it was a wish. A wish that it would be what was being photographed. A perfect father and daughter duo for everyone to see and admire. But even though the idealism of my pose fooled everyone, I was always on guard when wishing for your closeness.

We didn't know it at the time (film days, remember? No possibility to check and delete and retake to obliterate even more truth like today), but our deception was captured perfectly in one shot. Perhaps that's because there was so much beauty there too. Latent. Like the promise of alpine flowers beneath the snow.

Decades later, during our last few years together, I can tell you with absolute confidence that all of my smiles with you were completely pure. And yours too. We had earned the photographs that told the truth. As you struggled so much on your last Christmas, long deprived of your ability to walk across the kitchen, not to mention achieve a mountain summit, you said to me:

"I'm glad you don't have to go through this."

"I am sure I will have my own particular brand of suffering at the end of my life."

"Not if I can help it!!"

"But Dad. You'll be dead then."

"That doesn't matter."

December 21st, 1994. Around 4 p.m. The Arizona Desert.

One of my friends said that I had told her John Linnihan had an underwear collection. I had shared this detail when the story was fresh, sharp, unlike this process of recollection from twenty-five years later, where I am tapping back into the sequences and picking up the fragments left behind by memory's mysterious process of selection. Some details have become muted, some deleted but, when reminded of parts that have sunk into my subconscious over time, I can pull them up if I close my eyes and imagine myself as the twenty-eight-year-old woman I was then. What is the story now that it wasn't then? What was it then that it can never be again? What has been lost, and in the process of that losing, like a shedding of skin, what is being found?

For some reason, I forgot all about the underwear collection. Why do we forget some parts of our lives and remember others so clearly? I remember now that he told me about it quite late during our time together. It may have been the last time he raped me. Yes, I think it was. I was pretty numb to it by then to the point that it was almost becoming irrelevant. I said to him once, having achieved a state of glib to override the relentless sexual assaults, "If you're going to keep raping me every few hours, at least have the consideration to change the scenery every now and then." And this was also part of my strategy, another jab at him that he couldn't hurt me, that I was out of his reach, that the rapes were blasé so that he would, instead, chase after my affection, hold me in esteem—and I could continue to get the upper hand.

Yes, I think it was just before he decided to let me go. Or maybe it was after he had said he would. And I had to let him do it again in exchange for my possible freedom. Or maybe, for him, it was one more time until we were together again. My false promise. The one necessary for him to keep his.

After the act, he announced that he had a collection. He had a pair of underwear from every woman he had raped. I remember now that there were quite a few, although I didn't have the interest to count and didn't want to let such an atrocity puncture the shell I had built with any acknowledgement of such sickness, even to myself. I had to continue to block out where I really was. To ward off panic. Indifference maintained my iron.

Like any collector who hauls out their precious repetitions, he was very proud of it even if the onlooker is uninterested. Even if their victim's eyes are glazed and they start to nod agreement in the wrong places, collectors are so obsessed with the importance of their horde that they are oblivious to the darts of disinterest flying their way. He was as enthusiastic about his raped women collection of panties as a teenager showing off his prized stack of Marvel Comics. He fondled and smelled each in turn and then arranged them prettily on the bed for me to admire.

By that point, I didn't find it strange—the object of his collection, I mean. In the last twenty or so hours, even the most unbelievable predicaments had become normal. In his rape memoir, *The History of Violence*, Édouard Luis comments on how quickly we can adapt to danger. For me, it was also a survival strategy, this seamless adaptation to danger as a way of living my lie so that my captor would believe it. I had no choice but for danger to become normal.

Of course, he wanted mine as the next addition to his prized collection. And I pretended to be happy to be a part of it. Even grateful. Besides his Little Girl on the String nickname, he also called me Pretty in Polka-Dots. My contribution were white with small black polka-dots. I don't remember how many other pairs he had. Even though he showed me, I didn't really care to look. And he didn't care to really notice.

December 25th, 1994. The Apprehension of John Linnihan.

They picked him up in Laughlin, Nevada. Christmas Day 1994. He was alone. He was on his way back to Arizona after he had burgled a few houses in California and left a sixty-five-year-old woman for dead.

I have never been to Laughlin. I wonder sometimes about the last place where he was a free man. I know it's small. On the border of Nevada and Arizona. Maybe it's like a mini-Reno. Google tells me that Laughlin is known for gaming, entertainment, and water sports. "A real family place." It's on a river in the desert, a small town with between 7,000 and 8,000 people. Being in Nevada, the main industry is casinos. Besides brothels, that is.

Linnihan's luck ran out in Laughlin, a small Nevada gambling town where nine monstrous hotel-casinos rise like blocky castles out of the mash of houses surrounded by an indifferent desert. They told me how his vehicle was spied in a parking lot and the cops waited for him to return. I don't know where he was returning from, probably a brothel. Linnihan told me once, with the reverence of someone in the presence of a saint:

"There is nothing like a good whore. The good whore with the golden heart." It was as though this statement was advice he would pass on to anyone willing to listen. I guess he had no choice but to seek satisfaction through the services of prostituted women when his luck had momentarily dried up coming across abduction victims.

But what exactly is a good whore, John Linnihan, to you? This Good Whore with the Golden Heart. As a proverb, most of us have heard of her. But what is she really? I never had the opportunity to ask you. You died too soon or too late. However one would like to look at it.

Either way, I didn't get your personal take on this quintessential patriarchal romance with the buying and using of women's bodies. The myth that justifies male entitlement. Not to mention the clichéd excuse that prostitution is the world's oldest profession.[2] And, the same way that the so-called 'profession' of prostitution is the most common justification for women's bodies being bought and used by men, how convenient it is that she also likes it; she loves serving men! She has a saintly golden heart to prove it. Good girls. The good whore with the golden heart—the goddess of a serial rapist.[3]

Early 2000s. A Tale of a Failed Online Stripper.

Even though in times of desperation or cocky banter in my late teens, 20s, and 30s, I sometimes seriously considered selling my body for sex to gain some antithetical form of security, I only acted on this impulse once. Like all women who sell their bodies for male pleasure—even if they claim that it is a chosen occupation or that they gain satisfaction from helping the poor, emotionally repressed men obtain relief—the underlying motive is almost always money. My 'choice' was made out of a form of desperation. I was broke. I was behind on my rent. I couldn't find a job. I saw an ad in the newspaper for online stripping.

I had never stripped before. I have always been a bit shy about my sexuality (undoubtedly due to my ingrained fear of men). That said, the ensuing foray into my exceedingly short-lived career as an online stripper is akin to a farce of the Don Quixote kind where an aging nobleman roams around Spain as an outdated knight errant, ludicrously committed to a single-handed revival of chivalry: both tales are a product of innocence and madness.

I decided to dress in a tuxedo and top hat. I borrowed a cane from an elderly neighbour who happened to have a spare one. I thought I would do some kind of Marlene Dietrich/Mr. Peanuts dance and then, somehow, take my clothes off. I had no idea how this was going to happen. I had no music and I thought I would dance around somehow in a sexy way. And it would all just happen. Ta-Da! I would be a stripper. All would go well. And I would be paid $40 after I carried on in this fashion for an hour as male spectators masturbated. I tried not to think about that part.

I will never forget walking through the industrial park where my great debut was about to take place. Even though I had lived in this East Vancouver neighbourhood for years, I had no idea this area existed. I still don't. I can't remember the direction I took to get there. It was like a spaceship had landed and unfolded into a chunk of frowning warehouses. I don't recall seeing any activity at all around these building blocks. It was incredibly lonely. As lonely as I felt. I was the only one moving through a destitute grid of streets. I walked through still air like a dull knife cutting through claustrophobia. It was a day when the outdoors was actually stuffy.

I know I was depressed. I had that heavy doomed feeling I used to always get in my young womanhood as I trudged along with my top hat, tails, and cane in a big bag that felt like a hobo sack. I had that doomed feeling because I was doomed. Even though I was doing my best to be upbeat and cool. No problem! I can be a surface! I can be but-a-body! A saucy shell! I do it all the time!

As I walked, counting down the numbers on the stringently arranged warehouses towards my sad destiny, I planned my routine in my mind. It would be some kind of "Ya da da da da da da da DA da." Had Mr. Peanut done that across the TV screen in 1970s Planter's Peanuts commercials? Thinking I could actually do what I was told by a culture that sexually objectifies the female body and sells it was a complete farce. So much so that the only thing I could think of doing was try to imitate Mr. Peanut. I had no idea what I was doing. And I am happy now to know that I hadn't been that impeccably trained after all and that I never fully fit in. Or obeyed. In a way, this failure was part of my training ground for dissent. And my feminism. And my vigilance.

So, yes, the whole thing was fabulously ridiculous. The guy who I had talked to on the phone opened the door. He was a stereotypical porno kinda guy. Or maybe that's just how I remember him now: what I thought a stereotypical porno guy must be like. I felt something that I can only describe now as misogyny. A heaviness, an insidious stench.

He had a big gut and a droopy mustache. A shifty, danger-ous gaze, and exuded an aroma of beer and salami. Kind of like John Linnihan now that I think about it and perhaps remember completely incorrectly. Maybe he was an arrogant clean-shaven white guy in a baseball cap. A young entrepreneur getting in on the early days of the Internet and the possibilities of this new market for online porn, strutting around sternum first like a capitalist peacock. Chin up, always on the offensive. All I know is, whatever kind of porno guy he was, he must have thought I could do it. I was a woman, after all. Young. Blond. Slim. Big enough boobs. Broke. Perfect.

Whatever he looked like, he led me to an area with a cam-era and a computer. It was all very casual. Like this was a completely normal job like any other, but, unlike even working at a fast-food restaurant, no training was involved. I was just supposed to know what to do. Like all women would. The area was just that. An area. Nothing more. There were no walls. I had no privacy for performing my impending failure. I think there were some other women around. Appearing fully confi-dent in their conditioning to serve the male gaze. Looks easy enough, I deluded myself and felt painfully inadequate at the same time.

The man would be watching me. It was my first day. He had to make sure I had what it took. That I would represent his company and brand of stripper. He must have had a logo. Undoubtedly some kind of boobs-falling-out-of-a-skimpy-top thing. Or a woman bending over with her butt in the air, looking provocatively around her thigh, fingers poised to spread her labia for the climax that was guaranteed. The logo would certainly not be of a young woman dressed like Mr. Peanut. I put on my tuxedo. My stomach dropped. A bad sign. I became very nervous. I was shy about undressing in front of him. At least I had worn my only set of sexy underwear. At least I had some sexy underwear to wear that, in the end, I wouldn't be able to take off.

He told me I would not be able to see the men. I would be able to watch myself on the monitor, though, and I would be able to talk to them. He told me to say sexy things to turn them on. Of course, you know how to do that, he remarked. Sure, I said, after an awkward pause where I wondered if I actually did. I could feel him begin to doubt me. Sense the possibility of an intruder.

I stood in front of the camera, and I saw myself rise to the surface of the monitor like a ghost coming into focus. The reflection that I knew so well was foreign. Maybe that's good, I thought. I don't really recognize myself. Maybe I can be someone I am not.

As I stood there, stiffly, staring at my frozen body in the monitor, I heard a man's voice coming out of the speakers. Hello there! Who are you? What's your name? Marlene, I blurted, instantly feeling bad about bringing the great Marlene Dietrich into such a sleazy scenario. I hadn't thought of a name. I didn't want to use my own. I don't think anyone did. Something like Randy Ryder, Destiny Rose, Silky Diamond. I had never considered the fact that I should have come up with one of these names of my own, some kind of branding, personality, all balled up in this new life of easy money I was apparently embarking on.

The voice reminded me of the Wizard of Oz. All-encompassing and ominous. Whose wishes I had to fulfill. His demands. And, come to think of it, I was a bit of a Dorothy, certainly out of place in a dank stripper warehouse. Maybe this was illegal, my goody-two-shoes Dorothy side thought. The whole thing did seem kind of secret and was sparsely thrown together so they could pack up and leave pretty quickly if need be. But, unlike Dorothy, the wishes I was commanded to fulfill were not anything as grand as killing a wicked witch. They were sordid and simple. I just had to somehow make this invisible guy cum. How hard could that be?

I took hold of my cane. I turned my back to the camera and attempted to give a sexy look over my shoulder. I think I tried to wiggle my bum a bit. No idea if I succeeded in either of these moves as there was no comment or lascivious noise emitted from the speakers. Only the silence of unknown eyes expecting something of me that I had no idea how to do. I desperately tried to think of something sexy to say and realized that I really didn't know any sexy lines, at least ones that I wouldn't feel like an idiot uttering. I turned around and faced the camera and, yes, you guessed it, I started to do the Ya da da da da da da da Da da across the screen, cane held in both hands, arms swinging it in a jocular motion back and forth, not even doing any fancy cross step, just kind of leaping side to side like a gawky, newborn deer. The invisible guy's mouth must have fallen open in whatever world he was sitting in.

You have to take something off now, said the voice, a bit impatient but also assuming the role of my teacher. Right, I thought. Forgot about that. I had been having quite a bit of fun hopping across the screen, the exercise releasing a few endorphins that were softening the edges of my anxiety. "Ok, right, yah," I may have muttered as I stopped my goofy rollick and might have actually succeeded in leaning on one hand on the cane, a bit askance like Mr. Peanut, undoing the snap of my tuxedo jacket. After that perhaps provocative gesture, everything stopped including me, as I just stood there, trying to be sultry and a bit naughty but completely uncertain of how to do what I was supposed to do next. What do I do with the cane now? Do I drop it with a thwack onto the concrete floor, dramatic, like I am becoming aggressive, about to lunge and jump onto an imaginary bed? Or should I strut over to the wall and knowingly lean it up against it, dramatically turn my head and look his way, lock into his covert gaze, bare my teeth a little, give an under-my-breath growl? To tell you the truth, I just thought of these options now, from within the safety of my writing and perhaps from a more worldly twenty-odd years later perspective. In truth, my mind was blank. I must have stood there staring straight ahead. The gangly fawn, stunned under the pressure of not knowing what to do when it is caught in webcam stripping headlights.

I have no idea what I did with the cane, but I somehow wriggled begrudgingly out of the jacket. It probably fell on the floor with an apathetic plop. And then I continued to stand there, horrified, half-naked in front of some unknown pervert, in my hardly ever worn push-up black lace bra.

"Well," I heard the voice say. "C'mon, get on with it!" I imagined the voice attached to a body. Once again, (I hate to stereotype, but in my mind, rapists and perverts always have a mustache), he had a mustache. Maybe even some stupid ball cap. (Stupid hats, we used to call them). Sitting open-legged, pants undone, cock in hand, in some unkempt room. I stared at this vision. My top lip may have started to curl into a sneer of disgust.

"Are you gonna take it off or what?" I heard him almost yell, cock definitely far from hard, "I am *paying* for you, you know!"

I couldn't do it. I stood there, not knowing what to do for a minute that felt like forever. Then, I bent over and put my jacket back on.

"Hey, what's going on? You're not supposed to put your clothes *back* on."

"I know," I responded. The first time I said anything during these excruciating five or so minutes. "I am sorry, I can't do it. I don't belong here."

"That's okay," he actually said and, despite the annoyance of not getting the relief the website had promised, his voice was almost kind. "You belong in Vaudeville."

I didn't say goodbye. I just walked out. Dead ahead. Unflinching. Not humiliated as one would think I was. I was proud. Ironically, it ended up that I was the one who was relieved. My head was high. I strode. I have no idea what the porno guy's face looked like. I didn't turn my head to care. I was gone so fast I guess he didn't have any time to formulate a response. Some cruel thing to say. Some, "Hey, what's going on here. You haven't finished yet!" I may not have been able to perform even close to well enough to make some stranger achieve orgasm, but I certainly performed an impeccable disappearing act that day.

As I imagine myself striding homewards through that mysterious and gloomy industrial park, I recall a breeze. My heart was light. I think I chuckled a bit at the whole inane scene. I felt giddy. As giddy as I did while I just killed myself laughing as I wrote this. And, to extend my Wizard of Oz metaphor a bit more: it's too bad the breeze didn't surge into a tornado and make this wicked area magically disappear. But maybe there was one because I never knew where it was again.

I can't remember now exactly what I did about the no-money thing. I probably called my parents. After all, I have always had that luxury of being white, middle class, and from the First World—even if I have had to humiliate myself periodically asking them for money. I have never had no choice but to sell my body. I have always had the privilege to tap my heels together, turn, sneer, and flip the bird.

I'm Not Cool

I remember in the 80s and 90s, all of the cool kids were Annie Sprinkle fans. I tried to be. I really did. Like most young people, I wanted to be cool.

Annie Sprinkle has done a lot of amazing things: she was a leading spokesperson in advocating for safe sex in the heterosexual porn industry during the AIDS epidemic in the 1980s; she works for the rights, safety, and health of people in the sex industry; in the 1970s, her pornography was revolutionary in that the female was the sexual aggressor, she prioritized the female orgasm, and addressed the viewer directly, or 'returned the gaze'—a feminist subversion of the 'male gaze,' a term coined by film-critic Laura Mulvey in 1975 as a confrontation of how "women have almost always been looked *at*, while men do the *looking*."[4] In *Public Cervix Announcement*—a performance that is described as infamous (it's interesting that her most important feminist work is her most shocking)—Sprinkle lies on her back, opens her vagina with a speculum, and invites the audience to look at her cervix with a flashlight to celebrate and 'demystify' the female body and break the misogynist fear of female anatomy.[5] By the mid-80s, Sprinkle's outrageous and controversial performances were applauded by art journals, mainstream media, cultural digests, and academics.[6] As one of the first women to inspire the term 'sex-positive feminist,' Sprinkle's celebration of an unruly female body and her irreverence towards the strictures of patriarchal female objectification was fast becoming the focus of the feminist revolution.

The sexual liberation of the female body is one crucial part of many crucial parts of feminism. From a big picture feminist perspective, however, Sprinkle doesn't go far enough. Like all sex-positive feminists (implying that the rest of us are 'sex-negative'), her revolution is about personal sexual liberation, the freedom of an individual where female sexuality is the priority of feminism—but feminism must go far beyond the self if it is going to make any long-term changes in the world. Through her focus on self-discovery within the inherently misogynist institutions of prostitution and pornography, Sprinkle not only reinforces the ideology of the individual—one of the pillars of patriarchy and its capitalist economy of self-interest—she supports providing others (primarily men) the ability to buy sex and fulfill their sexual entitlement in a male-defined system. Feminism exists to dismantle patriarchy; women who uphold the very system that the feminist movement is against are not feminists.[7]

Along with other sex-positive—or fun-feminists—like Carol Leigh, AKA Scarlot the Harlot, who is responsible for viewing prostitution as sex 'work' (and therefore work like all others) was "excited, intrigued and fascinated" by being a prostitute,[8] Sprinkle entered the sex industry out of, using her word, "curiosity." Unlike the majority of people in the sex trade, Sprinkle's decision had nothing to do with a choice coerced by race, poverty, sexual abuse, or sexual orientation. She speaks for the privileged women in the sex industry—the First World few—who claim that they have freely chosen sex work and that they have rarely (if ever) had experiences of violence.[9] For Sprinkle, such statements that everything-is-fine-for-me personally extend into claims that people in the sex industry are responsible for any violence they may experience. She confides: "I think that if I was a victim, in a sense I was just as responsible as the victimizer—that sounds harsh, but whenever that happened I'm sure I created a lot of it. So I take responsibility for any exploitation that occurred."[10] I agree: ironically, such a benign representation of the sex industry *is* harsh, not to mention irresponsible when one thinks beyond the self where "the majority of the world's prostitutes—like the rest of the world's sweatshop labour—live and die poor, never collecting more than a fraction of the profit made off their own bodies."[11] Despite her revolutionary intent, Annie Sprinkle candy-coats the sex industry and erases the exploitation of other women and children. In the end, Sprinkle's subversion serves the status quo.

In the 90s, I went to an Annie Sprinkle performance to find out what all of the edgy buzz was about. I will admit here and now that I was one of the uncomfortable ones. I didn't know why then, but I felt in my gut that something was wrong. And this wasn't because I have any connection to the Christian Right as pro-pornography and prostitution advocates commonly accuse abolitionists like myself of being. How is it possible, or even logical, to connect feminists who work for a world without any exploitation as having anything to do with protecting the Christian Right's ownership of 'their' women's bodies and maintaining the misogynist virgin/whore paradigm? As I watched Sprinkle's performance, I didn't get it. Or maybe, on a deeper level, beneath all of the orgasms and fun, I did.

It was a Friday night and there were a lot of couples there. I remember all of the boyfriends were especially into it, discussing at the end of the show how progressive and revolutionary Sprinkle was, like they were suddenly experts in feminism. The usual excuse of 'prostitution is the world's oldest profession' is touted by Sprinkle, all defenders of the sex industry, and by the men at the performance that night who pulled out this clichéd card as an example of their knowledge of the subject and to justify their sexually entitled status as males. Even though historian Gerda Lerner has disproven this patriarchal myth,[12] does it really make any difference if one of the first ways women could make a living in patriarchy was to sexually service men?

Some of the girlfriends were quiet. I know I was. Others exuded an edgy bravado and flaunted a mysterious wisdom that I didn't believe. These were the girlfriends who aspired towards Cosi Fabian's Holy Whore and 'sacred prostitution' where Fabian celebrates how she is (personally) the most alive when she is with "a client."[13] These were the most popular girlfriends. The most sought after by the men. While those of us who didn't participate in the trendy banter and felt something was terribly wrong risked being not-cool-prudes.[14] We were the wallflowers in this new, titillating world of hip and cool pornography and prostitution. I remember I slunk away that mid-90s night, feeling somehow ashamed because I wasn't into it, as though I was missing out on what I couldn't articulate yet as being connected to my personal experiences of sexual exploitation—and to all the others who will never claim to like it.

Third Wave Feminism of the 1990s prioritized women's sexuality as liberation. Not only did pornography and prostitution become acts of freedom of expression, the agenda to decriminalize or legalize prostitution became premised on the argument that prostitution is a job like all others. Used by the police, the media, health workers, pornographers, strippers, and those directly selling sex, the use of the term 'sex worker' is now the politically correct must.[15] Abolitionists of the sex trade who defy this culturally implicit rule and choose to use the term 'prostituted person' have been reduced to and demonized as "prudes and pearl-clutchers." In truth, we are feminists who take an expansive perspective that includes all forms of violence and power abuse; we are feminists who equate so-called sex work as culturally accepted sexual assault.[16] As one of the first who condoned prostitution and pornography as benign acts of self-liberation (and even goes so far as to call it a 'public service'), Sprinkle romanticizes the extreme minority of women who claim to enjoy selling their bodies for male sexual relief and, in Meghan Murphy's words, "drags everyone else under the bus."[17]

The debate between Sex Workers' Rights Coalitions/Sex Industry Defenders and Abolitionists is fierce and controversial, and yet, ironically, both sides are basically fighting for the same thing: safety, respect, and an improved quality of life for people whose way of making a living—most often barely surviving—is life-threatening. However, Sex Workers' Rights Coalitions claim that treating sex work as regular work will make those in the industry safer. Abolitionists believe that it is impossible for the commodification of bodies to be regular work precisely because it *is* life-threatening. Abolitionists advocate for the Nordic Model, where sex buyers are criminalized, and prostituted people are protected and offered education, counselling, and support while transitioning to safer, more respectful lives and alternative ways of making a living. It should go without saying that, if prostitution and pornography were not life-threatening, if it were work like any other, there would be no need to fight for the safety of those in the trade. As Victor Malarek comments in his book, *The Johns: Sex for Sale and the Men Who Buy It*, "[t]here is no other occupation—other than war—in which so many women are routinely beaten, raped, maimed and killed each and every year."[18] Equating selling bodies for sex as a job like any other, despite good intentions, condones violence and exploitation as an acceptable part of society and, therefore, puts all women and children at risk, even those who haven't and never will be prostituted.

When researching her book, *Slavery Inc: The Untold Story of International Sex-Trafficking*, journalist Lydia Cacho went undercover in sex tourist destinations. Being over thirty at the time, Cacho was viewed as a woman in charge of the human merchandise, rather than being one of the objects for sale. The younger the better is the general preference for men who pay for sex; exploiting young flesh and innocence are more readily fetishized as acts of conquest.[19] While undercover, Cacho was able to strike up conversations with the sex tourists. She reports how the majority were regular guys with wives, with daughters. But for the sex tourists, prostituted people cannot be another person's wife, mother, or child. They are no longer human; they are a commodity. This dehumanization of the prostituted person will persist as long as bodies are being sold. Period. This is not a labour issue. It's an ideology.

Let's face it: no young person, be they male, female, or transgender, thinks: when I grow up, I want to sell my body for sex; there is no consent that isn't tainted by circumstances. Meghan Murphy states the obvious: "She isn't 'consenting' because ... she's really into this guy and really wants to sleep with him. If she did, she wouldn't have to be paid to do it."[20]

Regardless of what Sex Workers Rights Advocates argue, for the extreme majority of prostituted people, it is not a choice. It is poverty, racism, transphobia, sexual abuse, drug addiction, mental or physical disabilities, and lives of violence without opportunity that coerce people into having what may as well be called the choice of no choice. As Detective Inspector Simon Häggström, the head of the Stockholm Police Prostitution Unit, says: "When it comes to people's backgrounds it is clear that certain groups are more at risk of ending up in prostitution than others."[21] The problem with using the term sex worker as an attempt to legitimize prostitution as a job like any other where, usually, one doesn't have to bang or blow their boss multiple times a day, is that it's *not* work like any other. As a sex worker, you *do* have to bang and blow your boss every day. And what kind of trade union recommends its members take a course in hostage negotiating skills, advises that one plans an escape route before any job, recommends parting the pubic hair of a client and looking for crabs, and counsels members to not wear chains or other jewelry they could be strangled with?[22] Does this sound like work like any other? Is it really a good idea to normalize such danger as just another job risk? No, I've never been a prostituted person. No, I've never been a person of colour. No, I've never been a woman of colour. No, I haven't been homeless. No, I've never had gender dysphoria. No, I've never been transgender. No, I don't own any pearls. Yes, if I owned some pearls, I would either sell them to pay rent or buy books. Yes, I've always been white. Yes, I've always been relatively privileged (I say 'relatively' because, in Canada, I've lived below the poverty line all my adult life). Yes, my gender has always corresponded with my sex. Yes, I've always pretty much been straight. Yes, I did try and be with a woman a few times after getting sick of the non-stop parade of asshole men, but I realized I was basically straight, for better or for worse. Yes, I've been raped a lot. Yes, I have a mental illness. Yes, I went to university. Yes, I've read lots of feminist theory. Yes, I live with trauma. Yes, I've always been a radical, intersectional big picture let's always connect as many dots as we can and be self-aware of our positioning in the society we have dedicated our lives to dismantling feminist. Yes, I agree wholeheartedly with Mikki Kendall: "we are part of the society we are trying to change, and we can't absolve ourselves of our role in it" and that "everything that affects women is a feminist issue."[23] Yes, I would add that everything is a feminist issue, especially bodies being sold and exploited, be they literally exchanged for money or raped for free. Because these are the same thing. The rapist just has to go to the bank first to rape the sex worker.

Exit strategies need to be offered to people in the sex trade. Ways out. Because the fact is, if prostituted people had other opportunities than their current anti-opportunity, if there were a safe way out, the majority would take it. When Lydia Cacho interviewed prostituted women and children around the world, she realized that fighting for sex workers' rights was only a Band-aid, and worse, it didn't provide prostituted people with opportunities beyond the sex trade. After years of research, she explained how she "became absolutely convinced that all forms of prostitution are just a way of normalizing gender discrimination and violence against women" and how, even when she was talking to the women who were in more paradoxically 'privileged' positions of sexual exploitation, "[a]fter a while, when you get in depth in an interview, [the women] start telling you how miserable they are, how they are mistreated by clients, how they hate the smell of them, or the way the clients behave. [The women] start giving you little stories that are stories of violence."[24]

This is all about logic and far-reaching, long-term thinking and acting. Utopian? Unrealistic? Impossible? Nope. Just think about the millions of women and children with no choice but to be paid next to nothing (or just fed) to be raped multiple times a day for their 'job' right now. As you read. The reform they deserve is a way to make a living that doesn't include being raped. A way out. Opportunity. If our culture prioritizes giving opportunities to people who don't have any, it can be done. Dystopia doesn't have to be reality.

Meanwhile, in the 1997 collection of essays *Whores and Other Feminists*, Annie Sprinkle shares her "13 Tips to Cure Sex Worker's Burn Out Syndrome." The anthology was written by those who call themselves sex workers, porn writers, producers and performers, dominatrixes, and their allies—all voices that need to be heard. However, these voices should not demonize those who want to engage in a deep critique of hierarchy, which includes patriarchy, race, class, the environment, and speciesism. Everything is connected.

Whores and Other Feminists is one of the texts that contributed to the trendy movement of fun and sex-positive feminism that serves to further violence against women. It is also one of the foundational texts that made the sex worker mandate the rule in academia. Now, one can be an empowered poledancer[25] as long as they ignore the fact that the source of this empowerment is still rooted in attracting male attention and that the male continues to control the woman's body because he is buying it. This is how capitalism works: the consumer has power over the consumed. Kat Banyard sums it up in her book, *Pimp State: Sex, Money and the Future of Equality*: "Perhaps the single most effective strategy [sex workers rights coalitions and pro-sex feminists have] hit upon so far is to pump out the myth contained in the term 'sex work': the myth that it is possible to commodify consent."[26]

Abolitionists—who are also referred to as 'radical' feminists—are apparently so extreme because we are against a culture that is built upon power abuse by the few (typically white men), privilege of the few (white people[27] in general, including myself, but when talking about the exploitation of women and children's bodies: men), and exploitation of whatever those at the top of the hierarchy can literally and symbolically rape (in contexts of Western colonization,[28] white men, but any man in a patriarchal culture who is powerful enough to have the ability to exploit the bodies of women and children). When advocating for sex work as just another day at the office, radical feminists (I prefer to refer to us as logical feminists) are the dangerous fighters against the exploitation of women and children's bodies because a toxic, misogynist culture that condones violence against women and children has resulted in an ethic of exploitation. We are deemed dangerous because our goal is to upend an ideology of take-and-exploit for personal gain in all of its manifestations. Kings and their beneficiaries don't like being toppled from their castles.

Back to Annie Sprinkle's "13 Tips to Cure Sex Worker's Burn Out Syndrome." She encourages the apparently empowered sex worker to "admit you are burned out." She consoles her sex worker sisters whose only challenge in the sex industry is burnout and who are never in danger of assault, rape, or murder (unless it's their fault): "Our egos, as well as our incomes, are invested in feeling good about our work." And yet, because they are so busy being happy sex workers, she expresses how: "we are scared to acknowledge burn out, especially to ourselves." She advises: "Learn to recognize it, and see it as an opportunity to make positive changes in your life." Okay, I think I should follow this advice in my non-sex-worker world too! "Spend time alone, get in touch with your feelings, be aware of what colours you wear and, if the Sex Worker's Burn Out Syndrome is chronic, get the hell out of the business."[29] Yes, an exit strategy! If I ever had no choice but to have my body sold for sex, I, like the majority,[30] would get the hell out. But where? How? Can anyone imagine Sprinkle's 13 Tips being useful except to privileged call girls like Brooke Magnanti, the Ph.D. student who was paid £300 an hour and says she was very lucky to have had no bad experiences?[31] Yes, extremely lucky, I would say. The absurdity of this advice is actually funny if one thinks about it in the context of the sex slaves in Costa Rica who are sold to Canadian and American men for sometimes $3000—the price dependent on how young and 'fresh' the prostituted person is—and who get only get $5 or $10 of it[32]; the drug-addicted and sexually abused women (the majority Indigenous) being prostituted on the dark industrial streets in Vancouver, Canada's Downtown Eastside; the trafficked women from Eastern Europe literally being held hostage in legal German brothels.[33] Can anyone imagine any of these far-beyond burned-out 'sex workers' getting permission to go for a walk in the park wearing their happy colours?

"Hey, Pimp? Oh, Mr. Sex-Trafficker? I feel burned out from being raped most of my life. Can I have a few days off to get in touch with my feelings?" Yes, I know: Sex Workers' advocates work to improve the abuses of women and children, and, yes, this is very important *while* they are in horrifying and abusive situations. *While* being the key word. Must the prioritization of *now* negate the fact that we also need to focus on why and how such atrocities are happening, and, maybe even more importantly, happening at all? Shouldn't a big part of reducing harm (read: torture for many) also be offering a way out?

According to Sprinkle, her time working in the porn industry was the most fun she ever had: "No one forced me into it," she insists, "really... one of the things I especially enjoyed was you got to wear all these really fabulous costumes."[34] Sprinkle, like the Holy Whore Cosi Fabian, mentions payment as an added bonus, as though, unlike the majority who are coerced into having their bodies sold so they can eat, feed drug addictions, or support families, they don't even really need the money. I can't help but wonder, is this even porn at all? If it is, it sounds great. Where do I sign up? But what about young women like Jessie, who was told on set that she wouldn't get paid unless a speculum was inserted into her vagina to stretch it to the point of tearing,[35] an act referred to as gaping where the use of dental and medical equipment to spread open the vagina or anus gives the viewer a look inside while they are jerking off in front of their computers. And what about the fact that, because of the amount of online porn, there is fierce competition between producers as to who can be the 'sickest' and come up with the most brutal acts to attract the viewer into what was estimated in 2020 to be a $97 billion industry.[36] One of the latest most despicable trends in pornography is rose-budding (one can read a description of this horror in the endnotes).[37] Porn king Max Hardcore tells us how it is: "I force girls to drink my piss, fist fuck them, ream their asses and drill their throats until they puke."[38] Need I cite more?

"If you have any small option at all, you leave here,"[39] says a woman in a Nevada brothel. The key word being: option. If more and more women and children are able to exit the sex trade, more and more men will not have the option to commit sex crimes, and, even better, they will have fewer opportunities to justify rape as acts of philanthropy with excuses like: "She's poor. She's needing. He's poor. He's needing. I will feed them. They owe me."[40]

While watching Sprinkle's 'sex-positive' performance in the 90s, I thought: is this all there is to the life of the hip and cool? Of the so-called subversive?[41] Even though I couldn't name it at that time, I felt the celebration of pornography and prostitution all dolled up in a sexual revolution as something that really ends up maintaining the exploitation of women's bodies on a global scale. And supporting the belief system of a serial rapist: "There's nothing like a good whore," John Linnihan told me.

I was never cool. This sex-positive, my-life-is-all-about-my-sexuality attitude made me uncomfortable. And I never really knew 100% why. Until this writing. There is nothing fun about anything that contributes in even the smallest way to another's suffering. There is nothing positive about agreeing with a serial rapist.[42]

Summer, 2019. Lantzville BC.

He was there in my dream. My subconscious has been pretty lively of late. Taunting me. Haunting me. Through this relentless tilling of the soil of my now fifty-three years, I am excavating the archeological sites of my life and becoming accountable for the dead.

'He' is not the he who is John Linnihan, the man who abducted me, raped me countless times, but this is the man who was with me then and after, the he who doted, petted, adored, worshipped my strength, and exoticized my trauma.

I wrote the first draft of this manuscript using a different name for him. I didn't want to violate his privacy. He is a good friend. And an old one, too. So old, in fact, that I hadn't seen him for at least ten years before he died. I feel bad about that.

"Can you hear me, my friend!? I am sorry. I feel very bad about that. You were the only one who was fully there for me when I got home from Arizona and for all the close years after the abduction. The years when I was messed up and the years where I was bone-dry shrewd in using my trauma to my advantage. You were the one who dedicated yourself to saving me, and you were the one I could wring every drop of attention from to feed my gluttonous damage. I will honor you with your real name in this confession: Paul.

I told Paul once that I would kill him. This must sound like such a terrible thing to say. An unspeakable thing to admit. But I am speaking it because it's true. Life is never a straight line. Especially life after trauma. Like flesh growing over a wound that will never fully heal, victims can take from others what has been taken from them. I am confessing all. Even the parts where I, the abused, the victim, became an abuser. Where I used my victimhood, and the sympathy I could reap, the power I was given through what I had suffered, to my advantage. I am fleshing out the victim, digging into all the beauties, the triumphs. And making sure to not leave out the monsters, including my own. I didn't in the end. Kill him that is. But I liked to think I could. Like I had that kind of power. It took away some of the powerlessness that I had lived through when it was all taken from me. The suffocation of no escape.

I remember when I said—"I will kill you"—and Paul looked at me like it had never been said, even though we both knew very well that it had been. And then we denied it as the utterance lay beneath our everyday, an incomprehensible stain, like a bullet wound from a gun neither of us had known existed. Sometimes, after we'd had a few drinks, when his guard was down, and the stain of the utterance seemed to rise out of nowhere, Paul would chain smoke. Nervously. And he would attempt to assuage the jittery wound with sharp draws on cigarettes that feigned a cool edginess. At these times, Paul's eyes were those of a child, terrorized by a need that was always being snatched away. He would search my face for softness that wouldn't come until decades later when it was too late, and he would say, "You said ...."

And it would hang there. Those four words: I will kill you, an ever-present secret that we both knew was far from that simple. Like when I had been torn from my life in the back of Linnihan's camper/van, trapped in the unthinkable, and had crossed the line of 'it-will-never-happen-to-me,' with those four words, I crossed another line: the victim had become the victimizer. This is a secret I have carried for decades, one that I didn't even know I had, a secret that I'm finally growing to understand. And tell.

And when I think back on it now, in the instance of that utterance, what did I mean exactly? I had no intention or even thoughts of creeping up behind him or smothering him as he slept. I meant: I will kill you because I have your heart. I will kill you because I have your sympathy. I will kill you because you will do anything for me. I meant it because I knew that for certain. He had shown me. He had probably mourned more over what I had survived than I had myself. He had tried to save me when maybe I didn't need saving. Or as much as he presumed I did. Or as much as I presumed I didn't. I became an abuser because I had hardened myself to my own pain, and I stood tall and heartless upon the same foundation of the power abuse that had abused me.

When I got back from Arizona, no one could deny my need for attention because now I deserved it. It was no longer something I needed, something I had been denied, with the desperation that undermines its alleviation. I had a grand narrative that erased all my need for love. I remember a guy once told me that he would never love me because I wanted it too much.

"But I got it from you, Paul. Tenfold. Your desire to take care of me, rescue me, made you even more in love with me. And I always made sure to keep it unrequited, so you would do anything for me. I had no intention of giving you what you wanted and giving away the power you had given me. If I did, I would no longer get all of the proverbial cake and eat it too (I have never understood that idiom: why would anyone want all of the cake if they weren't going to eat it?). I devoured everything you gave me. I was starving.

We started the band together. Well, actually, I started the band, and he followed—sorry, Paul, I hate to say it—like an exuberant puppy. Paul was very useful in my fight to survive. Immediately after my return from the escape, songs started to surface as I processed the trauma, the assault on my system. Paul was enamored by every nuance of my newfound awareness of the pathology of violence that I effortlessly put into song. It was so exotic, so sexy, so raw. The unabashed victim. His guitar sang along with me and supported my rage, helped me mourn and embark upon my new life of always healing. And always telling.

"Did I ever really thank you, Paul?" No, he died before I began to realize all that he did for me. And all that my hunger took from him.

In the end, when I finally did acquiesce to his desire, years later, the clumsy sex we had that he wanted to believe in, I used to fill my ravenous need for affection. I had used him. Again. He knew it too, and our friendship ended. I broke the heart of the only one who tried to help me. I understand this now. I am sorry.

⸺⸺⸺◦◖◗◦⸻

Paul and I met at university in the 90s in a feminist literary theory class. He called himself a feminist and would proclaim this in circles of student debates that he always dominated. I found his proclamation of a full comprehension of feminism to be arrogant. I would cringe. In those days, I wasn't sure if it was possible for men to be feminists. What did they know about oppression and assault when they have been conditioned to do just that? And he demonstrated those tendencies with his know-it-all ego and the love of the sound of his own voice as he exercised the very domination he was lecturing against. His air of superiority as he stroked his goatee. His zealousness for the cause made me uncomfortable. I didn't believe him.

Now, long since those formative years of my feminism, I have made the decision to respond, "Yes, of course! C'mon in! Everyone is welcome! We need all the help we can get!"

As Robert Jensen says: "[f]eminist critiques of patriarchy emerged from women's struggle and are key to women's liberation, but a critique of patriarchy is also part of a larger struggle for a just and sustainable world for everyone."[43]

Everyone being the key word. But, I would add, learn to leave patriarchy at the door.[44]

It wasn't only that; even though Paul meant so well, he was an authoritarian feminist and a man to boot. It felt as though he had appropriated the discourse of women's oppression because it was so darn interesting, something to get his newly sharpened critical theory teeth into. And I wonder: can women be authoritarian feminists? Was radical feminist trail-blazer Andrea Dworkin 'authoritarian' in her unapologetic and uncompromising stance? Am I one because I don't want to waste my time conversing—not to mention trying to convert—feminist backlashers, people who jeopardize what is all so blatantly obvious? Do I want to engage with the twenty-first century, reactionary men's rights groups who claim that women are not fighting for equality at all but for female supremacy?[45]

I am not going to say her name. I don't want to give her any more attention than it's criminal she already has. You can look it up if you're one of the lucky people who haven't been polluted by it yet and if you really want to witness such a re-violation of sexual assault survivors. Or, you can just take my word for it.

When I first heard her smug tagline, "Hey everyone, it's been over two minutes and I haven't been raped yet," I was horrified. Such an irresponsible and attention-grasping statement—especially made by a woman—is as unbelievable to me as the existence of date rape drugs. And, because of the fear and misogyny that is still so rampant in our culture, this sensationalized statement has made her a YouTube celebrity with 94.4 subscribers as of October 2020. Sometimes it's really hard to be hopeful.

When I first heard her smug tagline, it was at that moment that I fully felt how deep the backlash is against not only women's rights but also against our safety. To the point that women are attacking us too.

When I first heard her smug tagline, I experienced a crash of re-traumatization. The rage surged. The shock. I stormed around the apartment. I felt nauseous. I was poisoned for at least a week. How could this be possible? And, if things could get even worse, she also proudly proclaims: "I don't care about a lot of women" and then snubs the entire feminist movement with her glib segment of "Feminism LOL." How could a woman hate other women so much that she puts us in even more danger by undermining the urgency of violence wielded against us and mocking the small gains we have made in the First World that will hopefully, someday, cross over the boundaries into the Third? When I first heard her smug tagline, I was heartbroken. She claims to be defending the extreme minority of men falsely accused of rape, and I say again—the extreme minority. Can you hear that? The extreme minority: 2-8% to be as exact as possible when attempting to nail down some solid statistics where it is estimated that between 64% and 96% of sexual assaults are not even reported.[46]

Fine, help out. Defend the few but, in so doing, don't de-legitimize the majority of real rapes, of women and children—including boys—and, again, a very small, but still important, number of grown men. Undermining and making fun of the prevalence of rape in our culture is unforgivable. If her goal is to re-traumatize victims and survivors, she has succeeded, with this one anyway. With this twisted gesture of misogyny and internalized sexism, she re-victimizes survivors and turns against women who fight for justice against the male violence that rapes and murders at least one woman or child every two minutes around the world.[47]

And I ask her: "Have you ever been raped? Are you one of the extremely lucky women in the world who somehow has escaped this trauma? If so, lucky you. And, if you actually haven't lived through what 1 in 3 of us have and will, you have no right to comment on something you have no idea about. And, if you actually have been raped, I just don't get it."

Do I really want to engage with such behaviour? No. But I probably have to. We have to face down the enemy to undermine their power. Expose their pathology, their toxic absurdity.

There has been a lot of talk of matriarchy these days, as well there should be with patriarchal exploitation and feminist backlash continuously revving their engines, poised to smash up all our gains.

This twenty-first century backlash has entrenched itself as the new and improved neo-patriarchy. It goes hand in hand with neoliberalism that has been tightening its grip on the globe since the 1980s and intensifying the rift between the exploited and the exploiter, the smug haves and the suffering have-nots.

And yet, the matriarchy that should be discussed is not the impending devastation of the rights of men, the take on matriarchy that is called upon to justify men's rights activists who call for a 'return' to patriarchy that, believe it or not, some say no longer exists.[48] Societies where women are respected and have a central role in communal decision-making are not an inevitable subjugation of men. If male backlashers think of women's rights as a women-defined system that now oppresses them, it is merely an inverted hierarchy, a male system of exercising power through exploitation of the classes below him; what can be paradoxically viewed as 'male-defined matriarchy' is nothing but patriarchy turned onto its head. Ironically, this victimization of men is caused by the patriarchy, whose apparent loss they are lamenting.[49]

But, look out anyway, men who think women are rising up to crush you (and, according to men's rights activists, already have)! Some of your absolute power will be taken away, so let's get everyone all wound up with: Patriarchy is gone! Matriarchy is returning! Here she comes! She's already here! There is a record 29% women in the 2019 Canadian parliament and 23.5% in the American Congress; there are currently eleven women heads of state worldwide; there's a smattering of 5% of women CEOs in Fortune 500 companies.[50] This is all evidence that women are going to snatch you up off of the side of the road![51] You won't be able to walk alone at night; we will trick you, tie you up, and rape you with our strap-ons. We will get long-overdue revenge on patriarchy by re-inventing slavery and basing it on the subordination of men rather than the subordination of women.[52] And, even worse, we will castrate all men with their own patriarchal myth of labia-dentata, our vaginas merciless, temptresses with teeth.

But, again: am I an authoritarian feminist? Does my determination make me contradict myself? Does the violence I have survived and the trauma that will always be a part of me push me into the realm of the enemy as I raise myself supreme in my lived wisdom and want nothing to do with he who self-righteously exploits, not even to discourse with, not even to share air? Does my complete lack of interest in interacting with ignorance, hatred, and misogyny (all part of the same package) put me into the realm of dictator, pointing and wagging my finger from on-high and cursing all of those who don't think like I do? Am I an authoritarian feminist when I emphatically argue that ideas and attitudes responsible for maintaining the ideology of exploitation are just plain wrong? If I am accused as such, that's fine: I stand upon the reality of a symbolically and literally raped world. I am unapologetic.

Paul's heart was in the right place, but, like so many men, he had been conditioned to dominate. He was completely oblivious to how his behaviour contradicted his words. When writing his book, *The End of Patriarchy: Radical Feminism for Men*, Robert Jensen explained how he was "writing because he thinks he has something useful to say, based on decades of teaching, research, organizing, and critical self-reflection." He tells us how he is not explaining women's experiences to them but using the work of feminist women to make sense of his experience in the sex/gender system in which he lives.[53]

Critical self-reflection is the key to any fight for equality: be aware of and critique our positioning in the monster we are tearing down; be mindful of what has been internalized, even to the point of, as in my case, becoming abusers ourselves through the power that can be gleaned through our victimization.[54]

At the same time, as long as they are willing to participate openly and not be shut down by taking the critique of their propensity to exploit personally, we need to listen to those who have been conditioned to not have a heart, to take, be they men or women. The abusers are also victims of the very system that conditions them to abuse.[55]

Robert Jensen shows his commitment and ability to critically self-reflect when he simultaneously admits and enlightens:

"I was socialized in patriarchy into a toxic masculinity that not only subordinates women but also crippled my own capacity to be fully human."[56]

According to the World Health Organization, Western men are three to four times as likely to kill themselves as women, and men who were deemed to be at high risk of suicide reported that seeking help could be construed as a threat to masculinity, including "a loss of power, control and autonomy."[57]

In her book, *Prostitution and Trafficking in Nevada: Making the Connections*, feminist psychologist and founder of the non-profit research institute *Prostitution Research & Education*, Melissa Farley,[58] points out how Peggy Reeves Sanday makes the connection between the well-being of the land with violence against women. Sanday studied 156 rape-free and rape-prone cultures and found a strong relationship between the way that women are treated and the way the land is treated. The destruction of the ecosystem caused by nuclear tests and military training is paralleled by the quieter destruction of the women in Nevada's legal brothels.[59] With its prerequisites of domination and exploitation, patriarchy is not only bad for women and men; it is bad for our shared ecosystem. In the end, patriarchy victimizes everything.

⟫•⟪

In the dream, Paul and I are roommates again. As is typical of dream logic, the house is a hodgepodge of what seems normal while dreaming but must be deciphered upon waking.

In the setting of this dream, random rooms are taken from my real life. The stairs are the stairs of my hairdresser's house; the living room is a warehouse with stacks of wide shelves, each one the perfect size to slide in my recently deceased father's kayak, or a corpse; the two adjoining bedrooms are very familiar and are splayed like the wings of a butterfly stuck in a collector's book, each held in place with a pin. There are white lace curtains, bedspreads to match, and bedside tables that remind me of the white dresser my dad built for me as a child with the jolly round knobs the diameter of a child's hand. The curtains are fluttering through open windows—which one would think would evoke feelings of innocence and purity—but, with a dreaming gesture of foreshadowing, these open windows contain the disquiet of an abandoned house.

As usual, Paul has done everything: found the apartment, signed the lease, arranged the move, found a roommate while I sat back as a princess, eyes deadened by recent trauma. Despite the dream's sinister essence, the roommate seems harmless enough, but I wonder how the men will fit into such virtuous, frilly bedrooms. Not literally in Paul's case; he was a small man (I often thought that was the reason for his need to over-compensate with his over-determined largesse) and will have no problem tucking into the child's bed, but the new roommate is exceedingly tall, and his feet will undoubtedly stick out over the end.

I am coming home from some now-deleted dream event. I start climbing the stairs. Halfway up, the carpet has been folded back as though to keep a door from opening. The thing is, there is no door.

The carpet is short shag. An off-Pepto-Bismol pink. The yanked back triangle exposes yellowed foam padding, reminiscent of nicotine from the endless chain of cigarettes Paul smoked to feed a wound that pre-existed me and all my self-centred damage. I remember how he told me a story countless times about having been seduced by a thirteen-year-old girl at the age of seven. Over and over again. He told the story with pride and painted the picture as a romp, in a chicken coop no less, and how they would roll around and become covered in feathers in throes of precocious sexuality. But, now that I think about it, despite the bravado, maybe this was a form of sexual abuse, buried by the socially conditioned male's need to shield his vulnerability.

As I dream, I can see right through this non-door and its sorry attempt at keeping the unspeakable behind it. Paul is there. Off to the side, kneeling in the legs akimbo position kids naturally sink into when they sit in a circle for story time. The roommate is there too. He is on his back on one of the beds, having pronged a young Asian sex slave with his long hard penis. Her body is spinning around; his cock is the center bolt of this reprehensible tilt-a-whirl. It is uncertain whether he is spinning her around or she is gymnastically doing it herself: being forced to and happy about it or both or being forced to and having to pretend she is happy about it and, in reality, is whirling round and round in an inescapable cycle of abuse.[60]

What is this? My anger is rising in my dream. A sex-tourist house-call? John Linnihan would be all over this!

There are other girls and young women positioned like nymphs in a Botticelli painting. Like pieces of fruit placed decoratively around the room, one is perched on the windowsill, another with legs dangling from a dresser, others sitting demurely on the floor and on the beds like a flower girl's scattered petals.

There is one girl on whom my dreaming gaze becomes fixated. Well before even pre-pubescence. Naked. The innocence of an androgynous flat chest shared by all children. She sits dutifully on the bed, seemingly oblivious to the horror going on next to her. Like Paul, she is sitting in this child-like way with her feet turned out. The little girl's eyes are glazed to shut out what is far from story time. Her hair shines as glossy down adorned with a barrette of tiny white roses. As you may have already guessed, I freak out.[61]

The dream becomes a kaleidoscope of smashing. I become hysterical and rage to an apex of catatonia and am suffocated by my quashed yells, yells that accelerate into an anvil inside my skull. My brain is ready to forge pieces of metal into new forms.

The pimps gather up their child merchandise. There is no fussing about. They are all just gone. Transported elsewhere with the ping of an invisible wand.

I run down the stairs and out into the street. All is silent. It has been dark for a long time. The light of the street lamps is patchy, like detached universes, each separation a piece of the fragmented morality that makes such a dream possible. Out of the black, from a void between the solipsistic circles of light, a white stretch limo peels out. It, too, is composed of pieces, coming together as they fall apart, the decadent ambivalence of our age that could go either way: forever stalled in a state of further destruction or moving towards a possibility of hope.

Early 2000s. The Marble Arch. Vancouver, Canada.

Besides my triumphantly failed attempt at online stripping, the only other time I have been anywhere near the sex industry in my personal life is the two or so hours I waitressed at a strip bar (or peeler bar as they are quaintly called in my hometown). As with the usual reason women get involved in the selling of female flesh, I applied for this job out of desperation. Well, as desperate as a First World, white, middle-class young woman can get. At that moment, this was the only job I could get. I didn't want to work there. I would have taken any other job if I could have found one. Working in a peeler bar, in any capacity, had never been something I had aspired to in my life. I had never wanted to have anything to do with the degradation and selling of bodies, even if I were only the one serving the drinks.

This anecdote is very short. And I am proud of this fact. I started my shift. I can't remember if we were supposed to dress scantily or not. I have a faint memory of myself not being dressed scantily at all, but rather in the black and white dress code of working in a fine dining restaurant. But that may be my memory having a good laugh at my expense.

I was given a tray. I asked for a float. Now that I think back on the details of this memory, there was something weird about how the drinks were sold. It was a system based on absolutely no trust. Unlike the usual system where a waitress is given a float of mixed bills, a roll of quarters, half a roll of dimes, and half a roll of nickels when she starts and then gives the establishment the sales plus the float at the end of the shift and keeps the extra as her tips, in the peeler bar, we had to pay for the drinks first before taking them to the customer. I hadn't brought any money with me (most likely because I didn't have any, hence the working in the peeler bar). Right away, I was out of place as I had to borrow twenty dollars from the surly bartender to start. Like the demarcation between the male voyeur and the female victim, the taking subject and the taken from object, even the monetary transactions had a severity that imposed separation and mistrust.

I felt dirty. I was anxious. I hated the place. The women on the stage were acting as though they were enjoying themselves, as if they liked being salivated over by predominantly disgusting men who were undoubtedly thinking disgusting thoughts about what they would do to the woman if they could afford to or when they would buy her and take her upstairs to the equally disgusting rooms that smelt of Lysol and had soiled drapes that were never opened and stained bed spreads that were never pulled back.

I didn't believe the women. I didn't buy their act. And even if they really were enjoying their all-out objectification, even if they were using the money to put themselves through law or medical school as is often claimed, I still knew there was something wrong. How could anything so ugly be okay? A woman must really have to work hard to convince herself that there is nothing wrong here, even something good. Or, they would have had to not know any different, always having lived in such emotional squalor. Violence hung in the air. Misogyny was never mentioned, so it was never questioned. I gulped down my repugnance and walked towards the customers.

None of them looked at me as I plonked their pints onto the table; their gazes were glued on the stripper. Hands with cash poked in my direction. I took it and placed their change into palms that seemed to float there for that purpose. Pinky white fleshy cups. Sometimes these palms flipped over and waved me away like an annoying insect or jabbed a contemptuous tip in my direction. Who was I? I wasn't important. I wasn't the one on stage, the adored object of degradation. There weren't many tips, though. I wasn't the one they were saving their money for. I was an invisible entity only meant to respond to their unfriendly grunts of 'Yes' when I asked if they would like another drink.

I carried on my role as an accommodating phantom, moving back and forth from bar to table, magically producing drinks and giving change for an hour or so as the strippers stripped one after the other. Then, there was a break. With the last flash of flesh disappearing behind the curtain, the men's heads were released. Boing. The heads all changed direction, and either looked at each other and commented on the hot titties on that one or how they'd sure like to bang that box, or lit a smoke, or looked at me. I was stripped of my invisibility; they didn't like what they saw; I wasn't the kind of woman women are supposed to be. Especially in a peeler bar. Maybe that was because I was wearing clothes. Or maybe because there wasn't an ounce of promiscuity emanating from my already offensive clothing. But wait (I soon discovered), there was something even worse! Something even more wrong with me! A fat, ruddy, be-jowled man looked at me in horror with betrayal and disgust; his goopy mouth drooped open.

"You've ... you've ... you've got chubby cheeks!!" he gasped, and the others glared at me as the imposter I was. They were right. Good. The jig was up. I was an imposter. A critical, threatening, burgeoning young feminist I-hate-you-all kind of imposter. The snarl I had been repressing since I first entered the peeler bar curled my lip. I reached over and grabbed one of his red, debauched neck flabs and squeezed. I leaned towards his face and glared like a hellion into his piss-in-a-snow-bank bleary blue eyes and hissed,

"So do you!" Then, yes, just like the time when I tried to be an online stripper, I spun around, marched towards the exit, plunked the tray on the bar, tossed a twenty into the vicinity of the surly bartender, and left. No one even noticed enough to call out "Hey wait" or "Where the fuck do you think you're you going?" or maybe I was such a nonentity on this edge of exploitation that I was able to leave as though I had never been there in the first place. I had the choice to liberate myself, oh-so-aware of my privilege that I can always do just that and the fact that I don't have to go to any of those places ever again because I have never been a truly desperate woman trying to feed my kids or get my next meal. I have never had to swallow their filth and pretend I like it. I have always had the option to leave. Unlike my friend Lisa.

Buffalo Head. A Police Station.

Lisa told me a story of one of the times she was arrested. She had been acting out, doing something untoward in the street, behavior that could not be tolerated in civilized society, inexcusably out of bounds. I have no idea what she was doing exactly. I am sure she wasn't robbing anyone or causing any harm. Except to herself. Along with disturbing the agreeable doze of denial. A young woman being terribly unpleasant.

She was sitting in the cop shop, handcuffed, and waiting for them to decide what to do with one such as her—one of the systemically abused; one who has not had the ability and good fortune to psychologically survive; one who no longer fits in with the sane, even though the sane, sick men who abused her and still walk around free are the ones who put her there. This was long before her absolute demise, her sitting in the cop shop on this particular day. I would like to think she would react the same way now—but I know I am mistaken as I have been told that all of her fire has long since been put out.

I don't know if she was being prostituted or not yet. I don't know if she had started to use crack yet to assuage the demons that had been implanted within her as a child. But she was on the street. Alone. On her own with the damage. Well on her way to the world of disposable women.

They made her wait a long time, Lisa told me. A good five hours. Even though there was no one else waiting. Maybe because they had no idea what to do with her or maybe because they were trying to teach her a lesson by neglecting her: let that unruly woman-whacko sit there for a few hours and realize the wrongs she has committed. How it's all her fault. Like her drug-addicted, prostituted sisters on the street who don't even bother reporting rapes and bad johns because the police most often do nothing, ignore her like she doesn't exist. Don't get me wrong. The same way I have been stressing that the majority of men are not rapists, there are good cops. Kind, caring people like the police who were so kind to me. Kind, caring police officers like Detective Inspector Simon Häggström who show prostituted women that they are as entitled to help as anyone else. Kind, caring police officers like Detective Lori Shenher who eventually had a nervous breakdown because she was given no support from the Vancouver Police Department or the city when investigating the decades of unacknowledged disappearances of poor, predominantly Indigenous, drug-addicted, and prostituted women from Vancouver, Canada's Downtown Eastside. However, these kind, caring police officers who strive to revolutionize a sexist, racist system from within, are the minority. And who knows how the ones who were so helpful to me would have behaved if I were Indigenous and drug-addicted and not cisgender. Much differently. I'm 98% sure.

When telling me about her time on the street in Vancouver's DTES, ex-prostituted woman and abolitionist Trisha Baptie explains how: "there was this deep understanding, gradually over time, that we just didn't matter. I know it was the police that didn't take it seriously. I know it was the police who didn't start an investigation. But it was also, they represent society. And society was saying: I don't care. Why do I care?"[62]

"We don't look for junkie hookers" was the attitude of the Vancouver police during the ten years of the ignored slaughter from the late 1980s into the 2000s. "We don't investigate rape," say the Mexican police. "It was their fault anyway." Femicides are suicide, is the typical verdict by the Mexican authorities. Untried. Uninvestigated. Sex trafficked women and children choose lives of often ten rapes a day. Sure, she's got some bruises, johns have been known to say. None of my concern. I'm paying. They had nothing before we came to abuse them, after all. She must have done something to make him mad.[63]

Sitting in a small-town police station that day, Lisa, who had been sexually assaulted by numerous men as a child, was but another global statistic of why-should-I-care about these women who put themselves there. Ignore her. Do her good. All she wants is attention. Yes, no doubt: she has been neglected all of her life. Ignore her, along with all of the toxins that she has been forced to swallow since she was a child. Good idea.

Lisa told me that above her head hung the head of a buffalo. Mounted on a plaque the shape of a coat of arms, glass eyes staring straight ahead. A species that had been virtually wiped out in the North American prairie due to the system of male supremacy that had put her there too. In the police station. Restrained.

The buffalo head is a trophy that marks the glory of conquest, of the subjugation of a species, and Lisa, like all abused women, is an anti-trophy, hidden by her neglect, her value her progressive dissolution. Patriarchy's murderous misogyny would be exposed if the heads of exterminated women were mounted and hung on the walls of public institutions.

Lisa felt the suffering of a fellow species with all of her traumatized being; the preserved and celebrated injustice that was stuck stunned on a lawmaker's wall called out to her. Here was a symbol of victimization that had silenced the oppressed to the point of near extinction. There was only this symbol now: the conqueror's vessel made of the flesh of his victim to be filled with his mythology of conquest. Just like the good whore; just like a rape victim. Just like Lisa.

She started to scream. She started to thrash about. She screamed for the plight of the buffalo. She screamed for the totality of injustice that emanated from this one memorialized example. Her life-long victimization gave her the physical awareness that surpasses reason, the same reason that orchestrated her abuse.

They knew what to do with her now. She was completely out of control. She had transgressed all boundaries of civility. They put her in jail. Overnight. And, the next day, she was returned to the psych ward. Sedated. Disciplined. Silenced. Out of sight.

Cheràn, Mexico. 2011.

There is an Indigenous village in Mexico called Cheràn. It's in Michoacán, one of the most violent states in Mexico. I have been told that half the state is so dangerous no one goes there except the cartels. Ironically, if you are a non-Mexican reader, you may have heard of what happened in Cheràn in 2011. There was an article in Vice and one in the Guardian. The triumph of Cheràn isn't talked about much in Mexico, though. If at all. The Mexican government and the mainstream media covered the event vaguely as 'some sort of internal problem.'[64] The majority of my friends in Mexico City didn't know anything about it until I, an outsider, told them. This coup, in the middle of Mexico, has been kept quiet so that it doesn't happen again. No racist, sexist hierarchy likes it when those at the bottom achieve justice.

Like the majority of Indigenous communities in the world, the people of Cheràn were terribly oppressed. Like all of the Indigenous towns in Mexico, the people of Cheràn were under siege.

In 2011, the women elders decided they would no longer sit by and continue to succumb to the daily extortions as friends and family disappeared, their daughters and granddaughters were raped, and their forests clear cut. Unless. They stopped. And took up arms.

Under the direction of the women, the community banded together and armed itself with pieces of wood covered with nails, rocks, sticks, machetes—whatever they could get their hands on. They donned balaclavas and kicked the cartels, the police, and the politicians out of town. Once the criminals had left, the people claimed all of their weapons for themselves. To keep their oppressors from coming back, they appropriated the very weapons that one would think would have been used against the uprising, but somehow the ferocity of the people united was a success in this enclave of triumph over injustice.

"Michoacán is one of Mexico's most violent regions," the Guardian reported in 2018, "but local officials say that not a single kidnapping or extortion attempt has been reported since the uprising. The people have also had success in protecting the environment and reforesting the region."[65] The citizens take turns sitting, on the periphery of their town and forest, armed, in balaclavas, keeping watch.

Bethel Pañeda is a young artist from the community of Cheràn. During the time of the uprising, she was a teenager. Pañeda is part of the new generation of a liberated Cheràn. One of her paintings, *Nanuka*, is of a young woman training to become a shaman. *Nanuka* represents Pañeda's generation of an exultant Cheràn and, yet, she carries with her the wisdom of centuries. And the wisdom of eight years ago.

Like the community encircling and protecting their town, *Nanuka* is fully contained, coherent, and unified by circles that maintain a new-found liberty, and yet she looks beyond these symbols. Like the town of Cheràn, she is keeping watch. She is always prepared to fight again, to resist. Her expression is fierce and defiant, irreverent towards what lies beyond her emancipated community. What threatens return. *Nanuka* is vigilance. She is the victim. She is the survivor. Far from defeated. Irreverent. Fierce.

The painting attests to the fact that never forgetting that which has been overcome is a key component to any revolution, to any survival. *Nanuka* shows me how I must not attempt to erase the scars of my victimization: I must have the strength to honour them. So that they won't happen again.

One of the main effects of my personal victimization has been an acute awareness of injustice, especially regarding sexual assault. Whenever I watch or see or read or hear about rape, prostitution, or pornography, I feel like I am being raped all over again. But, the interesting thing is, it's not personal anymore; it's not just about me. And, it may sound strange: it's not all bad. It is as though, through an experience that is perceived as—and is—horrifying, there is more to it than that. Instead of being weak, passive, and defeated, my experience as a victim kicked me in the ass. It made me start doing something about it.

Don't get me wrong: I certainly wouldn't wish my particular form of initiation into the realm of righteous anger on anyone else, but this is a good anger, a healthy anger, an anger that motivates. I mean, shouldn't we all be angry about the sexual exploitation of women and children? Shouldn't we all be angry when more than half of the people on earth are under siege? Shouldn't we all be angry that these realities even exist in the first place?

> Blow Bang #4 is a video tape made and sold in America. It is a videotape that American men watch and masturbate to. It consists of eight different scenes in which a woman kneels in the middle of a group of three to eight men and performs oral sex on them. At the end of each scene, each of the men ejaculates onto the woman's face or into her mouth. The copy on the video box describes it this way: 'Dirty bitches surrounded by hard throbbing cocks—and they like it.[66]

What follows is a story about a child sex slave in Cambodia that was told to Lydia Cacho during her research on international sex slavery:

The girl was known only as 'the doll.' She has long since been murdered, so no one will ever know her name. She was simply 'the doll,' an empty vessel for the fulfilment of what many men travel across the world for. Paying money to exercise their entitlement, satisfy their needs, and not have to care about any damage they are directly responsible for. Not have to give a damn about psychologically killing a child.

But the doll did not agree. The traffickers were never able to condition her to believe that being exploited by sex tourists is what she was born to do. They could never break her to the point where she said she liked it. The doll always wanted to escape. She misbehaved on purpose. She spat on the men. She was always angry. She was beaten and locked in her room. Somehow, she finally managed to escape. The other girls could not imagine how. The doll was magic, her determination giving her a power they couldn't comprehend. Unfortunately, there is no happy ending for this magic child.

A few days after the doll's escape, two men came to the child-brothel. What the doll had done was very bad, the other girls were told. They were ordered to eat while the men stood by and watched. When the girls had finished eating, the men said they had just eaten the doll's body, and if anyone else wanted to escape, they would be chopped into pieces for the other girls to eat.[67] A sex tourist responds, "But when you're on the other side of the world man, who cares."[68]

Chimamanda Ngozi Adichie tells us that: "Gender as it functions today is a grave injustice. I am angry. We should all be angry. Anger has a long history of bringing about positive change."[69]

We are all complicit in acts of rape because we are all complicit in the society that allows such atrocities to keep happening. More anger, a motivational anger that is fueled by awareness and empathy, is what is needed.

Like in the small town of Cheràn, being victimized does not have to end in defeat; we do not have to give the oppressor his victory. We guard ourselves. We guard others. We don't let him win.

The majority of women in the world have and will experience sexual abuse—if not all-out rape—in their lifetime[70] unless they stay home with their mothers, as per Camille Paglia's advice. In a recent YouTube discussion with Jordan Peterson, Paglia relates how her generation chose to have "the right to risk rape."[71] Sure, it's true. Pathetic and tragic, but true: women do risk rape by daring to be free, by going outside, by having

146

the audacity to live our lives with freedom of movement, as men do.[72]

Should this reality be accepted because it has always been that way, as espoused by Paglia, and the risk we will always have no choice but to take? Outdoors or in? Yes, every woman needs to carry this knowledge that it could happen to her and that it does, has, and will happen to others. We all need to be on guard. Be prepared to fight back. As Susan Brownmiller continued to warn women in 2019: "You're not equal, and you've got to remember there are predators out there."[73] The reality of rape has not gone away. Not yet. If ever. But that doesn't mean we should ever give up and that we should accept it and not work towards exposing the dysfunction that lies beneath.

However—and here is the revolution we can tease out of the oppression—if we refuse to accept the daily violation of risking rape by going outside, we are all already warriors. We need to be acutely aware of the risks, of our very real vulnerability in a (still) male supremacist society, but, at the same time, fight to not have to put up with it anymore. Without denying it, we need to learn to get beyond the fear inflicted upon us by no longer allowing it to have power over us. In other words: like Nanuka, like the people of Cherán keeping watch for the return of their exploiters, stare down the daily threat of assault with a relentless gaze of Fuck You.

Lethe. An Art Installation. To be continued.

It's a different story; it's the same story, every time I lie bound in the crime scene police tape in a public space. People don't see me at first. I blend in with the rest of the installation and, perhaps, they don't notice me right away because I am a part of the culture they are looking through. I am too recognizable to be immediately acknowledged.

In 1999, five years after the abduction and escape, I started to create a photography and performance art piece called *Lethe*. In Greek mythology, Lethe is the river of forgetfulness. It is a tributary of the River Styx that one crosses over before going to Hell so that they can, well, forget. I hadn't forgotten what happened to me all those years ago. The violence I had suffered and the ensuing trauma were fully lodged in my being as an artist and a survivor. And a never-ending victim. The forgotten, in my journey of Lethe, is what society brushes aside, doesn't care to listen to, doesn't bother to notice. *Lethe* is a reminder of what we cannot forget. It is a call to remember what is so often disregarded as lying beyond the self, beyond society, but is really at the core.

As I lie in the middle of the gallery, I am a cocoon corpse: both dead and alive, a femicide about to resurrect. Resilient. Reborn. Irreverent. I am the little girl on the string about to spring, bursting with the revenge that comes with the knowledge gained when having lived through extreme violence. By being a victim. By being a survivor.

After a while, people come up to me. They may wonder at the human form. The human length of the object. The shape of a mummy fully bound in blasting yellow plastic inscribed with: "Police Line. Do Not Cross." In my version, the well-worn phrase swirls and cuts and cancels out the traditional line, the line that contains a murder scene, the line that imposes no involvement in the aftermath of violence. Wraps, criss-crosses, shreds, knots, loops, and spirals are synthetic sinews that fuse flesh with surveillance, a different combination with each performative wrapping.

It is the same story; it is a different story every time a woman's body is found face-down in a field or burning next to a river. No one is just a "viewer" when we are all part of the same culture. Do they know, as they stare down at me, that looking into this darkness can lead to light?

Some of them think nothing of it. Heads tilt my direction while walking past. Give me the cursory three seconds of attention that is the average when viewing art. Others actually do look down. Really look, long enough to witness an inevitable blink. My blink. I have been able to see them all along. I have been watching. They don't expect this. The thing, the object, the objectified, looks back. One eye is exposed through a slit of tape wraps. One wide, mischievous laughing, loving, staring eye striving to exude empathy and hope. Yearning, pushing out to pull them in. You have taken the time to look down. Taken the time to greet me. Thank you.

"Oh my God! It's alive!!" the ones who look down often exclaim. Or, "Hahaha, there's a person in there." Some jump back, terrified by the fact that I am not really dead. I am far from it. This is just the beginning.

I am claustrophobic. I must breathe deeply through my nose and out my mouth to ward off the panic. Yes, I remind myself, you must lie here for one hour. This is the ritual. You have only begun. You must remain calm. The police tape cuts into my wrists. They were tied first, then my ankles. I have to make sure that I can't get away easily. That would be unrealistic. The performance requires the angst of authentic imprisonment.[74]

"Look at what is always here,"[75] my pseudo-corpse invites. The: she asked for it. The: what did she expect. The: it was all her fault. The: not-valued. The: she chose her life. The: not my problem. I have wrapped her in these crimes that she did not commit. I close my eyes.

The claustrophobia brings back the trauma. I am back in Linnihan's camper/van. My eyes are wide in the dark. Duct tape robs me of my ability to call out. My mind is wild again with how to get out of this. My being struck by the shock of what-the-fuck. This couldn't be me here, now, trapped in this far too common nightmare. Lying in the back of a vehicle. Being taken. Oh my God! I have been taken. I can't get away! I am racing down an invisible highway. How did I get myself into something that so often happens?

As when I fought for my life in Arizona, I call on all my strength and start to shred myself out.

I will never forget the story he told me. I doubt he will either. Twenty-odd years ago, a man was walking his dog down by the Fraser River, British Columbia. It was early. Around 6 a.m. In the late fall. Before the beginning of light. He smelled a barbeque.

"Why is someone having a barbeque down here at 6 a.m.?" was his first thought. I can see his dog on its haunches, nose pointing upwards, sniffing.

They walked towards the smell until they saw something smoldering in a clearing close to the river's edge. As I remember his story, I can see the smoke, as a fugitive, slipping between the mesh of branches above, becoming a part of the mist hovering above the cold river, clinging to the trees and sometimes, this time of year, hanging around all day. As a child, I always imagined unspeakable things happening down there. Next to the river. Terrible things that leave open wounds in their vanishing. Here was another crime scene of yet another disappeared woman set in a British Columbia November's heaviness of chill and grey.

He told me how, voice low, in a tone that the details of this story were only for me, upon the sight of the smoldering form, he and his dog stopped at the edge of the clearing. The dog knew more than the man. He immediately knew evil. I hear his low growl and see him start to back away.

"That's a strange-looking barbeque, that's for sure," the man told me he had thought. And I wondered about how we never expect what is so often happening. It's too terrible to be true.

I can imagine the dog starting to bark. Alarm warnings. Like an evil contained in the thing was about to spring through the trees and cause some unnameable harm.

The sun would have started its slow rise. Almost pointless this time of year with a soggy brightening that only lasts a few hours. There must have been an eeriness that accompanied its painstaking speed that day. As if it were reluctant to illuminate this scene.

He told me how they crept closer. They must have looked like hunters who don't dare to snap a twig, even though there was nothing and no one around. Except for the burning. That lay there. Prone in its smolder, exuding an aura of both holiness and hell.

They moved closer.

The smell of roasting meat filled their nostrils. The man coughed. Choked. Seemed to gag momentarily as he told me his story. His face greyed slightly at the memory but quickly reinstated detachment as though he was fighting off its inescapable effects. Make them go away. Show me that this big deal hadn't affected him as much as it had.

As soon as he could make out what it was, he jumped back in horror. In the swift sight of recognition, he had seen all that he needed to see.

It was a woman's body, naked, her features no longer recognizable. She had been burning for a few hours by then, he said, and he assumed that the fire had been raging at first, most likely started with gas.

After a while, the density of the dew rising from the bog and the mist descending from the cold sky had compacted the funeral pyre into this slow smolder. No matter. The fire had done its job, he related. Face blank. Blotting out the scene as he performed this unnameable duty of telling me.

No one will ever know who she was, where she was from, her story, her family, the details of how she had ended up here. She was but another Jane Doe. Another murdered and missing woman. Even though the plot leading up to such a death varies from woman to woman, the story is always the same. The theme. An undervalued life. A piece of trash to be used and disposed of. No bad conscience afterward. Why would there be? For the men who used her, this is what she was for. Drug addict. Cheap whore. Woman. She asked for it. It was all her fault. What did she expect?

The man called the police. He waited until they arrived. Gave his report. Went home.

He confided that he often wakes up at night seeing her, lying there, wrapped in the slow smolder, a grey mass that had once contained a life that deserved to be lived. Inconceivable in the brutality of her demise.[76]

⸺⬤⸺

I may still have the piece of crime scene police tape from that time. Maybe it's crammed into a box in my storage locker. Maybe it's wound up with all the others: the used and the waiting. Maybe it's lost.

It wasn't very long. Six feet maximum. A bit longer than the corpse it had surrounded and cut off from the world that had made her so. A corpse. An oddity to be wondered at. Police Line Do Not Cross. Do not cross over what happened to her as we think that it will never happen to us. We have nothing to do with it. She chose the life that put her there. Keep everything separate. She and I. You and me. Us and them. A curiosity. Maintain the line. Walk away.

The man told me how the piece of police tape was dirty from having lain in the mud for a few weeks. He had to wash it off when he got home. It was becoming buried. As though it had been trammeled upon by indifferent feet. Late November. The season when the rain pummels for days and causes the river to slop over its banks. Mud, always irreverent, smears the line between water and land.

A week or so after he had found the body, on his early morning walk with his dog, the man took some of the police tape. The body was long gone, but I imagine the horror still hanging in the air, palpable, adding a thicker pungency to the smell of late autumn decomposition. He tugged a piece from the mud, shook off the chunks of dirt as best he could, crumpled it into a ball, and shoved it into the pocket of his raincoat.

He told me later that he took it because he knew I would know what to do with it. And he was right. I did. With this shred of evidence, with this dulled spark of another taken woman, was born my first act of feminist resistance.

I had no idea where it came from, from where the idea and the energy had sprung. It was just there. Having lain latent for four years, waiting for a trigger to jolt me beyond my personal pain into what is much bigger than me, waiting for me to heal enough so that I had the strength to dive back in. Alive in the wisdom of what I have survived. Fierce in not accepting what doesn't have to be true.[77]

PTSD and the Sex Tourist. Summer, 2019.

Sometimes, I get angry, and it's not always an anger that motivates in a positive way.[78] Even though it's justified, it's an anger that hurts me and doesn't help anyone else.

I started to watch the Netflix series *Unbelievable* a couple of months ago. I was riveted. I felt like I was going to throw up, and it wasn't only because of the rape. It was mainly because of the way the young woman is treated after the rape, by the police, by the authorities, and especially by the two male detectives. She is bullied. She is not believed. The authorities are biased towards the young woman even before the interview begins. I watched, horrified, as their bias starts to undermine what happened to her. My insides doubled up. In unison with her imposed doubt, I thought, "Oh no!" The worst part, the final blow, is when the detectives tell her that she will be prosecuted if she is caught lying on the stand.[79] The young woman retracts her statement. I close my laptop, incapable of watching the remaining episodes. Devastated.

I am certainly not saying that all male detectives bully and re-traumatize rape victims, but I know it happens. In her book, *Had it Coming: What's Fair in the Age of #MeToo*, journalist Robyn Doolittle reports how, in Canada, with some of the most progressive sexual assault legislation in the world, only 34 percent of accusations end in a criminal charge, and 19.39 percent are discarded as 'unfounded.'[80] Like the double entendre of the series' name, the statistics of rape crimes that are discarded as unfounded *should* be unbelievable. But, unfortunately, they are not.

If I had been bullied and threatened with a criminal charge—especially if I were in my teens—I could very well have retracted

my testimony too. Many young women are reluctant to report
sexual assault in the first place out of shame, fear, just wanting
to forget, it's too much trouble, and the vulnerability when a
person's system is processing fresh trauma and perhaps even
the knowledge that they very well may not be believed. To have
the courage to report the assault, drag out your victimization,
and then to be victimized once again by the authorities is, unfortunately, in rape culture, believable—but also unforgivable.

I am glad that such an exposé of the further assault of rape
victims when reporting their crimes is available, especially
on such a prominent forum for entertainment. However, as
a victim, a survivor, and someone who has lived with PTSD
for twenty-four years, I couldn't watch more than one episode.
I became really angry. I felt sick. I started to shake. Tears
streamed down my cheeks. I wanted to scratch out the faces
of the terrible men through my monitor. I wanted to hold the
young woman and tell her what was really happening. Sit with
her. Shut those men down. Fight back.[81]

The documentary on teen porn, *Hot Girls Wanted*, also
had a very negative effect on me. The young women buying
into their role as objects to be exploited for male pleasure and
supporting their own abuse is as horrifying as the power abuse
it condones. This documentary shows the success of internalized sexism, the triumph of patriarchy to the point that young
women objectify themselves and, in so doing, end up supporting
violence against women, violence against themselves.[82]

Normalizing the exploitation of female bodies is very upsetting—especially for those of us who have lived knowledge of
where the objectification of women's bodies leads: to rape, to the
use of another human's body whenever he 'needs' it.[83]

"Sometimes you might rape someone: you can go to a prostitute instead," a john confided to writer and sex trade abolitionist, Julie Bindel.

"A desperate man who wants sex so bad, he needs sex to
be relieved. He might rape," another entitled women's body-
buyer told her. Bindel concludes that "it's not feminists such
as Andrea Dworkin and herself who are responsible for the

idea that all men are potential rapists—it's sometimes men themselves."[84] Men admit that they will rape if they cannot get access to women's bodies whenever they say they need it. They have made violence against women a regular part of life.

If using prostituted women to prevent rape isn't bad enough, it is easy to become potentially *too* angry when one is aware of what the porn industry is really doing.

"All soft-core porn has migrated into pop culture," says Gail Dines of Stop Porn Culture. "The vast majority of pornography is hard-core Gonzo: the premise of Gonzo is that women are meant to be fucked, dominated, made to suffer, and humiliate and part of the thrill is that it hurts and she hates it."[85]

It is absolutely legitimate to be angry about such very real horrors that are happening right now, but at the same time, I cannot allow them to re-traumatize me. I always have to be mindful of how upset I get. I have to work hard to not be devastated by what is always happening.[86] Gail Dines calls us to action against something that is so obviously inhumane and just plain wrong: "This has to stop. We have to fight back."[87]

———◆———

He should be an alien. But he isn't. I would like to think they are but a fabricated species of mutants called 'The Sex Tourists' stomping around some post-apocalyptic B-Movie set. I can hear the reverberations now of their big Birkinstocked feet, the sputtering special effects of the 50s making everything kitsch. Here they come! A gang of Godzillas in Bermuda shorts, feigning the enlightenment of world travel but, in reality, grunting the primitive mantra of:

"Me-have-lots-of-sex. What-I-want-when-I-want. How-I-want. My-right-as-man."

"Get-laid-by-young-desperate-women. Best-deal-only-$3."

But it's not a movie, a bunch of guys in Hawaiian shirts screeching a cult film joke. They are very real, this mutant breed of Sex Tourists, and, there are so many of them, they could be anyone.

"Yes, he goes to prostitutes in Third World countries," a male friend said, oblivious to the effect that would have on me. I was horrified. I became hysterical. There is a sex tourist in my social circle! A holiday rapist who partakes in and upholds the torture of women and children! Arrogant. Oblivious. Inexcusable. Across the table from me!

I don't know if you have ever been hysterical. I mean, really hysterical where you whirl up into a tornado of freaking out and can't make it stop. I felt like my entire being was flying apart and I wasn't going to be able to put it back together again. Grief, confusion, anger tore out of me. Every time I tried to stop, I stood as a husk, gasping, and it wound up again. Afterward, when I finally did succeed in making it stop, I was depleted and ashamed that I had lost it by feeling too much. Some people have told me that they worry about me because I feel too much. Isn't the not-enough more worrisome?

Even though the extreme majority of sex tourists are men,[88] I am not demonizing men in general. I want you to know this. Really know this. I am demonizing sex tourists, punters, and johns, that is, anyone who goes to a Third World country and to the Third World that exists in the first (like Vancouver, Canada's Downtown Eastside, for example) and exploits desperate human beings for their sexual gratification. And selfishness. And greed. To fulfill their biological rights as men. If you don't do this, I am not talking about you. And if you do, yes, please: take this very personally.

As I have said, the extreme majority of prostitutes are women, and the extreme majority of johns are men; the extreme majority of rapists are men, and the extreme majority of victims are women. Men cannot take this indisputable fact personally. This is the most important thing men can do to make the world a better place for everyone. Again, 'everyone' being the keyword. And, no! Thankfully, the majority of men are not sex tourists, or johns, or punters, or rapists. But every man exists in a system that makes it possible for him to become one who exploits. The same way every woman negotiates a system that makes it possible for her to be assaulted.

Some people have told me that they think of themselves as impervious to social conditioning and may be cringing or guffawing as they read this. Or have tossed the book onto the bed. Or thrown it across the room. They would never have left the house, never watched TV, never surfed the Internet, never played a video game. They would have to have been homeschooled by parents who also have never left the house and raised by parents who were equally unscathed by any sort of dysfunction. Well, if anyone thinks they are one of these miracles, guess what: you don't exist.[89]

We are all of what we are in. We are all products of a culture that exploits. Yes, we need to be vigilant about what is going on outside of us—sex tourists creeping around, for example, only exposing themselves in their online chat rooms, walking down the street, going to the same bank as us, working in the same office, moving in the same social circles—but also what we are made of. How am I complicit in what I am against? What have I internalized? What do I deny? This is the dialogue we need to have with ourselves and with each other. How am I involved? What can I do?

Lydia Cacho confides in her book *Slavery Inc: The Untold Story of International Sex Trafficking*:

> I hope this book finds its way into the hands of people who really care about the lives of these women and girls; of men who stop to look at themselves and are able to see in these women their very own daughters, sisters, nieces or granddaughters. I hope readers realize that all of the girls whose stories I tell deserve safe, dignified, happy lives, lives that none of them got to have because there are not enough people in the world who worry about and work to prevent sexual slavery.[90]

And the first step: don't take anything personally. It's far from just all about you: it's about everything.

One of the closest men in my life told me this. About the sex tourist in my midst. I know. If this weren't so horrible, it could be kind of funny. Look out! Here comes a sex tourist! Duck! He's getting closer! Everybody hide! The latter of which I really wanted to do.

He is a long-term friend of my friend. The fact that a man I love can have a friend who assaults women and girls is incomprehensible to me. How can he not see his friend raping a woman or child when he looks at him? That's what I see. How can this unforgivable elephant in the room be not only ignored but, in so doing, forgiven? I hate to say it but maybe it's easier for men to hang out with rapists than it is for women. Especially for women who have been raped.

My friend eventually told me that he doesn't like that his friend uses women's bodies to fill his biological needs (Yay!) and that he just tries not to think about it (not Yay). He told me that if he crossed all of the men off of the list who have used prostituted women, there wouldn't be a lot of male friends to choose from. (Wow. I have no idea what to make of that. Are men who exploit women even more rampant than already predicted?)

When one really thinks about it and goes so far as to feel about it, it is quite rational to become hysterical when such a disclosure hits you across the head. And yet, due to the atrocities we have to negotiate in a culture ruled by the mandate of exploitation, I, for one, am always working to keep a handle on it. On my rage. And it's never easy. Especially when you have PTSD.

Over the years, I have thought I probably had some form of PTSD and used to toss that fact off here and there. At parties. A juicy tidbit I could lob up into eager mouths as we related what we have survived in our lives, alcohol loosened lips passing small brags disguised as confidences around the table. Show us your cards. The winning hand was a royal flush of the person who had suffered the most.

My proclamation of PTSD was another badge of honour that kept people in awe. Another aspect of my victimization that gave me the upper hand. Like the heroin chic of the 90s where high fashion was modeled on literally strung-out women, my off-the-cuff confessions of 'Yah, sure, I have PTSD' played into the game of the glamorous victim. Look what she survived. It's so exotic: abduction, rape. Especially in the world of rock & roll, my victimization, the PTSD that I actually *did* suffer from, gave me power. The romance of life on the edge. Of course, there is no real power to be found in PTSD, and there is nothing exotic about having lived through sexual assault. In fact, it is the opposite of exotic: it's far too common.

I never took having PTSD seriously before. I mean seriously. Until I was in the middle of doing research for and writing this book and I finally noticed how damaged I can become when confronted with other women's suffering through my deep awareness of its causes. Immediately. Fly off of the proverbial rails and re-traumatize myself with what I am fighting against.

According to the writings of a lot of psychiatrists (and most likely my own as well but, apparently, I haven't been listening to her), I am a perfect candidate. I was surprised by how I fit into every category. Especially the life-threatening aspect. PTSD is more common among survivors who felt that their lives were in danger during the assault, which was the main theme in the abduction I wasn't murdered in.

I also found out that other factors that put a survivor at higher risk of PTSD include previous mental health issues like anxiety and depression and not having a strong support system.[91] This makes perfect sense, of course. Having genetic emotional and psychological vulnerability pre-trauma can certainly intensify its effects. My friend Lisa might not have to live with an untreatable combination of Bipolar and Schizophrenia if she hadn't been sexually abused by more than one man as a child.

When a child is abused, it is often repressed. Abused children typically don't ask for help because they don't understand what is happening. They know it doesn't feel good, and they don't like it. They live in constant fear of when it will happen again but don't tell anyone because they don't know if it's right or if it's wrong. They often feel shame and guilt, blame themselves for the violation and, at the same time, attempt to justify the abuse as somehow 'normal.' Survivors of childhood sexual abuse have told me that, even though it feels terrible, they think they are the bad ones. I made up excuses for him, confided a friend who had been sexually abused by his older brother for years. My brother couldn't help it. I forgave him and blamed myself.

Lisa didn't ask for help. Lisa didn't try to get away. She thought she was supposed to service these men. That it was what her mother wanted. Pay-back for the camping trip, she told me she had justified, as her body screamed in silence, unheard even by herself. Perhaps this desire to make such horror normal is because the child can't accept that the world could be so full of pain. They make sense of it by denying it. By making it not what it is.

The families of sexual assault survivors also experience trauma. And, like a victim of child abuse repressing their trauma because it's incomprehensible to them, families often can't accept that something so terrible has happened to their child, their sister, or their brother. They can't handle thinking about their loved one in that situation and so they repress. I have learned that the way victims are received by family and friends, post-violation, has a serious effect on the extent of the PTSD. For years after my abduction and assaults, whenever I saw my family, it was as though I had a tumor that I had to keep stuffing in when it showed itself from beneath the everything-is-fine surface. I was always gulping back what I needed to tell, a bile-coloured lump that saturated my psyche and spread to my finger-tips. I presumed it was because my family didn't love me. I found out ten years later that it was because if they thought about it, they would go crazy. I never expected that response: kind of a back-handed consolation as, when one gets down to it, the 'it's too terrible, we can't handle it' made my trauma all about them.

I realize now, though, that it did make me feel better knowing they felt so much they weren't capable of being there for me, the one who had literally been hurt. A bit. But it didn't negate the fact that I was abandoned for the ten years after the trauma. It was like it never happened. But making something never happen that did makes it happen even more.

Another part is also true.

The part about having previous mental health issues. I inherited that from you, Dad. Another thing we had in common! (A bit of affectionate, dark humour here!) Don't worry! It was certainly not your fault! Just a genetic make-up glitch in terms of unstable serotonin and dopamine levels exacerbated by emotional abuse and sexual assaults.

We come from a long line of depressives and closet alcoholics. People who self-medicated with booze and pills in private so that no one would know there was something wrong. Or so they thought. In the early twentieth century, long before there were antidepressants and mood stabilizers to—if we're lucky—straighten us out, mood disorders were even more shameful than they are today. They really had to be kept hidden back then or one would risk ostracization. A freak. It's a weakness when someone needs help. Something to be ashamed of. Especially for men.

You always slept on the couch the next day. All day. Failing at being a non-entity with a cushion over your face. Keeping out the world. What had happened that you may or may not remember from the night before. We would all walk past you, carrying on with our usual movements: up the stairs, to the kitchen, down the hall, into bedrooms, bathrooms, doing our homework. Having meals. But I don't think anyone actually went into the living room. Where you slept. All day. Swathed in the blatant denial of your misery, there was an invisible rope strung across the entrance to the living room: Do Not Enter Everything You Can See. Police Line. Do Not Cross.

I always wondered why you slept on the couch. In full view. Your shame out on display. Was it carelessness? Obliviousness? Or just the fact that it was your house and you could do whatever you wanted. An act of a man victimized by his need for dominance. Would it have been better if you had recovered in your bedroom, behind closed doors, the same way you hid your bottles of whiskey in the basement behind your stacks of firewood so that every time you went to throw another piece of wood on the fire, you could take another gulp? I imagined how you gulped or swigged, to put it less desperately. What did it look like? I was often tempted but too afraid to go down to look. You were very careful to hide this from us. The straight-up proof. It was always very hot in the house.

I remember my face being blotted with hives from the heat. And every time you went down to tend to the fire, you returned with more of a slope to your stagger, your face sagged by sadness and shame or sharpened by a feigned attempt at joviality. Sadness is so much more jarring in its desperate attempt to be otherwise.

You loved Kitty Wells when you were drunk. After the polkas that blasted at the beginning of each binge, on she would come with her country and western death march of "Searching. All my life, I've been searching." What were you searching for, Dad? Did you ever find it?

"Why do you drink so much, Dad?" I asked once.

"It tastes good." I was stunned by such overt denial. Alcoholism and depression reduced to taste buds.

Regarding my mood disorder inheritance, I am not sure where the mania came from, the extra twist into Bipolar. I have suffered from depression for as long as I can remember and, even though the memory is about everything being so dulled and hopeless, it's vivid. I would wander about, sensations tweaked by listlessness and confused about why I was this way and others weren't. Guilty. Ashamed. Three, four, five, six years old.

Did the mania begin after the abduction? Like all sexual assault victims, it's impossible to know what we were like before it happened. It is from then on always after.

"We have to do something about this. This has to stop,"

you said to me when the depression became so deep that I knew I wouldn't be able to live through another one. It was you who knew. It was you who made me say, "Yes, you're right, Dad," because it was you who understood. It was you who got me to finally try medication. Like all of the irony between us: your unchecked illness had exacerbated mine, but it was you who helped me to save my own life.

I don't like to condone big pharmaceutical corporations, and I don't like being dependent on psychotropic drugs. But they have helped me. Unlike people like Lisa, who suffer from much more complex cases of mental illness than I do, I have found one that works for me with few side effects. I have no idea what the medication is doing to my brain, though. I have come across some horrifying possibilities on the Internet that my psychiatrists have all denied. But how do they know when the drug is new and no one has lived out their life on it yet? Only life will tell.

There is always a sacrifice when you allow a chemical to lodge itself in your system. When you have to take it every day or you won't be able to function. When you are dependent. I dream someday of having the stability and unconditional love to be safe enough to try and go off of it. But, in the meantime, the medication saves my life. I may not be alive if you hadn't told me, as a father: this has to stop.

People who don't suffer from clinical depression have no idea what it means to fall into the pit of absolute hopelessness. In the midst of its darkness, you can think: "This will end, I will have hope again in a few days ... It always does ...." For me anyway. Thanks to the medication, no doubt. At the time, though, when I can barely drag my ashamed and poisoned being outside to buy milk, food, and try to go for a life-affirming walk, it feels like it will never go away. I am trapped. Again. Panic. How much longer can I live with this? My mind reels with how to get out of this trap, and there are no answers. No hope. I think absolute hopelessness is one of the worst feelings one can endure. It's what ends in suicide. Why wouldn't it? When you have absolutely no hope, when your being cycles in the impossibility of no escape, what is there to live for?

And the shame. That's the worst part. People who don't understand depression and have the good fortune to not live with mental illness insult us with: "Get over it. Go outside. Go for a walk." And the worst: "Everyone has problems. Everyone has things they need to work through. Bad days. It's not *just you.*"

These are the worst possible things you can say to a depressed person. The main thing that can help depressed people (besides exercise and having the good fortune to find a medication that works with minimal side effects) is—believe it or not, it's really easy, and it may even sound corny—a hug. A stroke of their hair. A kiss on the cheek. An: "It's okay. It will be okay. I am here for you. I love you." Don't judge. Don't say you understand. Because if you don't live with mental illness, you don't understand.

"Pull up your bootstraps. Get on with it. Get it together. That's what I do." When someone is clinically depressed, that is their greatest wish: to be able to do what you do.

I never realized that things were this bad (maybe that's because it had become so normal to me). I never knew that I was and am a walking time bomb until I found out about such symptoms of PTSD as 'hyperarousal,' and how the everyday is a 'minefield of potential threats' and how, "if a survivor becomes triggered by the news, or a scene in a movie, or a knock on the door, they might be thrown into re-experiencing the trauma."[92] This is what happened to me when I found out a friend of a friend uses women's (and maybe even girls' ... I didn't dare to ask this question) bodies from the Third World for sex. I have studied these mutants extensively. These men with blocked-out hearts. My stomach has churned with rage and tears have streamed, and my determination to keep fighting has become more firmly entrenched. But this has all been from a distance. From the safety of my desk or my reading chair. But here it was. In the living room. Lounging on the sofa. Scooping peanuts from the peanut bowl. Sipping an artisanal IPA. Participating in chit chat, ideas about art, sharing a meal.

This wasn't a chapter of a book or a scene in a movie or a knock on the door that I didn't open: the threat, the reality, the enemy, had stridden right in.

———◄◊►———

Sex tourists follow in the boot steps of the military. Lydia Cacho explains how, in Asia, the most popular (and one could say even the 'classic') destination for 'sexcations' were sex camps set up for R&R (rest and relaxation) between the Second World War and the Vietnam War to pacify the soldiers and provide 'relaxation therapy' by entertaining them with women.[93] Japan's military brothels in Korea during the Second World War enslaved between 150,000 and 200,000 women and girls as 'comfort women'; during the post-war American occupation of Japan, "the Japanese government received North American funds for the creation of new forced-prostitution camps ... for the occupation forces. In 1945, the Recreation and Amusement Association (RAA) was created, the RAA was really a euphemism for the military sex camps." To provide the necessary sexual relief for the men fighting the Vietnam War, "the US army invested

$16,000,000 in the Thai economy annually. In 1964, the population available for sexual exploitation had grown to 400,000. The Pentagon was responsible for creating what Senator James William Fulbright called 'an American brothel' in Asia."[94] Despite the fact that today's sex tourists aren't living with the constant threat of not knowing if they will live to see another day, does this sound familiar? First World men, having a bit of much deserved R&R in the exotic Orient, not to mention some respite from all the work that goes into relationships that involve effort, commitment, and empathy? As some sex tourists have expressed, they need some relief from those mouthy, demanding bitches back home. Through the gains made by feminism in the West, the poor, abused, First World men have had a few holes popped in their king-of-the-castle impunity bubbles. But not to fear. Within the greedy grasp of neoliberalism, the Third World offers millions of desperate women and children for the downtrodden johns to regain their beaten-down manhood.

"Women in Western countries are spoiled bitches," concludes a john.

"But there are many places in the world where women will treat you like a king for a fraction of what your Western girlfriend costs," says another. "Any woman living outside of the Western world knows that if she treats her man poorly he will walk down the street and have her replaced in less than fifteen minutes. Accordingly, when you tell your non-Western girlfriend to start sucking, she knows she better do a good job!"[95] Sometimes I wonder how it's possible that such creatures are of the same species. And there are many more. This next spokes-rapist should be behind bars:

"Go to where people are hungry," he advises his fellow johns on a sex tourist online forum. "Go to a poor country. Go to poverty plagued lands and find the women there. They will love you. They will take care of you. They will take it up the ass for you. They will suck it raw for you. They will massage you ... They will do anything for you ... for so little money. So little, just so they can have the next meal and live."[96] I don't think I need to cite more. These vile realities speak for themselves.

How are the attitudes and acts of sex tourists any different from the sex slavery in the military brothels and the gang-rapes committed by soldiers where the women are described as being—at gunpoint—"*forcibly willing* ... [because] they'd rather [be raped] than get shot"?[97] The women being used by the sex tourists, like the women being exploited by soldiers during wartime, have no choice but to be raped to survive.[98]

All sex tourists and many soldiers think nothing of exploiting Third World women's bodies.[99] Men need sex (men say). It is their right (rapists say). They are "acting on their natural instincts"[100] (johns state). A squad leader in the Vietnam War explained, in reference to just another gang-rape during wartime, "You can nail just about everybody on that—at least once. The guys are human, man."[101] During wartime, raping civilian women is Standard Operating Procedure (SOP). As in the everyday world of male supremacy, soldiers are only human, exercising their rights as men. The women are objects, without emotions, and, in one john's words, "they all die off after a while."[102] Lots more where that came from.

"Once you make people into objects, you take away their free will," says Lydia Cacho. "Clients in general, the ones who look for teenage girls and young women around the world to exploit for sex, tend to believe that they are not guilty of anything because these women and these girls have no chance." The classic justification made by holiday rapists—and international mining and forestry corporations that exploit the people as they rape the land—is: "They had nothing until we came here."

According to Cacho, these rapists "are not aware of the crime they are committing, but they are also not aware of how huge their participation is in this terrible crime."[103] They don't think they are doing anything wrong, and some even think they are helping the women and children they exploit.

These men are everywhere in our culture. In North America, they are called 'johns,' in the U.K, 'punters,' internationally, 'sex tourists,' amongst themselves, 'hobbyists' and, in countries like Germany, the Netherlands, Australia, and New Zealand where prostitution is legalized/decriminalized, 'clients.'

"There is no such thing as a typical john." Victor Malarek reports. "Few of them look like what most people imagine men who purchase sex to be: awkward, creepy loners fixated on porn before heading out for something more real. Many of these johns look like ordinary guys ... They are stockbrokers, plumbers, doctors, professors ... lawyers, judges, boy scout leaders ..., accountants ... soldiers, sailors, international peace-keepers, cops and other times they're men of the cloth .... What this brotherhood reveals is that, when it comes to sexuality and prostitution, johns' attitudes are remarkably consistent throughout the world. On these forums—whether in the U.S., Canada, Australia or Europe—it quickly becomes apparent that the search for paid sex is all about entitlement, power and control. What the john is looking for is a brief encounter where he can let go and freely express his most selfish desires ... His wants, needs and desires reign supreme. He doesn't have to worry about anybody else's."[104] Dipping into a stroll on their way to work for a morning blowjob, travelling to Asia, Latin America or Africa for a well-earned 'sexcation,' johns/punters/sex tourists/hobbyists/clients are the empty hearts that keep a culture of entitlement and exploitation beating. And they are everywhere.

It is impossible to know exactly how many sex tourists there are in the world but, seeing as "each year, 1.39 million people—mostly women and girls—are subjected to sexual slavery [and] they are bought, sold, and re-sold like raw materials in any given industry;"[105] "there is an estimated 10 million women and children ensnared in the sex markets around the globe and that most prostituted women report servicing an average of five clients a day; some see upwards of twenty;"[106] and, as Lydia Cacho reports, "the sex trade is the most profitable in the world, even more so than the arms and drug trades,"[107] this adds up to a lot.[108]

Men who buy sex *don't have time for relationships*. Men who buy sex *want a world with no human complications*. Men who buy sex consider it a bonus that *the woman leaves after*. Men who buy sex *take no responsibility for their direct complicity in the exploitation and suffering* of millions of women and children. Men who buy sex view *all women as objects* for their use. Men who buy sex *see all women as whores.*

"There's nothing like a good whore," said John Linnihan, a serial rapist. The good whore with the murdered heart—the woman who is raped multiple times a day. Everyday.

I wish we could just laugh at these terrible men. Because they are so pathetic. Because they are such cowards. Corral them away from the enclaves of our everyday and push them all up against a big-ass wall of shame and point and laugh and point and laugh and close in on them until they become crushed by the enormity of our irreverent mirth. Unfortunately, there is nothing funny about the collateral damage wreaked by these despicable beings.

As predicted, the sex tourist acquaintance has had his heart broken a few times (who hasn't); real relationships are too much work (that's your problem. Get a blow-up doll and leave living, breathing, feeling, loving, hurting creatures alone). He doesn't want to be hurt again (who does). He still has his entitled biological needs as a male in patriarchy (please leave women and children out of something you need to learn to control).

Obviously, everyone has had their heart broken, but perhaps those who are too afraid or unwilling to step up to the plate again should think about the onslaught of heartbreak that prostituted and raped people go through daily. Because of them. And those whom they are exploiting due to their own fear and weakness most often don't have a choice. They exist on a treadmill of heart smashing. Feel that. If you buy women and children for your sexual release, you are directly responsible for their suffering. You may not be literally murdering the women after you have had your solipsistic way with them as in war-time, but you are killing them nonetheless. Sabine, a woman who offers support for prostitutes from Eastern Europe in the legal German brothels, related how "[y]oung women, very young women ... say, 'I died here.' ... [T]he johns can damage the women to the extent that it is not possible for everything to go back to normal .... When they say 'I died,' it's true. Part of them truly has been murdered by johns. It wasn't an accident. It was a crime."[109]

In the long run, the outcome is the same: the continuation of the war against women.

I admit it! I am prejudiced against sex tourists. I am prejudiced against johns, punters, and hobbyists. I am prejudiced against child abusers. I am prejudiced against rapists.

The other day, I thought about the possibility of 'an intervention.' I felt like I had to try and do something.

Unlike the typical intervention where the intervenors are concerned for the well-being of the intervened, in this case of the friend of a friend sex tourist, my concern did not lie with him. My idea to try out an intervention was an act of cunning rather than an act of kindness for the suffering of the poor tortured perpetrator. Like my pretending to care for John Linnihan so that I could get away, my intervention idea was for all those for whom this weakness, fear, and unwillingness to empathize with has and will hurt.

I decided to try a subtle approach. A man-to-man approach. I asked my friend if he would send his friend a quote, something hard-hitting from the perspective of a man who had changed his ways when he became aware of the abuse he had been inflicting on women all of his life, something straight ahead, to the point, a dagger that should go through any heart. I thought maybe this man-to-man-to-man approach could be effective. Get one john/punter/sex tourist out of the circuit. I asked my friend to send this:

If I have one piece of advice, I'd ask you to look into the woman's eyes. That will tell you if she wants to be there or whether she's been forced into it. All drug-addicted hookers are forced to do it. All poor women are forced to do it. When I look back at the hundreds of women I've paid for sex, I know that most didn't want to be prostitutes. If anything, they should be called 'destitutes' and I used every single one of them because I didn't care. I would say that the majority of women don't want to be whores and men should think hard about what they are doing and quit deluding themselves with excuses and lies.[110]

My friend said he would send it. I don't know if he has. He hasn't told me. I must admit, I am afraid to ask.

———◈———

What are the statistics of sexual assault victims who end their own lives? It's impossible to say exactly, especially based on the fact that so many rapes go unreported, and then, even when the woman has had the courage to go to the cops, her complaint may be deemed unfounded. But women do. End their own lives. And many regularly have suicidal thoughts. Which I do.

A few months ago, I had a pretty serious meltdown connected to those symptoms of PTSD in combination with all the triggers I have just told you about in combination with Bipolar. I didn't tell anyone about it. I didn't tell anyone in my life because I didn't want to upset them. And, the usual: I was ashamed. I was embarrassed.

I didn't do it, of course, seeing as I am telling you about not doing it. I have never attempted suicide. I have never gone all the way to actually obtain the weapon, accumulate the pills or teeter on a ledge. But I have certainly thought about it. The latter especially.

I was staying on the eleventh floor of an apartment building. I couldn't stop thinking about it. Jumping. Jumping and then having the inevitable few seconds of Oh my God, why did I do that!! I would imagine hitting the ground. It was unthinkable. But I couldn't stop thinking about it.

I kept myself a good twelve feet from the windows at all times and never went near the balcony. I would feel nauseous and dizzy whenever I looked towards the windows, drawn to making a run for it and smashing myself through the glass (which was ridiculous as I probably would have rebounded, but you never know. Logic is not usually a part of losing it).

I was constantly trying to shove the thought and image out of my head. The image of making that dreaded leap. On the worst and final day, the floors began to tilt. I could feel myself being pulled towards the edge, starting to slide. I was horrified by how far this was going. I cried and moaned. I felt so helpless. I scurried back and forth around the perimeter of the apartment, packing my things. I left and didn't return until a friend was there too. Someone to distract me from my own obsessive thoughts. The very real possibility that tweaked me with anxiety. But I didn't tell him anything about it.

What is it about trauma that allows the culture that assaults us to win? Why does trauma make us very seriously consider and sometimes follow through on ending our own lives, on hurting ourselves when we are the ones who have been hurt? It is because we have internalized the hatred. The hatred that the rapist felt for us. It is because we feel judged by the same culture that assaults. That exploits. Whatever we do, we can't let them win. We must all stay alive.

PART FIVE

December 26ᵗʰ, 1994.

After the police nabbed him in a Laughlin, Nevada parking lot, Linnihan was booked based on my testimony and the license plate number I had given the cops. I assume that the vehicle was impounded. I wonder what happened to that strange camper/van combo with the mournful squeak after it had been scraped of all of its evidence. I wonder if Linnihan put up any fuss, asked what charges they had on him, denied everything, or just went with them. Guilty as charged. They would have put him in handcuffs. They probably took off his big cowboy hat exposing the limp comb-over. What shape of shadow would his hunched figure have cast as he was pushed through the sharp desert sun and shoved down into a squad car. Fiendish or defeated? Both?

The Other Victims. Ventura County, California. Sometime in 1994–1997.

After I got away, Linnihan headed back to California. It was Christmas Eve. Ventura County. A sixty-five-year-old woman was not home. She was having dinner with her family. I was told she had arrived home at around ten. When she got home, he was still in her house.

His violence was very extreme with her. Much more than he had ever been with me. How long did the ordeal last? I wonder. Was it because she was an older woman and therefore more disposable than I was in my want-to-keep-you-forever youth? When I first heard about it, I imagined that he was angry because I had betrayed him and he took it out on her. Maybe that's why he left her for dead, I thought. Maybe that's why he'd crossed the line into homicide. I felt bad. I felt somehow responsible. I don't know if I was unnecessarily flattering myself or ludicrously blaming myself. Or a combination of the two.

He would have heard her unlock the door. Did he panic or not give a damn? Did he know a woman lived alone there?

Had he cased the joint, or did he just skulk around and look for houses with no lights on? Was he hiding when she unlocked the door, turned on the lights, took off her coat, and went upstairs? Did he leap out of the shadows or confront her as she walked into the living room, grab her and start to strangle her, the same way he had subdued me, until she was on the edge of asphyxiation and croaking, "Please stop ... I'll do anything you want ...."

Was she unconscious when he beat her, raped her, sodomized her, and penetrated her with foreign objects? Just a sack of flesh on the floor for him to violate, getting off on the power of it all? I know she was still conscious during some of the brutalization because she testified as such. Well, that's what I was told by the DA in 1997, as I never got to hear her testimony. I was also told by the DA's office that she couldn't identify him because he was wearing a ski mask. She couldn't identify him, but I could. I could connect her with the man who had almost murdered her. For twenty-three years, I believed this. I was the one who could prove the attempted homicide. That was the main reason they needed my testimony. That was the main reason my life was on hold for three years.

Just before the completion of this book, a newspaper article was found. Long after I'd been flown down to California, met with the Chief of Police and the DA in the hotel restaurant, said, "Yah no problem. I can handle it" while I ate nothing; long after I'd panicked at my tawdry choice of shoes the next morning as I donned my credible victim outfit for the rape trial that wasn't mine; long after I'd been flown immediately back to Canada, I read it: The LA Times, October 8th, 1997: "Man Convicted of 1994 Sexual Assaults and Burglaries." In this article, I learned for the first time that the sixty-five-year-old victim, the woman Linnihan had left for dead, had positively identified him as the man who assaulted her.

"If there was any doubt about [the identity of] the mystery burglar," a juror told the press, "it went right out the window." As did my truth.

Why is it so important to me, this detail? So the woman who I was told couldn't identify Linnihan actually did? So what? I want to believe this newest addition to decades of memory is unimportant, but it appears to matter because I can't stop thinking about it. I feel re-victimized by what I was never told. Like the trial that was postponed for years, my truth had been postponed decades. I've lived the wrong story, and now stretched between the two, am about to snap.

After I read the article, I had to find out what had happened in that courtroom in 1997. I called the Ventura Courthouse for at least the third time since I started writing this book and trying to get the polaroid photo Linnihan had taken of me in the desert, the recording of my initial testimony, the court transcript: No No No. It's all gone. It happened so long ago. I was always told. This time, though, I was connected to the DA from 1997. He remembered me. The Linnihan case had been his. He asked if I would like to schedule a phone call. Yes, please, I responded. Ironically, even though the book was finished, I was about to get all the answers.

I found out that the crime against the sixty-five-year-old woman was more violent than I had thought. He had used brass knuckles to beat her to unconsciousness, to the point where she suffered from colour blindness and lost her sense of smell and taste. Those brass knuckles had likely been in the camper/van when he'd had me. He could have used them on me, but for some reason, he didn't. I felt in danger again. Sitting in the safety of twenty-four years later, I was terrified.

He tied her up with the phone cord from her landline phone, I read in the article. For some reason, he didn't use the rope he'd used with me. I guess he hadn't planned on assaulting a woman that night. It was a fluke that the woman he was robbing happened to come home. A predator's bonus.

He tied her up after the assault so that he could get away in case she wasn't completely dead. Did he know she was still breathing, or was he just not taking any chances? I see him scanning the room, ski mask on, looking for a way to make sure she couldn't get away until he was long gone. Once he'd sped off in the camper/van, the article told me, she gnawed through the cord. But here's the kicker. What changed everything for me: she had fought against her attacker so powerfully that the ski mask he was wearing came off enough for her to see part of his face. That is how she was able to identify him; that is how the story I'd lived for half my life was no longer true.

"Part of the ski mask was lifted when she was struggling," the DA told me last week on the phone. "She saw enough of his face to be able to identify him without a doubt. Everyone was shocked. Everyone thought she wouldn't be able to identify him because of the ski mask. As I was questioning her, I noticed that she kept looking in the defendant's direction. I asked her: is the man who assaulted you in this room? She pointed directly at him."

How interesting, I think now, how with sight damage and only having seen a portion of his face during the assault, she was able to identify him right away. While I, the one who had been with him the longest and had hunted his face for any vulnerability I could exploit, had scanned the faces in the courtroom for what could have been a full minute, couldn't see him because he'd aged so much in the three years in prison, and almost announced, "Where is John Linnihan?" The brutalization she had survived had been pounded into her to the extent where she barely needed to see him to know he was there. But for me, I had already begun to forget.

In the article, I am only the twenty-eight-year-old alleged third victim. Alleged. I know they have to say that because I didn't have a trial. But 'alleged'? No proof. No certainty. Even after all of these years, this hurts. It feels like what changed my life forever never happened.

There was another victim. An eighteen-year-old woman. Before I read the article, all I knew about her was that she was abducted and raped by the same man as I was. She was one of many he had assaulted and one of the only three who actually reported the crime. I've always wondered what happened to all the other victims. The article says nothing about them. The victims Linnihan celebrated with his collection of panties. Surely the police would have found the panties in his camper/ van. Another hidden stash of unreported rapes. Undoubtedly. I have more in common with these invisible victims now than I have always thought.

Apparently, Linnihan had kept the eighteen-year-old on a boat for six hours. I would have liked to know how she got away, or how he let her go. I still do. But, unlike before the article where I had no facts, I can now imagine her on a boat. The close quarters. The smell of mold rising from damp life jackets. The smell of the sea. The lonely lap of waves against the sides. The rocking to-and-fro as he assaulted her. A cradle turned into a nothing-will-ever-be-the-same-again death bed.

Did she psychologically over-power him like I did? Did she smash him over the head with a bottle or an oar and manage to get out of the cabin of the boat? Was the boat tied up to a wharf? Did she jump off and swim? The LA Times reported that she admitted to taking narcotics before Linnihan abducted her, so her testimony was deemed unreliable. I guess it was implied that she hallucinated the whole thing. The newspaper article doesn't say what kind of narcotics. This was another one of those "don't believe the victim" cases. Undermine her credibility however they could. Like the defense did with me when they tried to make me out as a slut. The only difference is that she told the truth. I know it's a sin to disobey "So help me God," a felony even, but I don't think God has anything to do with a rape trial, not to mention anything to do with the misogynist tradition of blaming the rape victim and getting the perpetrators off.

The newspaper doesn't say what kind of narcotics had discredited the eighteen-year-old's case. Only 'narcotics.' I wonder if this was taken into consideration during her testimony. Surely the prosecution could have gotten some scientific evidence as to whether a person can be oblivious to an assault when they are on whatever drug they don't say she was on. If she'd been on a hallucinogen, it may have made the assault even worse. If it had been on an opioid, maybe it would have made the disgusting experience less so. I tried to numb myself as much as possible with his beer and my sleeping pills. It didn't work very well. Some heroin would have definitely helped. But, like the attempt to discredit me as a slut and therefore a liar, I wouldn't have told the truth about that lie either.

This new evidence opens up a whole other proverbial can of worms. This is exactly like the consent and credibility controversies happening now in the twenty-first century with the newly disclosed epidemic of young women being assaulted on college campuses while 'blacked out.' The 1990s were a completely different time. An eighteen-year-old rape victim's reality was crossed out as soon as she fessed up to having taken drugs that night. Blacked out or not.

I have always wished I could have met them both. I don't know if it would have been a good thing or a bad thing or a pointless thing: three women who were brutalized to varying degrees by the same man sharing a cup of coffee and talking about ... what? Who knows. It didn't happen and never will. Maybe it would have led to empathy and support. Maybe it would have worsened the wounds.

I am pretty sure I asked, though. After my testimony. But I can't remember clearly. When I try to recall what happened after my time on the stand, the experience that was carved into my life, when I try to see all the other events during that forty-eight-hour whirl made up of an airport, a Holiday Inn, a courtroom, and then back to the airport, the images are so faded they could easily flip into fiction.

In terms of facts, even after reading the article in the LA Times, I am still left with questions. Maybe I asked if I could meet the other victims and my request was denied based on the legalities of talking to other witnesses during the trial. Maybe I had thought to ask and then been afraid to. Maybe I was just too tired and wanted to go home and forget. But I would certainly ask now. And insist. Twenty-three years later. Especially the artist in me who will pursue primary research even on her traumatized self. Maybe they would have liked to hear my story too. Maybe the eighteen-year-old, who would be in her 40s now, has wished for the same thing.

During our phone conversation last week, I think the DA had become aware of my silence, how my gut had plummeted when he stated that my truth didn't happen, and I was a victim again, I was a victim still, inconsequential when putting not only a menace to society away but the menace who had preyed upon me, too.

"We wouldn't have caught him without your testimony," he said after a pause. "If you hadn't gone back and gotten his license plate number, we wouldn't have been able to have picked him up that day. He would have hurt a lot more people." Invisible or not, it had, in a way, been my trial too. I was still the one who caught him.

A couple of years ago, I read Roxane Gay's *Hunger* and discovered that she thinks the same way as I do when it comes to being a victim vs. being a survivor. As I read, I was exhilarated. I put the book onto my lap, leaned back on the couch, and laughed. She agrees with me! Finally. Someone says what I have been feeling and thinking for decades. Thank you, Roxane!

"It took me a long time," she writes, "but I prefer 'victim' to 'survivor' now. I don't want to diminish the gravity of what happened. I don't want to pretend that I am on some triumphant, uplifting journey. I don't want to pretend that everything is okay. I'm living with what happened, moving forward without forgetting, moving forward without pretending I am unscarred."[1]

I would like to add to Gay's realization: I believe that *not* pretending everything is okay, both in ourselves and beyond ourselves, and *not denying our scars*, is a triumph in itself. By always remembering, we don't let him get away with it.

———————•(◦)•———————

I was flown to LA, did my duty of being an integral part of putting the serial rapist away for life, and was whisked back up to Canada. I had waited for three years for the trial, and

it was over and done in a mere twenty-four hours. Whoosh ...
like the magic of an airplane transporting you from one world
to another in a matter of hours, soaring over everything in between. No gravity to what happened when our lives have been
changed forever. Pretend everything is fine and it will all go
away. Shhhh ....

But things are changing now. Slowly. Since I started writing this book, Chanel Miller, who was sexually assaulted while
unconscious, published *Know My Name*. In her book, Miller focuses primarily on what happened during her trial. The tedium.
Her demonization by the press. The waiting for hours in what
she calls "the victim closet" before finally being called to the
stand; the waiting for years for the trial to even begin; the trial
stopping and then starting again when she had thought it was
done—her life being on hold for four years. She tells the story
of how victim-blaming closed in on her life. She tells the story
of the further trauma inflicted upon her when Brock Turner,
the man who had assaulted her and was in the process of all-
out raping her if he hadn't been stopped, is portrayed as more
of a victim than she is—the hardship he suffered when losing
the impunity of a privileged white male in white-supremacist
patriarchy is deemed more important than her losing her ability to ever again be able to live, in her words, 'unguarded.' For
Miller, it is the fact that she can't remember the sexual assault,
that her body was violated when she wasn't able to fight back
that torments and haunts her most.

But, there is a happy ending to Miller's story. Like mine,
as happy an ending as a terrible tale can have. In the end, the
victim does win. This is because outside the courtroom, the
public, our culture, listens to her. At last. We believe her. In
the thousands of emails and letters Miller received after her
victim statement goes viral—with the landmark opening line
of "you don't know me, but you've been inside of me"—people
believe her because they empathize with her. Many have been
victims too and, instead of being shamed and blamed even to
the point of blaming ourselves, we're not only talking about it
now: we're raging about it.

Emerald Fennell's 2020 rape-revenge film *Promising Young Woman* also tells the story of a woman who was sexually assaulted while unconscious. Just like in the Fraser Valley gang rape of the fifteen-year-old in 2010, it was filmed and then shared with classmates; the violation of a woman's body is laughed at, even by other women.

In patriarchy, rape is an act of discipline regardless of race or class. In Mikki Kendall's words: "rape has been used to repress, to undermine, and to control." However, in terms of the race of the rapists, Kendall also reports how: "statistically speaking, white men are most likely of all groups of men to commit sexual assault."[2] Maintaining power turns the privileged on. Like Toni Morrison says: "If you can only be tall because someone else is on their knees, then you have a very serious problem. And white people have a very serious problem." In the twenty-first century, systemic sexism and racism are now out in the open; our culture is starting to acknowledge this truth. Hierarchy, with white privileged men on top, is starting to topple. Slowly.

I'm not going to spoil *Promising Young Woman* for you in case you haven't seen it yet. But let's just say that the film narrates how common it is that men, and even men of colour, will sexually assault inebriated women. Instead of pointing the finger at women and how it's their responsibility to change their behaviour to put an end to the epidemic of sexual assault, the film portrays the rapists as buffoons, lethal, heartless, but buffoons nonetheless. Fennell shows how rape isn't a cultural problem caused by women over-drinking (as is claimed by male rights defenders and mainstream feminists who are not feminists if they participate in victim-blame). Rape is caused by raping. Sure, it's a good idea not to drink oneself to the point of unconsciousness—which young men do as well—but why is it the young woman's responsibility to not be raped? What about the rapists? Are they not involved? Does rape have nothing to do with the crime the young man—who (poor pathetic darling) can't help himself—is committing?

At the beginning of *Promising Young Woman*, the main character Cassie, played by Carrie Mulligan, is striding home from another all-nighter of rape-revenge. She's devouring a hot dog; the ketchup is running suggestively down her forearm. I was happy. Yes, I admit it. I thought: "Oh, this is going to be a happy movie! Like *I Spit on Your Grave*, absolute rape-revenge is going to be wielded!" As a victim, my mind just goes there: violence against rapists. Violence against the kind of man who imposed his violence within my body and my psyche. Don't worry. I wouldn't murder anyone. In cold blood anyway. But I would certainly fight if a man tried to rape me again. Who knows what might happen when you're fighting for your life. Let's face it: there is no guarantee that you're going to be raped by a rapist that you can psychologically overpower like I was. In so many ways, for me anyway, things could have been worse. And I'm always ready in case they are.

I haven't told you this part of my story, the part of my life where I'm always afraid. I take no chances of being raped again—or even murdered this time—to the point of paranoia with a heavy serving of Obsessive-Compulsive Disorder. Sometimes I can't sleep until I have peeked under all the beds, carried an empty bottle or a kitchen knife around the house, tiptoed upstairs, leaned against a corner barely breathing, listened for the slightest movement on the other side when the non-existent perpetrator betrays himself and, after a sufficient time of hearing nothing and still not believing the coast is clear, sprung around the corner like a member of a SWAT team. A boyfriend used to ask me, irritated: "Why do you always have to expect the worst!?" Well, I used to respond: that's because I've experienced it. *A* worst.[3] When I was abducted and thinking just that: "Oh my god, I'm being strangled; Oh my god, I'm abducted. Oh my god, there is a very good chance I will be murdered. This couldn't get any worse!" Extreme violence is a part of my life. It's always there.

In *Promising Young Woman*, no blood is shed—by the rapist anyway. I was a bit disappointed by this, but I got over it because revenge is had in the end. Unlike the ending of *Thelma and Louise* in 1991, where the only way the two heroines escape from exploitation and blame is to literally drive off a cliff, a legacy is left by Cassie's resistance. Like in *Know My Name,* the rapist's life is destroyed. As Miller's white privileged rapist says: "I just existed in a reality where nothing can ever go wrong or nobody could think of what I was doing as wrong."[4] Both Brock Turner of Miller's life and Al Monroe in Fennell's movie aren't allowed to have their culturally entitled fairy tale patriarchal futures. The smug impunity of those who have lounged about impervious at the top of the hierarchy is being chipped away.

The real-life Miller and the fictional Cassie are examples of progress. Ironic, progress, a tad paradoxical, where progress is based on triumphing over sexual assault. But progress nonetheless. In rape culture, a term that is now part of the vernacular, role models are women who have not let their culture get away with the violation of their bodies. Miller and Cassie are women who have learned (unfortunately the hard way) how to stand up to a culture of male—and especially well-off white male—entitlement. Unlike in my time, Cassie and Miller are warriors out in the open because the war is being acknowledged. Victims are finally being listened to; they are at long last being believed. As one of the would-be rapists laments in *Promising Young Woman*: "Why do you guys have to ruin everything?" Because it would be great if there were no need for rape memoirs anymore. That's why. But we still have a lot of listening, talking, and believing to do.

There are always differences of where, when, and how sexual assault happens, but it always amazes me how experiences of trauma, the aftermath of rape, are so much the same. In Miller's memoir, she talks about 'neglecting' the victim who is now a part of her. She discloses how she "didn't like her fragility, how quietly she spoke," but she "knew she was hungry for nourishment." The neglected victim needed "to be acknowledged and cared for," and she "refused to recognize her needs."[5] This changes, though. By the end of the memoir, Miller's victim is strong, triumphant, leading the way: the victim is the survivor.

Even though my experience of multiple rapes unleashed my wanna-be rock star, I denied my victim in my own way as

I thrashed about in my trauma. I shut down to the point of emotionally abusing another person; I acted as though I was okay; I raged that I was stronger than I really was; I eventually crashed and had to scrape myself up. Some women, almost always very young and in need of the most support, neglect the victim to the extent that they kill her as they kill themselves. In every case, the neglect of the victim is all about the shame that has been internalized, inflicted upon us from what a misogynist culture tells us to think of ourselves, what to think of our victim who is also the one who survived: that it was all our fault, that we could have stopped it if we'd wanted to, that we actually wanted to be filled with their filth. That we deserve to be disciplined or destroyed. Kept in a state of fear.

Thanks to victims and survivors like Chanel Miller and to Emerald Fennell's rape-revenge extravaganza, the traditionally impervious blue-blood rapists are starting to fall. But the men who raped me weren't privileged frat boys. Far from it. John Linnihan and the other two men (yes, there were others) existed on the margins of society in terms of class and race. Not to sympathize with him, but Linnihan wasn't well off. He'd never gone to university. He didn't have the comforts of the privileged classes and a well-paying profession. Thankfully, he couldn't afford shark-sharp attorneys like Brock Turner and Al Monroe could. Linnihan was a thoroughly pathetic person, glutted with demons and self-loathing, as he roamed back and forth across state lines burgling and then selling the ill-gotten goods in saloons. He was described as 'big John the Hustler' by one juror during the trial and a 'blustery, self-serving individual' by another. No one liked him. He couldn't seduce the jury like the well-spoken frat boy of Chanel's life could. When he strode into the Bird Cage Saloon, the jovial conversation ceased. Everyone knew he was bad news.

The other two rapists, the shadowy assailants soon to be revealed, were new Canadians, immigrants from Iran, working at minimum wage jobs. But, the high class, prioritized white, captain-of-a-sports-team kind of rapists and the ones from the margins all have one thing in common: male entitlement. The same way there is no one type of man who uses prostituted women and children, there is no one kind of man who rapes because, when it gets right down to it: he can. Society lets him. But this is starting to change. Slowly.

Some Things I've Learned in Mexico 2015 to the present.

I have my table. Table 104. The Lantzville Pub. British Columbia, Canada. An eager, early spring sun slants through a sky where every type of cloud has gathered. Cumulonimbus parade over the Salish Sea and bunch up against the mountains to the northeast; Stratus stretch across the horizon like deflated whales; and Cirrus, with their swoops and filigrees, make one fall in love with just looking.

In comparison to the majority of people in the world, I have everything. Even though I have suffered in my life, I have always had the opportunity to triumph. Regardless. And sit and watch and wonder.

And, believe it or not, what I suffered and survived in Arizona all of those years ago gave me a gift of knowing my strength and what I can survive. And now, resistance, fighting for justice for all, is what I live for. My life is far bigger than myself.[6]

One of the main reasons I moved to Mexico was to learn more about these things: privilege, violence, and resistance. I came to Mexico to study and feel the relationship between the First and the Third World—or the developed and the developing or the privileged and the under-privileged, or the exploiters and the exploited or the colonizers and the colonized (it is almost impossible to signify the placements of realities in a hierarchy without further denigrating the denigrated). I came to confront the global rapist.

Beginning with European Imperialism and its neoliberal legacy, the Third World is in a perpetual state of rape.[7] Even more so in a globalized world where international corporations exploit resources and the ideological pedigree of capitalism along with its mythology of 'development' reigns, we are more connected than ever.

Every country has a level of corruption. Even the pristine nations to the north with their comparably functioning democracies. But in the south, the level of corruption originates in the shacks that are actually houses. When a kid is alone. Slouching with machismo at eight. Young faces hardened into their impending lives of kill or be killed. Parents too busy working to bring in $10 a day if they are lucky. Or dead. Caught in some crossfire that they may or may not have been a literal part of. And the inner-reachings of the barrios exude an Animal Farm malevolence, as the kids are groomed to be cartel foot soldiers by the rusty corrugated metal that is the walls of their homes.

I have learned a lot of things in Mexico. I have learned that face-skinning is a semi-regular occurrence. A cartel act of discipline is to skin a person's face. This, the same as hanging the defeated from bridges, is an example, a warning that keeps a society obediently under siege.

It's always a young man. Most often, a cholo: a young Indigenous or part Indigenous man. It is always a young man who had no other opportunity but to join a cartel, become a foot soldier in the war on drugs and end up on the front page of a Mexico City newspaper as a faceless corpse. It could be anyone. It could be you, your kids, a friend, the warning proclaims. But this is a warning that more often than not cannot be heeded. Because in the countryside, in the small towns, and in the barrios that cling to the edges of cities, there is nothing else for young men to do but risk their lives to try and have something.

When I was in Monterrey in 2017 doing research on Nacidos Para Triunfar (Born to Triumph)[8]—an organization that helps save kids in the barrios from being recruited by the cartels—I was visiting the impoverished barrios on the edges of the city, and I saw a Hummer out trolling, flashing its hubcaps like diamond-studded teeth through the squalor. Kids born with nothing. Some resort to drinking paint thinner. I learned that paint thinner kills hunger. Literal hunger. That is the main thing they are escaping from.

The Hummers drive slowly. Their ostentatious width dominates the unpaved roads while dust billows in sordid plumes. They troll for victims, invisible nets cast wide to capture the willing prey. All trolling Hummers are black. How could metal shrouds that offer life through death be any other colour?

It was hot. Mid-forties. The street blared an eerie silence as the Hummer slunk by. From my worldview, the Hummer sighting was surreal, a phantom, as it parted the scorching air that made everything float and fade around the edges. But for the youth of this 'hood, there is nothing more real than their hunger. It is a slap in the face that offers everything. The bludgeons, the gunshot wounds, and the cocaine-coated possibility of power. Hummers represent the brutality of hierarchy. The prestige of the predator. Everything is out in the open in a Third World barrio.

Just before the Hummer sighting, we had driven past a house that I could not believe was a house. The man giving me the tour knows all these kids. Like the cartels that keep an eye on their potential recruits, NPT keeps watch, too. The cartels watch for a desperation they can corrupt; NPT waits for the desperation to lead to realization. Realization that they can get out if they take the life raft being offered. Besides being a literal one, the barrios are a psychological warzone.

The house didn't seem to have a front wall. Or maybe that's because I remember more clearly what was hidden. As we pulled up, two boys leaned in the doorway. Two prepubescent boys who looked like they were in their mid-thirties and aging badly. They wore rough leather masks that were their skin. Don't-mess-with-me masks. Forced to be so tough before their time. But what I remember most are two dangling, chubby little legs in the shadow near the back of the small room. The kind with dimpled knees and the creases around the ankles that look like they are made by a tightly wrapped thread. My eyes snapped in their direction like a mother who had just lost her child.

The little legs were illuminated by blots of blasting sunlight that raged through holes in the wall. The rest of the child was in the shadows. I squinted and focused, desperate to see, to find out something about this tiny, innocent creature surrounded by hell. A little girl. One or two. Wearing a white dress. Wavy black hair that just covered the nape of her neck. Bright eyes that I could see shining through the dark. Even though she had no shoes, I remember her wearing black patent dress-up ones with a delicate buckle on the side and a dainty strap. When I think of her, I feel a similar anguish as when I recall my last abortion. The abortion I didn't want to have. I found out later that the little girl's father had been shot and killed the night before.

And the Hummers troll. Dragging a silent death toll that promises Disneyland. The Disneyland of the Third World. From which, once you pass through the bewitching gates, there is very little chance of escape.

"Come with us, little boy who has already suffered as much as a man. Come with us, boy who will always have nothing unless you do. Come with us, child with the hunger that goes deeper than your hollow eyes and the unfulfilled status of your strut. You are ready. We have been watching you. All of your dreams await. Just by climbing into this magic vehicle, you will go from the bottom to the top. You can oppress and no longer be oppressed. You can exercise onto others all of the pain that has been inflicted upon you."

And as the boys in a Mexican barrio never settle all snug in their beds, visions of money, guns, and women dance in their heads.

———————————

She got away, eventually. Another child who was old enough now to be sexually exploited by the wealthy men from the north, living the future of the little girl in the shadows who I fell instantly in love with in the barrios of Monterrey. This little girl was from Guatemala, and, like so many children in impoverished countries, she was taken from her home. Just taken. Men came with guns and her mother had no choice. The girl was seven or so. I can't remember her exact age, and such details don't matter. The fact that she was taken is enough.

A little boy was taken, too. He wasn't her brother but was soon to become so. For three years, they clung to each other in fear and in mutual protection. As they were transported across the Guatemala/Mexico border, they became all each other had.

After she got away, she sought the safety of Mexico City. Funny that. People always think Mexico City is so dangerous. Yes, it is, but ironically, it's the safest place in Mexico. I often joke that if the cartels moved drugs through Mexico City, they would get stuck in a traffic jam. A friend told me that the cartels don't shit where they eat. The shitting goes on in the countryside. After she got away, she went straight to the safe haven of Mexico City and told her story.

She and the little boy were together for two or three years. She was raped right away. The beginning of the seasoning that, like 'the doll' in Cambodia, she would never succumb to. The little boy worked. And he comforted the girl and helped her to clean herself after the daily assaults. They slept together at night until this became a problem. This is the part I remember the most—the beatings and the raping and the locking in dark rooms is not as horrifying as this part that almost happened.

They decided that the girl was more valuable than the boy. She would bring in more money. She was already a sought-after item by the men who came looking for a child to destroy.

They decided that the girl and the boy were too attached. They decided it was dangerous to have any humanity going on, that the girl had an ally in the boy, that they took care of each other, that there was love. Love threatens torture. Love impedes the process of beating down someone's emotions until they are but a robot made of flesh. Somebody had to go, and somebody had to be disciplined. Somebody had to be physically exterminated, and the other had to be emotionally destroyed to become a fully compliant slave.

They took them to the country. They tied him to a tree. They made her hold the gun. They commanded her to shoot him. Her only friend. Her little brother.

They took them to the country. They tied him to a tree. They made her hold the gun. They commanded her to shoot him. Her only friend. Her little brother.
They took them to the country. They tied him to a tree. They made her hold the gun. They commanded her to shoot him. Her only friend. Her little brother.

⸻◦◦⟨◉⟩◦◦⸻

She didn't do it. Someone else did. One of the men who was forced to be a killer. One of the men who was once a boy whose face was hammered into a steel mask. And, yet, beneath the metal that had become flesh lies fear. As still as prey hiding in the brush. Silent.

When I read her story, I thought of him, too. I thought: how are the oppressed and the oppressor produced? What are the heartless components of the machine that is so skilled at banging out these shapes, relentless, as though it is the only way we can ever be? And, how are they one and the same thing? The killer and the killed? How are they the other side of the Janus face of a culture made of violence, conquest, and exploitation? Two-faced. I believe that the young man who killed the little boy didn't want to be a killer. How could anyone? The same way the girl didn't want to be a sex slave. The same way the little boy didn't want to be murdered.

She didn't do it. She told the story of standing there, gun in hand, being forced to point it at her brother. A brother who, in many ways, had also become like a son; and she, his sister and also like his daughter—so thick was the density of their need for each other.

She stood there. Aiming it at him as he turned his head to one side and scrunched his face in an attempt to ward off the inevitable, this savage ending that would happen whether it was she who pulled the trigger or not. They shouted at her:

"Fire! Shoot! C'mon, you stupid bitch, pull the trigger!"

"You had better do it," another sneered. "You think your life is miserable now, wait and see what happens if you don't kill

191

this piece of Guatemalan vermin." The leader moved towards her, his eyes hardened slits. He raised his hand as though to slap her across the face, the unexpected movement cutting the air. The hand stopped just before it reached her face. He traced her jawline with his finger, slowly, almost gently, until he stuck it into her mouth and commanded her to suck. Fingertips moving down her neck, a sharp, mock strangle at the throat, cupped her young breast, his head cocked to one side, quizzical, as though he were evaluating a future acquisition. She looked at the ground. Taking it. As she had been trained to do. No longer whimpering or stiff with fear. His hand continued, grabbed her ass. Gave it a proprietary pat.

"And if you do it," he oozed, "things will be so much easier for you. Maybe we won't lock you in the hole anymore. Maybe you can be with the commander. Have some chocolate. Some nice food. Some pretty clothes. Shoot him. Be a good girl. Be a good whore. You don't need him. He's not worth his miserable life."

Her arms had started to droop. The man shoved them back up, and another soldier hit her across the head with the back of his hand. Her head flew to one side; tears roared down her face. The boy hung like Christ, head heavy with grief. Tears rolled down his cheeks in unison with the torrent of hers. The paramilitary stood as chunks of shadow as the birds returned to the high branches about to resume their afternoon song. The world hesitated as though to ask, along with the children,

"Why is this happening? Why is this life?"

<hr />

Finally, a sex tourist listened. Finally, a man on holiday who had paid to abuse her had an accessible heart. Somehow, after he had gotten his money's worth, he was able to feel for a fellow creature: a young woman, a young woman who had been so recently a child, a young woman from a poor country, a young woman like all the others he had used whose eyes he had never bothered, or cared, or even thought of looking into. For some reason, he looked into her eyes, and like a miracle, she became human. This man who had exploited women's bodies for his individual needs began to extend himself beyond himself. Willing to put himself at risk. Willing to open himself to empathy. Willing to never go back again. Willing to get her out so that she wouldn't ever have to go back again either.

After she didn't shoot the little boy. After he was shot an unnecessary number of times and drooped in the ropes that bound him. After his blood ran down his legs and dripped from his toes and formed a crimson pool at the base of the tree. After he was left there to cook and rot in the sun. As he was being pecked at by birds and dug into by maggots until his tomb was made of ropes and bones, she was beaten. Just enough to almost kill her. They were professionals in knowing how to push brutality to the edge and stop, just soon enough to keep their prisoner not quite dead.

She didn't remember what happened for the next few months. Her body healed, but her heart never did. The brutal beating where she hung for weeks on the edge of life and death was nothing compared to the psychological torture of being forced to witness the murder of the little boy.

She told the interviewer how, over the years, she was moved from child brothel to child brothel, servicing men from the north, men who paid more to violate a child. Even though she hated them all, after each man took from her, she kept asking them to help her. She begged. She wept. After they had fucked her girl-body, she sat at their feet and lay her head on their laps, begging these men who were both her violators and her possible saviors. Some of them didn't tell the pimp. Overlooked the fact that she had begged them to help her, been a bit of a downer and an inconvenience. But some of them did, annoyed by this human suffering at the end of their entitled transaction, their well-deserved bit of holiday fun. And she was beaten. Or stuck in the hole. But she never stopped asking. She had a resilience that would never be broken.

Until, finally, seven years after her abduction, after her young body had been used by thousands of men, after she had lived for years in horror that she would be the next rape and murder package deal,[9] one of them finally heard her. One of them finally looked into her eyes, saw her humanity, and helped her. He got her out of the prison his selfishness had financed. One of the sex tourists found his humanity.

The Living Contradiction.

When Linnihan brutally raped the sixty-five-year-old woman and left her for dead, when he relieved himself in her almost-corpse, did he do it because he was simply a bad man, a sick person, and any possibility for empathy had been long corroded? Had he been 'just born that way'?

But I had seen some tenderness between these barbs of brutality. I had seen the innocence that was poisoned by his belief that he had been guaranteed something he was never given. I had seen the expectant eyes of a boy who had never been taught how to grow up. I had seen the foundation of the hatred—I had seen the living contradiction.

The day at the Burger King when he didn't kill me and leave me slumped on the side of a middle-of-nowhere Arizona road, I continued to walk down the highway towards the Greyhound Station. The telltale red, white and blue sign with its lunging dog spurred me forth and was the beacon that guaranteed my soon-to-be salvation: safe on a bus and watching this twisted heartland unravel and stream past. The vehicle I had less than half an hour ago been a prisoner of jiggled along with its furtive squeak and carried my captor farther and farther away from me. I was finally free.

"Everything is actually going to be okay!" I congratulated myself. "You got out of it! You escaped! You survived! Good job! That was really close." I marvelled at the fact that I actually wasn't dead; I hadn't been sliced up in the desert or kept forever as his sex slave. My life dream that the night before had been reduced to "get yourself the hell out of here!" had actually come true. I was almost skipping down the side of the highway until, much to my disbelief and horror, the vehicle looked as though it was going to turn. I stopped and watched as it leaned a bit to the right and the wheels, yes, the wheels of the camper/van were turning! My heart dropped. The horror came back as quickly as it had gone: he drove into the parking lot of the Greyhound station

Rape Baby

Arizona was the first and only time I was abducted, but not the first time I've been raped. I don't worry about it as much anymore and don't feel like as much of a target. It's a relief in a lot of ways to no longer be young. My mom told me this once, years ago, how she was happy that in middle-age, she no longer attracted unwanted attention. She felt freer to just be in the world. I thought it an odd thing to say at the time. But I agree with her now.

I am pushing menopause. I can no longer have babies. I barely bleed anymore. It is statistically proven that women in their reproductive age are much more desirable rape victims. This is odd: a victim and a rapist are obviously not going to have a future together. There isn't any happy-ever-after-having-a-family-kind-of-possibility.

A guy told me once that fucking fertile women is way more of a turn-on than fucking non-fertile women. He didn't want to have any kids, though. The strange fantasy of fertility based on the reality of fertility, but the fantasy not wanting to have anything to do with that reality, especially if she does the natural thing and gets knocked up. Twisted.

I decided to research the statistics of rape babies. It was a lot easier than I thought because rape babies are far more common than I thought: the national rape-related pregnancy rate in the US is 5.0% per rape among victims of reproductive age (aged 12 to 45); among adult women, an estimated 32,101 pregnancies result from rape each year. Among 34 cases of rape-related pregnancy, the majority occurred among

adolescents and resulted from assault by a known, often related, perpetrator. Only 11.7% of these victims received immediate medical attention after the assault, and 47.1% received no
medical attention related to the rape. A total of 32.4% of these
victims did not discover they were pregnant until they had
already entered the second trimester; 32.2% opted to keep the
infant, whereas 50% had an abortion, and 5.9% placed the infant for adoption; an additional 11.8% miscarried. Rape-related
pregnancy occurs with significant frequency. It is a cause of
many unwanted pregnancies and is closely linked to familial
and domestic violence. It is obvious that greater attention and
effort should be aimed at preventing and identifying unwanted
pregnancies that result from sexual assault.[10]

Yes. Good idea: giving greater attention to pregnancies that
originate in violence. I don't think it's possible for a baby to have
a good life with such a toxic start. I knew a guy once who was a
rape baby. My friend had a thing with him for a bit, and he told
her. She left him because he was really messed up. Intravenous
drugs. Violence. Assaults. Last I heard, he was in prison.

I remember one of the times I had an abortion, the
anti-abortionists were in front of the clinic parading around
with their smug placards of mutilated fetuses in all their gory
glory.

"Glory Glory for the Fetus! Hallelujah for the Fetus!
Glory Glory for the Fetus. The woman doesn't matter at all!"

They weren't singing that song or anything. I just made
it up now. Maybe I'll teach it to them the next time I shout at
them.

What really gets me about these so-called pro-life people is
that so many of them are men. That there are anti-choice men
out there at all. Yes, there are women out there too, and this is
disturbing, and sometimes it's difficult to decide which is worse.

In her book, *Living Dolls: The Return of Sexism*, Natasha
Walter describes twenty-first century culture as 'hyper-sexual'
and that it has co-opted the language of choice and liberation.[11]
As the legacy of the Third Wave 'Pro-Sex' feminist prioritization of women's sexual agency, young women are now free

to become empowered lap-dancers with the continued goal of satisfying the male, objectifying, gaze.

The women out there parading around with their horror movie placards hearken back to a much deeper tradition of internalized sexism, though, than the I-can-have-sex-with-anyone-I-want-so-now-I-am-free, all-dolled-up contemporary (non) feminists. The dogma of the self-righteous anti-abortionists is a continuation of the obligation of the female sex to fulfill their biological duty as dictated by the Christian, conveniently male, god. Anti-choice women uphold what Gerda Lerner tells us is "the traditionalist explanation that focuses on women's reproductive capacity and sees motherhood as women's chief goal in life."

Lerner, writing through the work of anthropologists, has proven that the inevitability of male supremacy is not inevitable at all. She explains how it is in the pre-patriarchal "hunter and gatherer societies where we find many examples of complementarity between the sexes and societies in which women have relatively high status, which contradicts the claims of the man-the-hunter school of thought." Citing Elise Boulding's essay for a non-sexist future, Lerner points out how Boulding "has shown that the man-the-hunter myth and its perpetuation are socio-cultural creations which serve the interest of maintaining male supremacy and hegemony."[12] Be they the pole-dancers proving their liberation in a lascivious 'gentleman's club' or the anti-choice women maintaining female biological determinism, these are women on the side of their own oppression.

It can be surprising that women are out there impeding their sisters' right to choose; however, when it gets right down to it, it's not surprising at all that men are. And that they make up the majority.[13]

The control and ownership of female sexuality was the beginning of patriarchy and male supremacy. Friedrich Engels tells us how the first act of class oppression was of the female sex by the male; Claude Lévi-Strauss argues that it was the 'exchange in women' as the leading cause of female subordination and that it took many forms such as bride-stealing, rape, and negotiated marriages; Gerda Lerner states that the oppression of women predates the creation of slavery and made it possible. Women were the first slaves, and as with all people who have been or are currently enslaved, to make a person into a slave, they must be made *other* than human,[14] which is exactly what happens when you take away a woman's right to choose whether to have a baby or not—but I am certainly not implying that it's always an easy decision to make.

This time on my way to get my second abortion, the raw emotion of choosing to surgically end a life I could never properly care for had put me in a pretty feisty mood. I lashed out at the anti-choice activists impeding my way with their arrogant self-righteousness and disregard for the life of the woman. Because of my particular disdain for the men involved and their insidious perpetuation of patriarchy, I went up to one of them and said,

"I have a question."

"Yes."

"What if it's a rape baby? A fetus created through extreme violence. Should a woman be forced to carry violence and trauma to term?" I thought I had a good point, that surely this would be an exception to their condemnation of a woman's right to her own body. He responded like an evangelistic zombie:

"It's not the fetus' fault." I was shocked. I got really mad. I shouted all kinds of things at him. Such a cavalier statement about another creature's body and psyche brought back all my trauma. It was actually amazing that I didn't take it all out on him. Grab a bottle from the garbage can and smash it over his head. Sometimes I commend myself on my self-restraint.

I had a rape fetus inside me once. I know I promised you a happy ending to all of this (and there is, I promise you once again!), but this part is worse than everything I have told you so far. For me anyway. When I started writing this memoir, I had no idea that I was going to write about this particular victimization. I try not to think about it. Even thirty-three years

198

later. And the funny thing is, the reason why I don't want to think about it is because I can't remember any of it. The during part anyway.

My biggest problem when I was the desirable rape victim age is that I was too curious. I had too big of a passion for life. I talked about this in Part One. Women aren't allowed the same freedoms as men. I am saying this again because it's really important because it's so unfair. It's really important because it's true. Over one-half of the species shouldn't be disciplined for having the audacity of wanting to be fully alive.

GHB. Montreal 1986

This is a testimony of one of the fifty percentile of rapes that are estimated as going unreported. I was too shocked to report it. I was too traumatized. I just wanted to forget it had ever happened. I was really young. The fact that this had happened to me was inconceivable. The fact that it had happened at all was unimaginable. I had never known about any of this kind of thing happening. I guess that's why it was easy not to ever think about: because for all my life, up until then, such an act never existed.

I was at a friend's birthday party. I was having a lot of fun. I was nineteen. I was living in Montreal. It was my first year of university. My life was full of non-stop adventures. But I certainly didn't sign up for this one.

There were two guys there. They were friends of my friend. They worked with her. Cooks in the restaurant where she waitressed. She was a classical pianist and was studying music at McGill University. I forget her name because I never saw her again.

The two guys were Persian. The new Canadians I told you about in Part Five. They knew a restaurant with belly dancers. They had some friends who worked there, so we could stay after hours if we wanted to. I had never seen belly dancers. The birthday party was winding down. They invited me to go with them.

"Of course! I would love to come! I've never seen belly dancers before!" They were friends of my classical pianist friend. Everything must be fine if it's connected to the purity of the symphony, shouldn't it? Everything will be fine when you know nothing about what is going to happen, won't it?

It ended up that I didn't see belly dancers until years later. We went into the restaurant. The belly dancers were on a break. The guys took me to a table near the exit that didn't have much of a view of the stage. I think I mentioned this, and they said we were just going to sit here during the break. I sat down on a brown vinyl bench with plastic plants hanging behind it. One of the guys asked me if I wanted a drink. I said vodka soda. He knew the bartender. They chatted and then he brought me the drink. I had two or three sips. The next thing I knew, I woke up in an apartment, having been raped and impregnated by two men.

It was 1986, and they had put GHB in my drink. The date rape drug. No one knew about it then. Except the rapists, of course. I knew they had drugged me, but I had no idea what GHB was or that it was about to become "a thing" for the inconceivably terrible men who put it into our drinks to fuck our might-as-well-be-dead but oh-so-cooperative bodies. When I think of the men who do this, I feel as though I am a different species. How can we be related? Why is what you did to me and probably to many other women acceptable to you? How is any of this possible?

I want you to know, though, that I have never had that many really bad things happen to me. Not like lots of other people. That's the thing. These stories are terrible, but they could be so much worse. Believe it or not, I think I got off relatively unscathed.

There was a guy I knew once who had a collection of books about serial killers. Some of them were biographies, and there were a couple of autobiographies. I know the names of the serial killers celebrated in these books, but I will not mention them again and add to their twisted notoriety.

"How can you read such terrible books?" I asked, horrified. "Books that sensationalize evil? Why should someone who has committed multiple rapes and murders be allowed to tell their story, and how can it even be published and the pain continued?" I knew it was all about the profitability of sensationalism and the guarantee that people like him would buy them, but I asked the questions anyway.

"Serial killers are interesting," he responded indifferently. "Why should I be interested in victims? Victims are boring."

I certainly didn't expect that answer. I left and never went back to his house. I didn't speak to him again except for the token 'Hey' when we walked past each other on the street

"I am a victim," I thought. "And I am certainly not boring."

I knew at that moment this book would be written someday. When I was ready.

December 21st, 1994. Around 6 p.m. A Small Arizona Town.

I stood on the side of the Arizona highway. The camper/van pulled into the Greyhound station. My view was blocked by the building. I couldn't see if he got out of the vehicle, if he went in, or if he was sitting waiting for me. Nothing. I waited, wondering what to do. The Greyhound station had been my lifeline for an hour or so now. It was all I had thought about since I saw it emerge from the middle of the nowhere I had been held captive in. Should I go back to the Burger King? I have no memory of thinking that. It would have been the logical option. Go back there and get help. I only remember the startle and disappointment. I waited. Didn't dare to move as though I was trying to hide in open view. I assumed the worst.

And then, as unexpectedly as he had pulled in, he pulled out and continued driving down the road. Away from me. I breathed. I started to walk again. Head down and marching. This was going to happen. I was getting away. I was going to make it to the station before he came back. I was going to buy a ticket. I was going to get on a bus and get the hell out of here.

And I arrived. I was back in public again. Safe. There were witnesses. There was a phone. I went up to the counter. The man looked up at me curiously and handed me the bag with the Whopper and the carton of milk.

"A man just left this for you."

Post-Rapes Ritual. Montreal 1986.

When I came to, one of the men was gone. The other one was still there. The apartment was a sickly cream colour scuffed with the long-ago need to be repainted. There were no pictures on the walls. No one ever lived there long. The soiled curtains matched the neglect of lives coming and going and the mangled lines of broken blinds looked like hacked-up innards. Flagrant morning sun blasted through the cracks as knives of light. I lay on a bed in the middle of an operating theatre where surgery had been performed on my young body, on my innocence. Soiled white paint closed in on me from the walls and from the ceiling. The emptiness was suffocating. A world stripped down to a brutal, soulless nothing.

He ceremoniously handed me my underwear.
Like a gift.
I felt as empty as the barren walls.
He told me what a great time he and his friend had had.
I stared through hollow discs.
He wanted my phone number.
Really? I still think.
How could this be possible?
Such an impossibility happening to me.
Then this insanity of thinking I would give him my phone number?
Like I had enjoyed what I had no memory of.
But started to have a horrifying idea about.

And felt like I was going to puke.
A sickly state of no recollection of what I knew had happened.
To me.
To my body.
Me as a halfway corpse.
Only a pulse.
Only breathing.
Some shapes of entitled violation.
Holding my prone body down.
Spreading my legs.
I said,
"Sure you can have my phone number.
Yes, it would be great to see you guys again."
He handed me a piece of scrap paper.
A pen.
I scribbled down a fake one.
"Thank you. I'll call you soon,"
he smiled.

I have no memory of finding the rest of my clothes. This memory is buried beneath the ritual of the underwear. Did he hand them all to me, piece by piece? In a scooped-up bundle in his arms? Or were they a crumpled mass on the floor that I had to humiliatingly dig through? I only have the memory of leaving. Carrying a shock that still hasn't dissipated. And never will.

The stairs were equally ugly and smelled of stale cooking. I crept down a lumpy strip of no-slip vinyl, concentrating on not tripping. My legs were jelly. I may have tripped on the final step and burst through the door as through a membrane onto the bustling morning street. That's how I imagine it now. That would have been the most appropriate exit: exploding out of a torture chamber through a sheath of flesh stretched translucent, my young being made of anguish. The surreal experience that every recently violated person has when they re-emerge into normalcy—a foreigner, a freak, a crude cut-out clumsily pasted onto the flow of the everyday. People racing to work.

Corner stores offering milk for tea when you wake up to an empty carton and have to dash out and get more. Newspaper stands. The streams and jams of traffic honking impatiently. People lined up waiting for buses. Early morning flower stands with their magnificence of not having been picked over yet.

I had no idea what neighbourhood of Montreal I was in. I just had to find a Metro station. Look at the map. Get back to a world I recognized. Get back to my little apartment. Close the curtains and sleep for days. Maybe when I woke up, none of this would have happened. Everything would be the same again. Like the people who rushed around in their daily patterns, I would fall back into mine. Without this illness that had suddenly become a part of me. Infiltrated my joy. I could feel sickness gagging me from the inside, rising up, lodged there as a mash of toxins from my womb to the base of my throat. I did succeed in forgetting. Dulling the details. Until now. In this act of writing, that makes me wonder why I am writing this at all.

A Girl in a Park. Anywhere. Any Time.

As I write, I am having a moment of doubt. Despite my revolutionary proclamations, through this painful act of remembering what I have intentionally forgotten for decades, a story that I have rarely told, I am wondering if it really is a good idea to remember such things in detail. To not just forget.

I am sitting at table 104. It is early autumn, and the leaves have begun to quiver with their impending descent. The light has softened from the saturation of summer, and I am immersed in the delicate transition towards the blocks of grey wet that are approaching in the north. Tears are streaming. Sometimes it can be so difficult to write this, to remember fully, to tell you everything, and maybe tell you something important that will open up your remembering, your telling.

I will continue this moment of doubt, another honesty that I won't hold back in the hopes that I will return to another reason for courage. I will ask you what I know many people *already ask.* I will get another jump on the inevitable attempts to undermine this manifesto.

Is it really healthy to express, to acknowledge, to surface pain and trauma to undermine the dangers of repression? Or is it better to keep it all buried. Maybe if it decays for long enough, it will decompose and go away. Maybe it won't fester. The fact that I was unconscious during the first rapes makes the memory virtually unthinkable. I have not thought of it for most of my life. But I know it's been there since it started. It is part of my body. There is never an absolute exorcism.

What is it about testosterone and the corresponding construction of the man in patriarchy that makes such acts even possible? So that victims often feel like we have to spend the rest of our lives not remembering—unremembering that we have been forced to contain another's rot.

A friend told me a story. His story was recalled through my story. My story triggered something in his life that had been forgotten. Something so horrible that he had blacked it out, too. Here is another good reason to tell our stories, no matter how painful: from within the brutality of the gender divide, the disparate worlds of the he and the she, we can connect through the disconnect and override the surveillance that is bent upon keeping us apart.

He told me how there was an unconscious girl in the park. He was fifteen or sixteen. She may have been dead, he told me he had thought. No one seemed to know exactly and it didn't seem to matter. He didn't know who she was, and that didn't seem to matter either. He found out because a guy a bit older came over and told him and his buddy,

"There's a girl passed out over there. Go fuck her. I just did. It was great."[15]

My friend told me about a sinister structure in the park. It was called "The Rig." It was originally intended for small children to play on. The small children never went near it. In their innocence, they knew it was a very dangerous place. And they were right.

It ended up being for the older teenage boys who hung out under and around it. My friend included. They climbed it recklessly when drunk or high. The long hairs. The hoodlums. The scary boys. The boys I would have certainly been afraid of when I was a teenager. But then I was scared of all boys. Young men and their burgeoning testosterone that buzzes with the unpredictability of going one way or the other.

It was three stories tall. Raw wood. There were platforms meant for the kids to climb around on. Ten feet by ten feet, he approximated. A kind of blocky monkey bars tucked away in the corner of the park. Hemmed in by poplar and shrubs. Railway tracks. A creek. The girl lay prone and ready behind The Rig.

They didn't see her, he said. My friend and his friend when they were walking home from school that day. They were creeped out and kept walking. Didn't think to look behind The Rig. Creeped out. Disgusted. Kept walking. He confessed.

They went home. Back to the normalcy of not being raped repeatedly on the edge of a playground. Back to the normalcy of not being brutalized amidst the damp sweet of poplars, face up or face down in cool, dark soil, immersed in the conflation of decomposition and life. Back to the normalcy of the poplars never witnessing such violation, with their leaves like silver dollars, whispering magic as they rustle and shimmer. Back to the normalcy of not being serenaded by the bright back and forth calls of children playing while a young woman's limp body is being raped. Back to the normalcy of a female body not being a vessel for the very hatred that hates her for no reason other than just being. Back to the normalcy of not thinking about what is. Back to the normalcy of ignoring denial.

He was nonchalant, my friend remarked. The young rapist. The guy who had told him about the prone girl to fuck. Another ordinary day with a bonus on the side as he happened by, or another guy was considerate enough to fill him in on, or a time-worn scenario he came up with himself. An 'of course' this is what we do. Go do it. I am giving you a tip. I didn't have to tell you. A between guys kinda' thing. A slap on the back. Go for it, homie. She's all yours. Go fuck her. An invitation. A command.

An entitlement. A convenience. A gift. Go fuck her. I'm done. It's your turn.

They never heard anything more about it, he told me when I asked. After they walked by and went home. Nothing was reported. No one talked about it at school. No one ever knew who she was. And no one cared to ask.

My friend told me he had buried it, the untold story he had walked past. The story with a well-worn plot. He and his buddy never spoke about it. Too terrible to think about even when it doesn't happen to you.[16]

December 21st, 1994 around 6 p.m. A Greyhound Station. A Small Town in Arizona.

I took the Burger King bag from the guy behind the ticket counter. I bought a ticket back to Las Vegas. I think the bus was leaving pretty soon. I don't recall waiting around the station for long or sitting in one of those cold, plastic, dirty, cream-colored scoop chairs attached in rows of five or six or eight, depending on the size of the waiting room. Staring at the clock. Suspended in my need to get as far away from here as possible. Watching the darkening desert. Feeling the harsh heat of day dissipate. My body ceasing to sweat. Watching other folks straggle in from the homely parking lot, dropped off in dusty cars or dented trucks. Seeing a car every now and then drive by and dissolve into the lingering heat. Some kind of country music coming out of lousy speakers, tinny, barely audible. The lonely nowhere of a small town bus station.

No. I don't remember any of this. I just got onto a bus. Stepped up triumphant and numb onto my magic Greyhound. That whisked me away through silver light.

PART SIX

The Newspaper Article.

I have lost the newspaper article from that time. This isn't the newspaper article that was found right before the publication of this book, the one that changed what I had thought was true for over twenty years, the one that I have bookmarked now in my favourites: this is the one that was lost long ago, the one I cast aside in my traumatized state of disregard for even the life-affirming.

I called Prescott to find out what newspapers there were in 1994. I was told the Prescott Courier was the only one. The article must have been in it. I have searched the newspaper archives. Again and again. Full of disbelief that I can't find it. I thought for sure it would be there. This tactile object I could hold onto amidst the slippages of memory, this irretrievable moment yet another layer in a life's ever-shifting backdrop.

But I can't help but wonder: if I were able to read it again, where would it take me? What words had the reporter chosen, what phrases, what tone? But I will never know. This part will always be forgotten as it has dissolved into the phantasmagoric world of late-twentieth-century microfiche.

I know it existed, though. It was mailed to me. The memory is in keeping with the spectral fate of the microfiche as it floats on the brink of disintegration. All colours are long forgotten. The scene is murky, one-dimensional. As though I am remembering through cataracts.

It was soon after my return to the apartment where Paul and I were roommates. The place of his loving but oh-so-cloying and paternal concern. Me, a pampered princess in this apartment on the hill with a surround of bay windows. A tower where I stood and kept watch for the return of my captor.

I had only been back for a couple of weeks. Paul wasn't there to immediately sense my alarm and run down to answer the door. I see myself stiffen when I hear the doorbell ring. Who could it be? I think. Why is someone here? I don't dare go down the stairs, descend from my tower to the dangers that lie beyond. Open the door.

There is a sharp knock. And another. Another. Impatient now. I tip-toe down. Peer through the peephole. It's a letter carrier. I open the door.

I see myself bending slightly forward, extending my hand to receive his offering, opening what may have been a manila envelope, a larger envelope than usual that would have pricked surprise, fortified concern. It was still so close to just after the abduction that everything held the possibility of re-imprisonment.

I opened the envelope and pulled out a piece of newspaper. Folded in half. It was the front page. I don't think I left the doorway as I stood and read an interpretation of my story from a public perspective. It had as big an impact on me as when I got the love letter from prison. But in a way, my ordeal and triumph being written about and even known about by a local paper, the local community, was a much greater surprise. Besides the cops, I didn't know that anyone else knew, that my story had most likely been talked about in a small-town coffee shop and maybe even at the Bird Cage Saloon amidst those same yellow beams of light slanting through the high windows as on the day of the abduction.

I remember touching the paper. The inky smell of it. Maybe I hung it on the fridge. Maybe I tucked it away somewhere for safekeeping or forgetfulness. Maybe it yellowed from age before it was lost during one of my many moves.

I hadn't expected anything. I was just happy to not be a prisoner anymore. Not having to withstand being raped every couple of hours. Not having to worry about being kept in some airstream trailer in the middle of the desert. Not having to fear for my life and constantly plot how to save it. Not having to be two people at the same time. It was as though everything was still reduced to that one way of being: don't be murdered.

Such things as newspaper articles were of a different world. A different universe. The straight world. Maybe that's why I lost it. It had nothing to do with my reality and I carelessly cast it aside, as I did so many things.

The headline read: "Canadian Hero ...." I can't remember the exact words of the rest. It was something like "Canadian Hero Catches Serial Rapist." I wish I could read it again now. But it's lost. I know it existed, though, because that was the first time this victim thought of herself as a hero. It was even written in a newspaper. Even though I didn't think much of it at the time, it did make me feel proud. I had made a mistake, but I had done something important, too.

These were the days when you were still drinking, Dad.

Long before the time when you were forced to quit. You had no choice. If you hadn't, you would have lost everything.

You had many death beds. You told me the story, as you lay in what could have been the third to last or the second, about the best time of your life. It was long before marriage. Long before kids. Long before responsibility. Long before having to quit.

You were with your friends. In the forest. Sixteen, seventeen, eighteen years old. The physical prime of all healthy male lives. You used to take a bus to the base of Hollyburn Mountain, you told me. You and your buddies. And it was the base. There wasn't the wide curving road that people speed up now for a zippy Sunday drive. You climbed up from what would have been a small highway then. Just above sea level. Pack-boards full of bottles of beer on your backs.

This was back in the days when there were cabins on Hollyburn Mountain. I don't know how many, but I think you told me there were five. Anyone could use them. If you made it up on a Friday night before they were all taken, the cabin in the woods was your party-down castle.

"I want to tell you about the best time of my life," you said as I sat next to you, devouring your every last word as your eyes travelled back in time.

"Gee, we had fun! We'd climb up Hollyburn! Get one of those cabins up there on a Friday night! Me and my friends! Climb up with cases of beer on our backs!"

"Wasn't it hard climbing all that way, Dad, weighed down by all those bottles of beer?"

"Nah. Prime of our lives. It was nothing for us in those days."

I imagine you and your friends inside the rustic cabin. Weathered boards and slanted steps. I see knotholes in the walls, moonbeams shining through. You and your friends sitting on creaking chairs or cross-legged on a barren floor. A coal oil lamp like the one you would always light at the cabin when I was a kid. Its warm hiss. A steady flicker as the flame never stays still.

I forgot to ask you if you had brought sleeping bags, maybe a gas stove. Some coffee for the morning. Some food. You didn't mention any of those essential items because the most important one was the beer.

These nights always ended up in euphoria.

As you confided the best time of your life that had been kept secret for most of it, your words were sparse, yet eager, as they reached out to touch the memory, summon it back to life. I saw the gang of flashlight beams, bobbing and streaking through the pitch black. Like a web of lighthouse beacons, sporadically cut up by trunks of Hemlock and whoops of delight, as a pack of unleashed youth leapt over deadfall and ploughed through dense stands of salal.

The best time of your life: racing through the forest rip-roaring drunk with your buddies. You lay back on the pillow. Your expression both serene and sad.

⎯⎯⎯⎯●⎯⎯⎯⎯

These were back in the days when your buddies still came around. Your drinking buddies. They mysteriously stopped coming after you had to quit.

You would all stand in your workshop, leaning against the work-bench, the lathe, the table saw, in a circle of drunken comradery. The basement. The scary place. The forbidden place. The place of men. I wanted to come to the party too. To your party. You didn't ever tell me this story, not even on your death-beds when you told me so many others and, as you were leaving, you were finally able to show me your love. But I have told it to myself countless times. This is another brick in the foundation of my life-long fear of men. My anxiety in their presence. Nerves tweaked. My desperate need to please that, as so often happened, resulted in my getting hurt.

So I did. I couldn't help it. I felt it was wrong, but I went down anyway. I came to your party. Even though I knew there was danger. Guaranteed. I yearned to be a part of it. To be a part of your laughter that I could hear as I stood at the top of the stairs, looking through the crack in the door I didn't dare open any further. Yet. Straining to see what I knew was wrong to enter. A gut feeling denied. Four, five, six years old. Learning how to not say "No."

Slowly. Holding my breath, I opened the door and placed one foot on the top stair. Then the other. Down one step. Two. A whole stairway until I would appear, stealth-like in my desire for you to love me. I can't remember if you and your friends turned your heads. I imagine myself wearing the pink ging-ham dress, shaped like a bell, from when I was around two, the colour of the tea-rose perfume your mother always wore, even though I would have long grown out of it by then. White knee socks that underlined my still dimpled knees. Black pat-ent shoes with buckles. This is how I remember it. Myself: a pretty-little-girl victim. All dressed up to lose a war I had no idea I was in.

I reach the bottom of the stairs. Did they look at me before it started? Their joking around interrupted by my need? Did I have to creep into the circle? Weighed down by being ignored? Humiliated before it began? Tug shyly on a pant leg?

Whatever way it happened, I was noticed. By you. Spotted as your convenient psychological prey in the crowd. Your

self-esteem scapegoat. And I don't remember why or when or
how it started. I only remember the starting. The burst of a
polka in 2/4 time. And you sang, pointing and laughing like an
overgrown bully:

"I don't want her, you can have her, she's too fat for me, hey!
She's too fat for me, hey!
She's too fat for me, hey!
I don't want her you can have her she's too fat for me
She's too fat, she's too fat, she's too fat for me! HEY!!"

Did you dance around? I know you swung your beer bottle
like it was some sort of sea shanty. Maybe kicked a leg out
drunkenly to the "Heys!" You thought it was funny. Harmless.
All in good fun. Your face was red. Shiny. And, as I remember
it now, your glowing cheeks had the innocence of apples. But
yours was a tainted innocence. Snubbed and clumsy and lethal.
That of a man who is still a child and begs "Pick Me" with a
joviality that tries too hard. And I, your daughter, became the
brunt of a big joke that you tried to get your buddies to join in
on. I don't think anyone did. I am happy to remember that now.
I had allies. Maybe they were as horrified as I was. Some of
them seemed uncomfortable. Squirmed. Scowled in your direction. Noticed the heat of my cheeks. The terror in my eyes. But
you didn't. Or maybe you did and it made you loathe yourself
more. I can't remember leaving.

Some readers may think, what of it? Big deal. What's she complaining about? That's not so bad. She's too sensitive. She could
have been sexually abused. Then she would have something to
complain about.

But they are wrong.

When reading Dr. Gabor Maté's book, *In the Realm of the
Hungry Ghosts: Close Encounters with Addiction*, the doubting of
the validity of the chronic emotional rejection I had experienced
into my 40s was lifted. I knew what I have always felt is true.

Maté diagnoses drug addiction as a result of dysfunctional
human development rather than anything innate or, more

typically, the addict's choice, the "it's all their fault," and "they could change their lives if they really wanted to." The majority of drug-addicted people were sexually assaulted in childhood—especially the women—who often continue to be raped in adulthood as they are prostituted to pay for their addiction; however, and here's where my personal trials were finally honoured, Maté also connects physical abuse to emotional abuse and explains how the cause is the same, and the effect is only a matter of degree. And good fortune.

"The very same brain centres that interpret and "feel" physical pain also become activated during the experience of emotional rejection," Maté says. He explains how on brain scans, experiences of emotional rejection "light up" when a person is emotionally ostracized in the same way as when triggered by physically harmful stimuli."[1] When I read this, I was relieved that what I have felt all of my life even has science behind it.

Yes, those who may accuse me of making too much about nothing, you're right: we always could have been sexually abused as children. And those who weren't are the lucky ones. Regardless of what I have survived and still struggle with, I am one of those lucky ones. But that doesn't take away the fact that the cycle of emotional abuse has a profound and debilitating effect on the abused. Like when I didn't listen to my gut feeling when being hunted by a serial rapist when the people at the Bird Cage warned me about him, said he was bad news, and I was still inclined to be nice. To accept the fated ride back to the motel, even though I was uneasy and I just wanted him to go away and my heart rose in my throat and made my voice small and I felt like I was floating, fading, and it was as though my limbs were dissolving in the air. I was afraid; I doubted the fear. I didn't have the self-confidence to believe myself. To take care of myself. To stand up for myself. I was a little girl again wearing the pink gingham dress, eyes wide in their deadly desire to please men, even men who I wanted to go away. I wasn't able to say: "I don't want to talk to you. Please leave me alone" like I am finally, at fifty-three, learning to do and am still not very good at. But at least now I understand why.

As I write these parts of this memoir, I wrestle with extreme guilt for bringing my dad into the story of my abduction and rapes. I have thought about deleting it all many times. I have paced around the house with a level of anxiety that I can barely contain, virtually pulling at my hair; the whole thing, the whole telling of my story, and how it is so much more than just about me and therefore nothing can be left out becoming nothing, cruel, ridiculous, selfish in my desire to write a manifesto for all. I have thought: I can't do it! It's too much of a betrayal! I must re-write my book. I must leave out the beginning. How this victim was created. Keep it all hidden like abuse so often is. Continue the cycle. But then I think: No. There is no story; there is no life without its beginning; there is no victim without a genesis.

I know I am risking deeply hurting and perhaps even losing some of my family. I don't want my mom to ever read this, and I don't think I would want you to either, Dad. But I have no idea what you would think, and I never will: whether you would be angry and ashamed by my telling your life-long secret, by describing the extent of your alcoholism, your self-medication, your untreated trauma. Or, would you understand that I have no choice? That this book, my life as a victim and a survivor, would not exist without you and that men cannot be left out of the cycle of abuse. Even fathers. I do know that you would want to read the ending, though. Our mutual triumph. How we turned out. And maybe you would forgive me for telling this story that is far bigger than both of us. I want everyone to know and you too, Dad: this doesn't have anything to do with blame. It's just the truth. And you were a victim and a survivor too. And, from your place of damage, you did your best.

Lisa

Unlike my story, there is nothing even close to a happy ending for my friend Lisa. The last time I spoke with her was so upsetting that I haven't talked to her since. I feel badly about this, and whenever I am in my hometown, I say: "I am going to find Lisa." I haven't done it yet.[2]

You always told me I should find her again, Dad. She used to phone your house semi-regularly looking for me. You were the one who talked to her. You were the one who had the patience to listen through her trauma. You were the one who cared enough to give her your time.

The last time I talked to Lisa was on a Christmas Eve. I don't remember exactly what year. Probably getting on ten years ago now. Since her early twenties, when all the sexual abuse she had suffered as a child came exploding to the surface, Lisa has been on who knows how many psychotropic drugs. I lost count as every time I saw her, she was trying another one. Her mental illness could never be diagnosed exactly. Was it Bipolar 1? Was it Schizophrenia? Did it have something to do with her thyroid? A combination of all three? She has been sent to an endless stream of specialists. The doctors and psychiatrists have never come up with a diagnosis they could effectively medicate, and Lisa has lived a life of going on and then going off and going on and then off on off on off a relentless combination of medications. None of them have worked.

Anyone who knows what it's like to go on a psychotropic drug, especially a cocktail of a couple in combination with lithium, will know that this is what your life becomes. You can do nothing else except adapt to one and then, when it doesn't work, go slowly off of that one and go onto another one, and then if that combination doesn't work either, the cycle continues. That is what it has been like for my friend Lisa: she has lived on a medicated rollercoaster for at least fifteen years.

She didn't have to be mentally ill. She didn't have to be condemned to a life of a futile parade of attempts at medicating the trauma out of her so that she would be sort of "normal," maybe hold down a job, maybe be able to pay rent, and have the home everyone deserves. She didn't have to have her life taken away from her before it had even started. She became mentally ill because of the abuse she had suffered. Because of what those four men did to her little-girl-being. The men who sexually abused her as a child inflicted such deep wounds that she didn't have a chance. They killed her before her life had begun.

"The major cause of severe substance addiction is always childhood trauma," Gabor Maté tells us when describing his experiences as the doctor for the drug-addicted and sexually abused residents of what is known as Canada's poorest postal code. "I don't know anybody in the Downtown Eastside ... who wasn't abused as a child. Not even by accident. And all of the women I treat were sexually abused specifically ... The more adverse childhood experiences a person has, the exponentially greater chance of substance abuse later on."[3] Just like my friend Lisa.

Back to the myth of free will: I have been told many times that some people can handle being sexually abused as children. I have heard that they are just able to 'get over it' and lead normal lives. Apparently, that's because they have the discipline to exercise the inherent free will that everyone can access equally. If they really want to, they just 'decide' and will themselves out of all the inevitable damage that has been inflicted upon them in their lives. Really? I have never met any of these miraculous people. The unscathed. I have only met their opposite.

These mythological people prove that the mentally ill and drug-addicted are (merely) weak and that they (simply) choose their lives of living with trauma. They actually want to continue to be abused and often homeless. Everyone chooses their lives, I have been told countless times.

Yes, it is possible for a person who has suffered sexual abuse, is mentally ill, and drug-addicted to get clean, access some solid counseling, and have the good fortune of getting on a psychotropic drug that is effective with only a few side effects, but there is no 'merely,' 'just' or 'simply' about it. And this real-life miracle is not very common.

Lisa started using crack. She told me the last time I talked to her. She told me in a matter of fact, 'of course,' kind of way. I was shocked. I was horrified. I instantly judged. And I started to cry.

Lisa started being prostituted to pay for the crack. She
told me the last time I talked to her. She told me in a matter
of fact, 'of course,' kind of way. I was shocked. I was horrified.
I instantly judged. And I started to cry.
"Why?"
"Crack is the only thing that grounds me," she said.
"Oh."
How can anybody argue with that?

———◉———

I am not home at the moment. I am not in the nurturing forest or just having walked upon the beach that has everything
and sitting at table 104 in the Lantzville Pub. Somehow, in
the course of writing this manuscript, I have learned to write
it elsewhere. I have learned to write it away from home. I am
learning to be strong in my vulnerability.

I made an art project once called just that: Vulnerable. I
went into the British Columbia rainforest and took self-portraits
naked amidst the ferns and salal and brambles and mud. I got
dirty, scratched up, bruised. For the performance, I buried
myself in dirt and lay there for four hours. Behind me was a
projection that stated: We Are All Vulnerable.

A woman thanked me. She told me that the world would be
a better place if we all acknowledged this fact, if we all could
have the courage to live within our inherently vulnerable beings. Learn vulnerability as a strength, not a weakness, and
begin to relinquish the pathological desire to conquer and take.

Others stared for a minute or so, with the same detached,
objectifying gaze wielded when one looks at animals in a zoo,
then abruptly turned and walked back into the safety of another
photograph of the sunset, an escapist landscape that claims to
be real. I hate to generalize, but it was mostly men who looked
very confused. Disgusted even. One man sneered at me: "You're
SO dirty!!" I was impressed by the patriarchal candor of this
utterance, such a juicy piece of truth that I am hauling out
right now as it hearkens back to the origins of misogyny. My

unabashed, female flesh immersed in the soil was a most blatant offence to the sterile sensibilities of patriarchal fear: keep out the dirt, keep out the blood, keep out the wilderness, keep out the woman. Keep out death. Keep out birth. And I am sure this man who cowered in the face of this most urgent of truths didn't like being included in my proclamation: "We Are All Vulnerable," which, naturally, included him. Ouch.

⸻⸻◆⸻⸻

The last time I was home was a week ago. I started to look for Lisa. Not very hard, but I started to take the first steps; I started to pluck up the courage to confront her most likely continued demise. I started to ask around.

A friend told me that another friend had seen Lisa recently. Bumped into her on the street. He used to be one of her best friends. They were roommates during their early twenties when he played in a ska band. Lisa always went to their gigs and danced. She was one of the most fashionable, the most original, the most full of fun, the most fabulous.

I will never forget the first time I met her. We were on the Seawall in Stanley Park. I don't know what I was doing there that day, but I certainly remember her. She was walking along the beach in love with everything. People stacked stones just to see how high they could stack them: Lisa took it as some sort of mysticism; mediocre musicians played in little clumps or on their own: Lisa thought they were all rock stars; someone was carving something unexceptional out of driftwood: Lisa thought it was brilliant. She shared her thoughts with everyone: "You are a mystic! You are a rock star! You are *so* brilliant!" She invited me into her magical appreciation of all.

"I'll blow you for $10," is all she said to him. An old friend from her late teens. From our days of dressing up in everything outrageous we could find at the Sally Ann, from our days of always being the ones who got an encore going at Violent Femmes and Red Hot Chili Pepper concerts, from our days of dancing our asses off (as she used to say, almost tripping over her words for the joy of relating tales of last night's romp), from our days where anything goes because we didn't know much of anything yet and, if we did, we had no inclination to spoil the fun and find out what it was. Everything was new, fresh. Everything was exciting. Especially for Lisa. But I always wondered at the intensity of her spark. I was attracted to it and it made me uncomfortable at the same time. It was too much. It was as though she was unconsciously overcompensating for what lay beneath. And what was about to extinguish her brilliant light.

Lisa's innocence, even though it seemed the purest, was a fraud. Hers was an innocence underlain by Hell. The hell of a small child being forced to live just that. Having no choice but to give men blowjobs. She never told me if they literally raped her. But the blowjobs were over and over and over. Make them cum. The most important thing. Forget about destroying a life. That's what she was made for. It was her job. She had been trained from childhood. And now, in her perpetually traumatized state, she is being kept alive by what she knows best, and what is killing her grounds her.

You always told me, Dad,

that I need to find Lisa, go and see her again, so she doesn't feel even more shunned. Know that I don't judge her. At all. The opposite. I promise you I will, Dad. In this moment of writing, I pledge to practice what I preach.

Crackpot. Montreal, 1986.

When I was eighteen or so, I read the novel *Crackpot* by Adele Wiseman. It boggled my mind; I couldn't believe such a thing could happen. The protagonist, Hoda, is a first-generation Canadian Russian Jew. Throughout her life, she is hounded by prejudice and persecution, both racial and sexual. She gains weight to protect herself, to create a barrier between herself and the perpetrators. She becomes a prostitute. She becomes a prostitute to try and fit in and be accepted by the culture and the men who abuse her. She hurts herself to please men. And, in turn, they hurt her back. She becomes pregnant and has no idea this is so. Neither does anyone else because the pregnancy is hidden within her walls of flesh. From out of nowhere to herself and to the reader, she is in labour. She has no idea what is going on. A baby appears. Just drops out of her. I was horrified. I had never considered the fact that a woman can be so out of touch with her body.

How could a woman have no idea that she had a baby growing inside her? I thought. How could a woman hunger to be accepted by her persecutors to the extent that she would hurt herself to get a bit of even feigned affection? Little did I know it, though, even when I was reading this novel and was so horrified by the thought of this, that I was out of touch with my own body. I had the same hunger. As I read this novel that shocked me with so many things I didn't know, I was living them too.

After the rapes in Montreal, after I'd slept for who knows how long, I got up. Undoubtedly begrudgingly so. I can remember lying suspended in a forced inertia, a triumph in tragedy as I willed myself to not be here. But nothing is ever perfect. Far from it as this not-being I was working so hard to maintain was underlain by guilt. Guilt that can momentarily be quelled by going back to sleep again but which only succeeds in compounding into more guilt. Deeper guilt. Any relief being fortified by its undoing. But I didn't give up. Drifting back and forth between reality and its denial and pushing myself back and back until I wasn't here anymore and more hours of escape were piling up and coming to and not daring to open my eyes and pushing back and back again and denying my bladder and denying my thirst until eventually, I had no choice but to come back, be here, at least for long enough to attend to bodily functions.

I know it was grey out all the time. And, even if it wasn't, that's the way it felt. That's the way I remember it. Montreal. People love it there. Anyone who goes there loves it. Can't say enough about how great it is. Yes, I remember when I first went there, that's how I felt too. The exotic of Canada. Like another country in the same one. Edgy. Exciting. French.

I don't love Montreal anymore. Those two men killed it for me. Killed all the fun: the overflowing bars, the grooviest nightclubs, the smoked meat sandwiches, the best bagels in the country, the croissants on par with those in France. The buzzing coffee shops. The vibrant conversations that put English Canada to shame. The feels-like-you're-in-Europe when you're in Canada. The renegade province with its nose snubbing essence. Punk rock all the way. Montreal. How I had always wanted to go there.

But I don't love it now. How could I? Sorry, Montreal. It's not your fault. But all you are to me now is blocks of drudgery. Cold. Loneliness. The wide indifferent streets that I wandered after my life changed so drastically. Waiting. Waiting. Waiting for my first abortion. The termination of an unwanted pregnancy. Not a baby. A rape.

I did end up leaving my apartment. Eventually. After days of lying there floating in limbo between semi-consciousness and semi-unconsciousness, not eating, not drinking, dragging myself out of bed when I had no choice but to get up to pee, my eyes open just enough to find the way to and from the toilet, after getting back that morning from being raped and impregnated by those two terrible men, those two terrible men who defy comprehension, those two terrible men that are most likely still out there living, those two terrible men who got away with it because I was too shocked to even think about reporting their crimes, I did end up leaving my apartment.

And when I found out I was pregnant, I was as surprised as Hoda. I had never considered that possibility to the extent that I had forgotten how it had happened.

My friend and I were walking along one of those blank, grey boulevards. One that would have been bursting with vibrancy and mystique a mere two months ago. I said,

"My nipples really hurt." I don't think I had told her what had happened. I don't think I had told anyone. If I had, I am sure something would have been done. Of course, something would have been done. But I didn't tell anyone. I lived with it alone by blocking it out.

I didn't know such an act existed. I can't process this. I can't cognate. This is not the world I know. What I thought life was. This is so ugly. I can't bear to think about it. It must not exist.[4]

"Sounds like you're pregnant," she stated flatly. I was amazed by her worldliness. How she would just know this and have an answer right away to what was a big mystery to me. I remember now that I actually wondered how it had happened. I was surprised. How could this be?

"I don't have a boyfriend," I said to my friend. "How could I be pregnant?" Right from the start, I was able to make it go away, make it not exist. Almost.

"We should go to the hospital and you can get a pregnancy test," she said. Like this kind of thing was done all the time.

"Okay."

We kept walking. The hospital was nearby, as though our original direction had been on the way to the hospital from the get-go, like it had been fated. The roads were apocalyptic. Bereft of life, even though I had it growing inside me. I don't recall any trees, or birds, or anything besides she and I and our march that echoed from the shut doors lining the abandoned streets, like eyes forever shut. It was a death march, now that I think of it: the beginning of the death of this life inside of me along with this continuing death of my innocence. As we approached the hospital, I had a sinking feeling that was so unbearable I eventually became hardened enough to feel nothing. And, along with that hardening that was reminiscent of the darkness that underlay Scarlett O'Hara's frivolous "Fiddle-dee-dee! I'll think about it tomorrow," I did, for over half of my life, make tomorrow never come.

I had an ulterior motive for going to your cremation,

Dad, being the only one there and seeing how this memoir has become a sort of confession, I may as well tell you: part of me wanted to be the one who pushed the button, who started the process of your cremation; part of me needed to take that power. But, at the same time, part of me didn't want a stranger to commit the act that you never wanted.

And yes, in keeping with the complex and contradictory nature of our father/daughter relationship, I also wanted to create a loving ritual for you. I wanted to give you this final gift. I brought a piece of every tree and every plant from the mountain where you had walked for forty years and buried you with your forest before you were burned. I gave you dignity amidst our culture's institutionalized relationship with death. And, yes, I wanted to live this story to the very end. With all its sweetness and blades.

Approaching the end of our story, Dad, when I started standing up to you and we would all-out fight, the years of my repressing my confusion and hurt finally surfacing as intolerance and anger, you would apologize by giving me a knife. How can the symbolism be more bizarre and truer, Dad? The intensity of irony when you get right down to baring all, to digging as deeply as possible in search of truth, understanding, peace.

You loved knives. You were a man, after all. And men love knives, don't they. The power. The defense. The status and, not to mention, the usefulness—the Boy Scout in men, so eager to impress and to serve. You always had to have a Swiss Army Knife in your pocket. Even when you couldn't go outside anymore. Just in case the something would happen that was definitely not going to, and you would be needed for your manly know-how. You would pull it out keenly, decide which blade or one of the multiple fittings would best serve the occasion with the bright pleasure that comes with pride. The final touch on your laborious dressing rituals of your final year was "Where's

my pocket knife?" And, into your pocket, it would go. Ready.
Just in case.

I have no idea how many knives you had. I know there were
at least two Swiss Army Knives. I took one. Just for the hell of
it. A just for the hell of it that now resides in my jewelry box.
Another piece of closeness that I may or may not ever use. In
the physical sense, that is. You had a lot of other knives, too,
because after you died, all your grandsons were hauling them
out of drawers, finding more tucked away in the backs of cup-
boards, claiming them for their own lives as men.

You had the best cooking knives. Immaculately sharp. It
was very important for you to always keep them that way. I
learned this from you. I don't like cooking in a kitchen with dull
knives. I require the beauty of an impeccably sliced tomato, the
joy of being able to effortlessly dice. To create sustenance. To
feed myself beauty.

You always gave me cooking knives. I am a woman, after
all, and I just so happen to love cooking. This could have something to do with being in the kitchen most of my childhood.
With Mom. Because she was my protector. From you.

It's always been you who has sharpened my knives for me. A
ritual. I would bring them to you from wherever I was currently
living, even if it was another country, for you to ceremoniously
sharpen. You were always pleased by this gesture, by this connection between us. By still feeling useful. And this is one of
the reasons I did it: I always asked you to sharpen my knives
as you descended into the agony of a man losing his power. So
that, for those minutes, you could be a man again.

You would take them down to the workbench where you had
three knife sharpening stones. You were very well prepared for
all your rituals. You would always use the one without the lid.
I suppose that was because it was the best one and the lid had
been lost one of the hundreds of times it had been taken off.
The stone was worn down, concave, while the others sat lidded
and linear. Waiting their turn that never came.

You've been dead for four months now. My knives are getting dull. Before your death, I prepared for this moment, this

time in my life when I would have to sharpen my knives myself. I asked you to teach me. Such pride in your near-death existence of not being able to do much of anything anymore when I made this request. I helped you down the stairs.

As usual, you slid your most well-used stone across the workbench. Poured oil on it from an oil can that is so old it could very well have been your father's. You squirted an elegant zigzag down the center of the stone, a flip of your now frail wrist and a well-practiced flourish as you placed the oily brown can back in its spot where it has always sat underneath the windowsill. You were a man again. In control. You most likely looked over your shoulder and winked at me. Always a bit of a show-off. Always liking to be the center of attention. And this was the last time. Sharpening my knife. Maybe you knew it too. Every moment together had the weight of religion then, compounded by all those decades of lack. Unrequited love. At long last expressed.

You took my knife in your right hand.

Gently. Precisely. You started to swirl the tip of the knife on the top of the stone. Then the edges, gradually moving up from the tip. Then turn the knife over. Test with your thumb. No, not sharp enough. Do it again. No, not sharp enough. Again.

I tried to listen to what you said. Your careful instructions. Your personal tips. Your philosophy behind maintaining a perfectly sharp knife. But my eyes were full of tears. My ears were ringing. I fought back the sobs that clawed within. I didn't want to disturb you. I didn't want you to know that this would be the last time you ever did this for me. I heard nothing that you said. Until, you turned to me, triumphant, with:

"That should do it!" and placed your gift back into the palm of my hand. And I still hold it tight.

I must admit, though, during your epic celebration of life, I was getting pretty annoyed by everyone talking about how great you were. Yes, of course, you were: but you were human too. One of the speakers said that you never asked one of your work crew to do something you couldn't do yourself, how encouraging you were and so emotionally supportive to your apprentices. I flinched. It may have been how you treated them, but that wasn't how you treated me. For most of my life anyway.

One of the speakers said you were always happy. I thought back to the hidden bottles, the abrasive joviality that soon sank to despair, the sleeping on the couch all day the next day incapacitated by shame and denial. Happily, at that moment, there was a crash of thunder. The sky opened. Torrents poured. It hadn't rained in months. I had to contain a burst of laughter as the rain thundered on the roof. Either you or the universe was on my side. Or both.

What is it about the surface of a life? The life that is remembered at memorials? The life that is preserved in photo albums, digital files now stored on external hard drives always ready to be retrieved and celebrated posthumously with a proclamation of 'Lo! Here is the life!' The evidence is displayed in reception rooms of funeral homes as proof of a perfect one, its impossibility buried by: Look at him on top of mountains! Look at him alongside his co-workers! Look at him on a boat! Look at him next to a campfire! Look at him, look at him, look at him. Always outwardly smiling. A life that is so easy to know. So easy to love.

What is it about the surface of a life? It is but an edge that hasn't been sharpened by reality. And beneath lies the body of the knife.

———◦((◦))◦———

I know a photograph that was left out of your memorial slide-show. It was one of those photographs that never made it into the photo album. Never had the privilege of adding to the narrative of your life. Was never on display as "this is how it was." Too.

I found it tucked in the back of a photo album; it could have slipped out at any moment in its perpetual state of almost lost. There were others. Others that hadn't made it onto the pages of condoned memory, inserted into their yellowing photo corners determined to keep things straight. No, it was one of the renegades. One of the ones that loitered precariously on the sidelines, narrating the edges, poised to fly out anytime as long-cloistered moths or ghosts. If invited. If the manicured real were opened up, held upside down, and shaken. Look at what would fall out: the retrievable forgotten.

I am surprised no one threw this photo out. I mean, what would be the point of keeping it unless there was a desperation that there weren't enough photos taken that year. Or negligence. Or indecision. Or not looking at it closely enough to notice it should have been censored to keep up appearances.

"Oh, I'll keep it just in case," my mother may have thought. Just in case of what? Just in case she wanted to expose some of the other side of how it really was? Why hadn't she thrown it out? Destroyed the evidence so that this instance of memory could be forever erased. But she didn't. For whatever reason, she didn't. And it was just there. Waiting for decades for me to find it.

It was taken on one of those special occasions: Christmas, Easter, Thanksgiving. It's a fascinating photograph. One of those inadvertent masterpieces that leave out just enough so that the flat image catapults into what could be behind that door and, in this case, there really is a door rather than only a metaphor. It's both: reality and a symbol that can propel the viewer into representations of a door: open/closed, being the most immediate, an opening into a journey, a discovery, a slamming shut in your face, and the vibrations, the ruptures produced by the severity of the force—oppression thwarted by overkill, creating more gaps, more openings in the repercussions of denial as closure.

You stand, on a threshold, thirty-six, the same age I was when I found it, looking into the space that the photograph doesn't give us: the behind the door, probably into a kitchen. You are shouting in that direction, shouting through the open door. Your expression is an exact dramatization of the word 'belligerent.' But one can read that the hostility didn't come from without. It came from within. It came from self-loathing; it came from fear: the origin of any war.

I'm very familiar with that face. Not just because of you, but also because I worked as a cocktail waitress for many years. Every night, I would witness the sad men who'd had too much to drink. With every drink too many, their faces would contort further and further into a volatility that could snap into rage at any moment. Even just looking at a woman could cause a stream of debasing comments to put him back on top, back into the position of power, even if only said to himself, under his resentful breath. In hierarchy, he has no choice but to do this; it is his role, his place. He knows that the young woman doesn't desire him. He knows she would humiliate his manhood by not fulfilling his desire, his right. So, he hates her, the young woman. And all of the hers that have come before. And she deserves it. She's had it coming. Precisely because she takes away his power. By coming over to see if he's alright. By calling him a cab. By listening to his self-pity and blame. By existing.

My family is on the other side, sitting around the table. Posing for the photograph. Pretending nothing is going on to the left of their domestic circle of posed civility. There must have been noise. After all, the photograph contains a man shouting. Was the happy holiday music cranked to drown you out? Everyone is doing a really good job of keeping up the act. Except me. I hadn't been taught yet.

I am in the middle of the photo. Two or three years old. Sitting on my mother's lap. Wreathed by grandparents, great aunts and uncles, my sister, cousins, all smiling and focused on this act of dutiful documentation. But I am not yet aware of the importance of pretense for the sake of a well-maintained posterity. My eyes are traumatized circles; my face is frozen in terror. I look like I am about to be sick.

"This is my father when he was the same age as I am right now," I thought when I pulled out the yellowed portal. "This is the creature I was afraid of. This is the evidence. Look. It has been hidden in the edges of the book."

The Abortion of a Rape Baby. Montreal, 1986.

I know it may sound a bit clichéd, but one of the main things I remember after the pregnancy test were playgrounds. I can't remember the season, but it was chilly and grey. It wasn't freezing cold like Montreal gets in the winter when one rarely dares to go outside, but it exuded an inhospitality that makes one not so keen on going out and is only prodded by the alternative of becoming increasingly depressed due to the guilt guaranteed by not leaving the house.

The sun may have been out some of the days, but to me, every day was grey, and a sharp wind penetrated my coat. Everyone had left, all the friends I hadn't told. It must have been the end of the spring semester, and they had all gone home for the summer. But why do I remember it as being so cold?

I was staying in a house that had been rented by friends. The friends who were no longer there. I remember the house felt unbearably hollow as I wandered around, poking my head into abandoned rooms, surprised by how even the air echoed absence. I have no memory of why I wasn't living in my apartment anymore or when or how I'd left. Maybe I moved as soon as I found out I was pregnant with a rape baby and was waiting for the abortion. Then, after that was done, after the thing was out of me, I could go back to Vancouver, back home, and forget.

I had to wait a long time for the abortion. The Montreal abortion clinics were very busy in 1986. This was most likely because there weren't very many; it was still pretty dodgy getting a safe abortion in Canada in those days. At the time, I had no idea how lucky I was. Montreal was one of the most progressive parts of the country in terms of women's rights. I wasn't forced to have a rape baby, and if I had been in another part of Canada, I might have had no other choice. Even though it was Montreal where these rapes had happened, it was the same city that saved me, too.

When it was finally my turn, they did it at the latest possible moment. Most likely due to the backlog. The need for women to be able to choose what they want to do with their own bodies.

I think I was about three months along, the beginning of the second trimester. I can't remember exactly because I don't think I even knew then.

I most likely didn't find out I was pregnant until well into the second month. I never kept track of my menstrual cycle. I was true to the unspoken patriarchal legislation of young women being out of touch with their bodies, inadvertently contributing to the undervaluing of those sexed female by not valuing ourselves enough to pay attention.

I wandered the streets of Montreal for a month or so. University had finished, there was no point getting a job when I would be gone as soon as this job was done. Alone, bored, depressed, dreading the start of another day when I would resume my pastime of haunting playgrounds, sitting on swings or on benches, watching kids play, and hating myself for doing so. It was making things worse. I knew that. But I really had nothing else to do and nowhere else to go and, if I did, I had no inclination to do it. I was just drawn there. Out of boredom, out of desire, out of self-punishment. This was certainly not my fault. I had done nothing to deserve this. So why did I feel like I had? Why did I treat myself like I had done something wrong?

I remember I felt dirty. And empty. The low self-esteem that had been bashed into me since childhood took full advantage of my beaten-down state. I became too shy and insecure to talk to anyone. I could barely go into stores and buy food. That would mean I would have to talk to the cashier. Good Morning, Bonjour, Merci, Thank You were all too much for me. I really can't remember how or what I ate.

Amazingly, we get through these things. Somehow, we 'soldier on' and can exist until it's over. As long as we still have hope that we will have a future, that there is brightness ahead. And I must have. I got through it. I was still so young. There was a certainty that things would be better. That I would be able to get back on track with what I had planned for my life.

And I did. The time passed, as time thankfully does, even when it feels like it never will. It was finally the big day. I went there alone. Terrified and pretending to be otherwise, in a state of numbness, going through the motions with no idea what to expect. There were women there who had been there before, who filled me in. I found out how far along I was. I remember one of the women said I should have a general anesthetic. I thought:

"Whew! Yes, that will be good. I will literally not be here." But when I went into the room and they got me to put my feet into the stirrups, shimmy my butt down to the edge of the examination table, I was only given some local anesthetic and, right away, the machine started. No messing around. Get the show on the road. There were other women waiting.

The sound of the machine is a sound I would hear three more times in my life. This was the first one. The middle two begotten out of recklessness and having been conditioned to not care enough about my body—or myself—the last wanted by me but unwanted by the father. And I knowing that I wasn't capable of having a child alone.

I felt a tube enter. And the suction began. Pulling the thing into pieces. Did it feel anything? Did it have any kind of consciousness? Did it feel the violence and sickness through which it had almost come into the world? Did it know this was for the best?

Afterward, I went into the recovery room with all the other women who'd had abortions that day. I remember that there were a lot, and I wondered at all the lives and scenarios that had brought them there. I wonder now, considering the turmoil that was happening with legalizing abortions in Canada at that time, how the safe abortions that day even happened at all. Somehow, abortions were being performed at McGill Hospital. I still don't really understand how or why. Whatever the reason, I didn't have to risk my life giving birth to a rape baby. And I know I would have. Even though I have no desire to ever go back to Montreal, I will always be grateful for this. Thanks, Montreal.

As soon as I could, probably the next day, I boarded a plane and went home. I had called my mother numerous times while I was waiting. I couldn't and never have told her what happened. I was too ashamed and didn't want to upset her. I just told her something terrible had happened and that I wanted to come home. In the end, I was right not to tell her then because I found out later that she didn't want to know.

She bought me a ticket and, like the embryo being suctioned out of my womb just the day before, the plane popped the membrane of my trap. I felt tension release as we tore out of the Montreal sky. As I flew west, the hell that those two terrible men had filled me with began to dissipate from my skin, from my soul, from my heart. But it has never left completely; it still exists as nausea at the base of my stomach, in my womb, where that child had grown for three months. It is there now as I write this, thirty-three years later. The young woman who was so brutally violated will always be a part of me. We can play tricks with our minds, fool ourselves, enforce forgetfulness, but a body's memory remains. A body never forgets.

When I went to the bathroom, as the plane curved up to skim the Arctic Circle, I was so happy to see the red chunks from the walls of my uterus falling out of me. I remember I picked one off the thick, soiled, post-abortion pad I had been given at the clinic. I held it, smelled it, turned it around in my palm a few times, and flushed it down the toilet.

It all gets down to the mountains with us.

The greatest gift you gave me. The greatest gift anyone has ever given me. The gift that you tried to take away but always returned when we were in the mountains. And still do. A year and a half since your death.

I am alone now. And strong. Most of the time. As I marvel at the hues of green that descend from brilliant to mossy brown and back again, ride a symphony of bird song, immerse myself in the cycle of decomposition and birth, raw and perfect, I feel you ahead of me—and sometimes I can even see you—tending to the trail with the snippers you never forgot to put in your back pocket before leaving the house. Leading the way.

Like the granite that builds the peaks and cuts the crevasses of the ranges where I am from, I feel immovable when I am there, exultant on a summit or standing in a forest one can only access when they have the determination to push through weakness. The peace that one achieves as they allow themselves to decay and grow, to surge and erode. To be vulnerable. To be strong. To stand fierce. Vigilant.

It is this connection to the raw of existence that built the fighter in me. The gift you gave me that I never knew I had until I was forced to fight for my life. The edges of the void one skims when climbing a mountain face. You could fall. It is undeniable.

Stare down fear. Keep to beauty.[5]

A Fugue of the Unfounded. Me: Prescott, Arizona, 1994/ Another Young Woman: Edmonton, Alberta, 1994.

Edmonton, Alberta 1994:
She walked into the trailer.
Prescott, Arizona 1994:
I got into the vehicle.
I had pepper spray in my pocket.
The police report didn't say she did.
She was seventeen.
I was twenty-eight.
She was applying for a job.
I accepted a ride back to the motel.
My gut said don't do it.
I wonder if hers did?
He tricked me.

He tricked her.

Does that mean we were guilty?

I shifted the pepper spray to my right-hand pocket. I knew it was a risk to do so, for him to potentially see the pepper spray. I was on guard as soon as I got in, and I knew, deep down, that it had been a mistake. It was all so foreign. Even though I had sensed danger, I had no idea what it would feel like when it actually happened. When the danger became absolute. Climbing up into that vehicle, closing the door, I had crossed a line. I had entered another world, the underside of this one. Like she had.

She was so young. Still a teenager. Only seventeen. Did she know, yet, that things are often not what they seem? I did. But not as much as I did afterward. As I do now.

Hurry up, I thought, this ride that I wished I hadn't accepted. But I was too polite to say anything. "Hey, I decided to walk after all. It's such a nice night. I realized I could use some exercise. Sitting all day. Writing the letter to my ex. Thanks anyway."

The darkness pressed in. I felt trapped, even though I didn't know that I was yet. I was caught in a limbo of what was about to happen. The air was static, like a TV sputtering between reception, or that shrill, relentless beep when a station has gone off the air. This could be okay; this could be the worst. Bzzzzzzz bzz bz bzzzz bz bz ...

I had never experienced the worst before. Or been conscious for it anyway. The worst it had ever been for me. I had no idea how far it could go. The velocity with which the worst can blast into oblivion, unmoored and floating in uncertainty and the possibility of never standing on solid ground again. The void: what one immediately learns they very well may not return from. Back to solid ground. Back to before I had stepped up into his vehicle. And the door was slammed shut.

Did the sound of metal upon metal ring out into the night in the motley parking lot behind the bar where drunken patrons lingered and frayed? G-bye. See yah tomorrow. Fuck you. These were my final connections with the outside world, the outside that might have helped if I had called out and bashed my fist against the window right after the door had clicked closed. Decisive. My fate sealed. It was only a matter of minutes and the gap between my liberty and my imprisonment would no longer exist. And I would have no idea where I was, what I was going to do, and then amaze myself by how quickly I could adapt to this possibility of death. My strength as competent as a perfectly sharpened knife.

My chit-chat tinkled on the surface of foreboding. The foreboding I denied as it climbed up my spine in the brooding dark. His brooding-being hunched as an outline that I could only make out as street lights flashed past. A steady heartbeat of light. Flash. Black. Flash. Black. Flash. Slowing down.

Was he psyching himself up for it? What was he thinking just before? Just before the moment when my life was hacked in half. I have no idea what goes on in the mind of a predator pre-attack.

"Hey, you have the same bag as me!

Why are we turning here? This isn't the way to the motel!"

She walked into the trailer. Maybe she could have gotten out. Maybe she could have spun around as soon as her two feet had landed on the floor of a space that I imagine is sealed up in ice and snow until the spring thaw. Musty. Close.

As I read, I saw a warped floor swaying in the middle and bent up towards the outside. The outside. The place she should never have left. The place I should never have left. Perhaps the sagging floor was soft beneath her feet, being eaten away by mold, closing in as it was about to hold her hostage for the next two hours. Maybe she felt the same static as I did, the same tension in the air that builds before a storm. In unison with the forlorn squeak of John Linnihan's camper/van, I imagine the trailer floor creaking, too, whimpering as she paced nervously in place. From the cold. From the fear. From what was about to happen.

Apparently, she could have left. It said in the court transcript that she "believed" he had locked the door. She wasn't sure. This detail was used against her credibility even though the man weighed over 200 pounds and she a mere 105.[6]

"Am I just being paranoid?" she may have thought, as I did. "Is everything on the up and up here?" She, but another young woman who hadn't learned to trust her gut yet. To know her body. Like me. As I still doubted what I knew to be true. In that split second when I lifted my second leg onto the runner and hoisted myself in. My last chance to change my mind. Good girl. He pulled over. Why? Why are we stopping? Why did he turn? Oh my God. That bag is the same as mine because it *is* mine!! My hand scoured the inside of the door. Again. Up down back and forth. Disbelief. Again. This can't be happening! There is no handle on the inside of the door! There was some kind of winch between the driver's seat and the passenger seat that he used to crank the door open with. There was absolutely no doubt that I was locked in! Could I have twisted myself around and grabbed the handle of the winch? Wrenched on it with all my strength? I could have tried if I had known it was there. I didn't notice it until I was sitting up front, again, when the pawn had become the queen, and it was used to crank open the door to let me go. But, even if I had known it was there during the process of the abduction, it would have been no use as he weighed well over 200 pounds and I a mere 125.

She told the court how she became frightened. She said she didn't want him to know. Her decision for self-preservation. As I read, I hear her narrative in counterpoint with mine. I want to get out! I changed my mind! It was a mistake coming here. A terrible, terrible mistake. A mistake I know now to be true.

I don't know if I was frightened. Or terrified. Or so shocked that I didn't feel anything at all in that moment. I can't even remember if I struggled. There was no time for terror or struggle as everything had become his hands as clamps. No reason to fight back because it wouldn't have done any good. Maybe made things worse. The same as where her mind had gone. The decision she had made, like when one of Linnihan's hands held my wrist and warded off the pepper spray. The other around my neck. My world stopped with the cutting off of my breath. He asked her, "Are you a friendly and affectionate person like me?"[7] Did she say, "Yes." Or did she remain quiet? It didn't say anything about that in the court transcript. How does one respond when a job interview lurches towards rape as the company owner moves in on you? About to violate. His breath hot and wet on your cheek. His was a rhetorical question. With no intention of getting a reply. No purpose of getting her consent. Just asked for effect to maintain his delusion that there could be affection for a person who has been lied to, tricked, trapped, and about to be assaulted. His dark fairy tale.

"I was so patient. So loving ..." John Linnihan's face trembled like a neglected child's. "I gave everything. And she just took! That's all they ever do. Those bitches! Take. Take. Take!!" How readily the victimizer can make himself the victim.

"I have an airstream trailer in the desert. I'm going to take you there and keep you forever. It will be your new home," Linnihan extended his affectionate threat. I recoiled but forced myself to lean forward. Touched his arm affectionately. Thanked him for the offer so that I could get away.

He asked for a massage, the Edmonton rapist. She decided to play it cool. "So as not to egg him on," she told the court. His advances became more aggressive. He ordered her to take off her clothes. I see his bulk blocking any possibility of fighting to get to the door that may not be locked. Out came the penis. Deprived of its entitlement, treacherous with self-pity. Like all rapists. Otherwise, they wouldn't rape.

No, No, No. She said she had said.

If there had been a handle on the inside of the door of Linnihan's camper/van, if I could have opened it, I would have hurled myself out and ran. And yelled. And ran. And banged on the nearest door. I imagine panicking lights being switched on. The house immediately ablaze. Who could be banging on our door at this hour? Just a minute. Hurry, please hurry! A man tried to abduct me! Hurry. He is following me. Please let me in before he sees me. Call the police!

Would the door have opened? Suspiciously. A startled face
haloed by the lights in the house. We don't want any trouble
here. A tight mouth. Or, oh dear, what has happened to you? A
concerned brow. Please. Let me in. I can hide under a bed. You
can call the police. I think he may want to kill me!
He didn't listen to her. After all, she had been saying 'Yes'
all along by not saying anything, by playing it cool. Giving him
the massages he had ordered. Taking off her clothes. The little
slut. She wants it. Pretending now that she doesn't. Leading me
on. Who does she think she is? My imagination spun as I read:
he shoves her against the wall. The trailer shakes.
I grabbed my pepper spray. He grabbed my neck. I began to
spray madly, desperately aiming for his eyes. The red stream
only grazed his neck. His ear. You little bitch. You have pepper spray?! Squeezes harder. This can't be happening! I can't
breathe!
"No, No, No,"
She said.
"Please stop. I'll do anything you want,"
I managed.
We beg.
Unspoken.
Not believed.
Unfounded.

I read her story. The account of the Ewanchuk sexual assault
case that happened in Edmonton, Alberta, Canada, in 1994.
I looked up from the book, my body lead, my eyes unblinking
at the thought. There are so many similarities. Between her
story and mine. If I had had my own trial, could it have ended
the same way?

The young woman's strategy to conceal her fear to try and avoid
making the terrible situation even worse turned out to work

against a sexual assault victim in the mid-90s. When reaching his verdict of not guilty, Justice John Moore explained: "She is a credible witness, and I know that she was afraid .... However, she successfully kept all her thoughts, emotions and speculations deep within herself. She did not communicate most of them"[8]—even though she testified that she had said 'No' multiple times. But no matter, the majority of the time, she did everything he asked. No meant yes. A sexy game of cat and mouse. None of this had anything to do with the fact that she had no idea what the man who was assaulting her was capable of. The judge stated that this was a case of 'implied consent.'[9] Apparently, believing a lie, making a mistake, and doing your best to not escalate the violence of the situation, means you consent to being raped.

Like her, I had no idea what the guy was capable of. Who does? Some freak of nature preys upon you, tricks you, and locks you into a confined space so that he can assault you? He very well could be a rapist *and* a serial killer. How are we supposed to know? You need to adapt; you need to show no fear. Humans are animals; rapists are predators. Predators are turned on by fear. The smell of blood. Having power over someone, a woman, a creature they hate because of a lifetime of conditioned misogyny. A creature they hate as much as they desire. A creature they hate because they desire. They're all a bunch of lying bitches, John Linnihan confided after I had taken control by bringing myself down to his level, orchestrating his trust. Everything you are doing to me I have done many times before. We all make mistakes. I used to do all kinds of terrible things. I forgive you. I know you don't want to be a bad person. You have had some bad breaks. I understand. I lied, I lied, I lied.

By abducting, raping, and sometimes reaching the apex of murder, predators achieve the heady thrill of absolute domination and feed their emptiness by violently taking from another. In this tooth and nail context, if there is no way to literally escape at that moment, no weapon conveniently left lying around in arm's reach, playing it cool and deceiving the captor may be your only option. It was for me.

How is one to know what kind of rapist they happen to have been abducted by? Whether or not he is a rapist and a serial killer? Or only a rapist? But of course, I didn't know that he wasn't going to murder me when his hands were around my neck and his gun was to my head. Shucks, we hadn't gotten to know each other yet. And, lucky me, in the end, he was not an all-out sociopath: he had remorse that I was able to claw into. I became his ultimate lying bitch. You ain't seen nothin' yet. Asshole.

I was not sliced up in the desert as I had feared. Obviously, one expects the worst when finding oneself in the midst of it; survival instincts immediately kick in when there is a very good possibility you will be killed. It isn't like you know the guy or anything. You will do anything, acquiesce to all his demands to get the hell out of there. Unfortunately, the state may not see it that way. Especially in the 90s.[10] I could have been punished for saving my own life.

Apparently, this young woman and I didn't resist the assaults, that is, in a socially condoned way, as in by vigorously and physically fighting back. We were supposed to shout; we were supposed to be sufficiently hysterical when reporting the crime so that we would have fit the criteria of being 'ideal' or 'real' sexual assault victims. Instead, according to Melanie Randall's study "Sexual Assault Law, Credibility, and 'Ideal' Victims: Consent, Resistance and Victim Blaming," we were 'bad' victims, and our accounts would be subject to the most scrutiny, our credibility attacked, and we would be less deserving of legal protection.[11] We would have been blamed.

The clench of rape mythology, which keeps women in their blame-worthy places, stretches as far back as the beginning of patriarchy, until the moment identified by Susan Brownmiller when penises became weapons and rape became a justified act of discipline. Keep those women down. We must control them because we can't live without them. Don't you know that:

1. Women secretly want to be raped. (Thank you for fulfilling my dirty little secret. I checked that off my bucket list. Couldn't have done it without you, sigh. My dream rapist).

2. If we truly don't want to be raped, we can stop it. (No problem. The guy isn't being violent or anything, and I always pack a gun, one of those deceptive feminine types that I can hide easily beneath my please-rape-me clothing. The rapist is rarely bigger than the woman and unable to pin her down or strangle her. And, if he is bigger, women have hidden superpowers when our devious fury is unleashed! We cannot be trusted and must be disciplined by mythology—ideologically burned at the stake.[12])

3. We ask for it. (Yes, I already admitted: he fulfilled my fantasy. And the other guys too. Pity I wasn't conscious for the first ones).

4. Even if we say we don't like it, it isn't so bad. We just have to relax.[13] (Yes, ladies. Simple as that. Enjoy! He's your knight in rot and rancour! It's your lucky day!)

5. If we don't want it, as former Canadian Justice Robin Camp instructed, we need to simply keep our knees together.[14] (Yes, rapists have never been known to pry legs open or tie us up. Beat us up first. Maybe you should go to the gym and strengthen your quads if you really want to keep them out. It's your fault for not beefing up before going outside).

6. We must know that 'No' actually means 'Yes' or 'Try again' or 'Persuade me.' And if No really does mean NO, it's our responsibility to make that clear. (Perhaps bonk him over the head if there is something in arms' reach—if your arms happen to be free—to bonk with).

7. If we have had sex before, rape isn't so bad. (Not a problem. C'mon all! I'm broken in and ready to serve you!).

8. We often deserve to be raped because we've acted a certain way or dressed provocatively. (Back to the poor darlings theme again: the rapists are the victims of their own rape myth. They are but walking hard-ons being tugged hither and thither with no control over their actions. It's a Pac-Man game gone terribly wrong. The women are wreaking torture with their control

button of just existing! Look out! A woman looked in a hard-on-led man's direction and smiled! She's wearing lipstick. The Harpy. And he can see her legs. She has breasts. How dare she! He's going to explode! He's really out of control now! Oh No! The horror! She got up and left ... maybe had the audacity to go to the bathroom. He banged into the side of the game! What a mess! He is trapped: I love her I hate her I love her I hate her. When you think of it this way, this particular rape myth looks far worse on men than it does on women).

However, it appears that I didn't fulfill a very integral qualification of being a 'good' victim: not only did I not comply with the woman's responsibility (while being strangled, lest we forget) of screaming, thrashing about, and making a NO clear enough for a rapist to cease the realization of his predatory plans, I didn't say 'No' at all. Not even once.

She did. The seventeen-year-old Edmonton woman in 1994. She said 'No' three times. And that still wasn't enough. The poor rapist didn't understand (perhaps he was hard of hearing). Boo-hoo, poor guy. The treacherous women lead him on while he tricks them, locks them in, and ties them up. How dare we! And then, we lead him on even more when he abducts us! And we comply with his demands to try and make it easier on ourselves. To try and ward off more danger. Get him to hurry up. And that means we are into it when we only want the disgusting creature to finish. Blow his entitled load. How twisted is that?[15]

Yes, I never said No. Instead, I thought:

"Oh, great. I have to get through this and escape somehow. I just have to put up with all of this raping, and hitting, and forced cock sucking until I can figure out how to get away. Maybe moan a bit so he will get off me sooner and stop making me suffocate and gag as he shoves his grotty tongue down my throat. I just have to do everything he says after he forced me into compliance. 'Please stop ... I'll do anything you want ...' as my system started to shut down. But that wasn't a No to the 'sex' doncha' know. No, that was a No to being murdered. In a court of law, that may have been considered different. A different category. The please don't murder me category and the please don't rape me one. In my case, the judge may have said he actually didn't rape me. Kept everything separate even though everything is connected. She is guilty. Because never once did I literally say 'No.'

I have realized, though, in a First World country where rape victims can get justice, unlike in countries like Mexico where there aren't even rape kits,[16] I never gave my testimony as mine and not only as evidence to prove someone else's. For years, I didn't think about prosecuting personally. Why was this? Why did I try and let it all float away? Why did I not truly value and legitimize what I had survived? Why did I not acknowledge the abduction and rapes as crimes against my person and my body? And I succeeded for many years, or thought I did, at pushing it away.

Ten or so years later, I phoned Arizona. I asked. I said I wanted to have my trial. I said that I hadn't thought of it until now. Silence on the line. I am sure they couldn't believe a person would phone them up ten years after a crime and want their trial now. They said it was too late. There was nothing they could do.

I wonder now, after reading about the Ewanchuk case, if I had actually had my own trial, if the elderly woman had not been left for dead two days after I got away, or he let me go, however you would like to look at it, or both, if the trial had *only* been about abducting and assaulting me, would I have won? Would this particular serial rapist have been put away? And, if so, for how long? A few years? And then he would have been back out there burgling, abducting, and raping.

There is a good chance that if the trial was in 1994, like the Edmonton woman's was, when there was still the ruling of implied consent, he could have gotten off, or gotten one of those almost equally insulting 'slap-on-the wrist' sentences. It is very possible that the defense attorney could have succeeded in representing me as a slut, a divorcee, and careless and foolish for not taking responsibility for navigating my own safety, for being in a bar, for travelling alone, for, in Melanie Randall's words, not taking it upon myself to manage men's sexual attention and aggression, and also for not accurately assessing and avoiding risk.[17] The internalized shame that I have kept buried inside of myself for twenty-five years could very well have condemned me externally as well.

And, as a very real possibility, his accusation that I had had sex the night of the day I got away would have carried more clout if the jury had not been swayed by the attempted murder of an elderly woman. If it had been my own trial, and there wasn't this escalation of the case into homicide, maybe the defense could have been successful in turning my testimony against me, maybe even making the leap that after I was subdued through strangulation, I got into the whole thing, liked it because women enjoy being taken by force, especially an 'unconventional' woman like me. Bad victim. All my lies to the rapist could have been used against me. All the ruthless lies that I told to play on his heart, make him believe we had a relationship. I had led him on. Yes, I most certainly had. Maybe the serial rapist would have become the victim and I, the perpetrator. Maybe, like with so many rape victims who try to get justice, I would have been assaulted all over again.

"Did you say no to his sexual advances the first time he raped you? And all the times after that?"

"No! No! Please don't rape me!!" the good victim proclaims.

"Oh, yah, sure, honey. I'll stop. Sorry about that. I don't know what got into me."

"I know a good counsellor. I think you need some help."

"Yes, you're right. Can you give me the number? I'll call right away. Really sorry about this."

Yes, it was horrible and disgusting, but being a sexually mature woman, I could put up with it. Just barely. Perhaps one rape myth is true: as I said before, I am always so grateful I was never raped as a child, like my friend Lisa and, now that I think about it, like my dad was, too. The strangulation and constant threats on my life were far worse than the rapes. That was what I was really fighting against. When a person is being held hostage, getting away is the bottom line. You have no choice but to just endure the rest, keep your eye on the prize, so to speak. Being sexually assaulted every couple of hours was the least of my worries.

But I know very well if the trial had only been about the crimes he had committed against me, Linnihan definitely wouldn't have been put away for life. It wasn't enough. I wasn't left for dead, and, to make matters worse, on the outside, I was as cool as the proverbial cucumber. Both during and after the crime, I maintained the charade that I was not affected at all. No problem, I said to the rapist and to the DA. I fulfilled many of the pre-requisites of patriarchy's rape mythology. I had had many sex partners in my life—certainly not healthy interludes, mind you, but so-called promiscuous sex that I had because, ironically, I was looking for beauty, for love, for acceptance. Most of my life, I lived a pathology of rejection, setting myself up for it by being too 'easy,' by being too desperate. I hurt myself out of grasping for what I needed. I was perfect fuck-and-throw-away prey. I lived a roller coaster ride of devastation, and my hunger always left me open to another dupe, another string of: "You're so beautiful. You're so special. I've never met anyone like you before." And my falling for it. Over and over again. How could I have explained all this to a jury? It is the fling-the-muck-at-the-slut that would have much more readily stuck. Than the complexity of truth.

To make matters worse (I already told you but brace yourselves anyway): I'd had abortions. If there were so-called prolife people on the jury, I would have been toast. In the context of rape mythology and victim-blaming, I would have had a lot working against me if the defense had been looking for dirt on me to clean up a filthy rapist.

Twenty-odd years ago, rape myths had even more clout to blame sexual assault victims, and as recently as 2010, Melanie Randall wrote of the continued potency of rape mythology to "disappear" perpetrators.[18] Regardless of the fact that sexual assault laws in Canada and the US have technically eliminated such ridiculous legislations as "implied consent," in 2019, Robyn Doolittle comments how "we didn't necessarily do a lot to change the underlying attitudes."[19]

And I ask, *wouldn't the bruises around my neck have been enough?*

I have often thought about the fact that I didn't get my own trial. Felt kind of sorry for myself. But maybe it was for the best that I didn't. Maybe I wouldn't have gotten the acknowledgement that I have craved all these years that I assumed, based on the brutality I had lived through, I would have received. Maybe it would have made things worse. Maybe it would have been an assault upon an assault like the experiences of one in five raped women whose cases are cast aside as unfounded.[20] Maybe it was best that I just did my job of putting the fucker away for life even if he didn't serve a single year for the crimes he committed against me. And, write this book. Tell you everything. Maybe I was blessed by not thinking to fight for my personal retribution until it was too late.

And, if you still want to blame me and say I asked for it, at least, now, through this book, it's on my terms.

December 22nd, 1994. The Las Vegas Police Station.

I don't know if they were ever photographed. The bruises around my neck, that is. I forgot to tell you about reporting the crime, giving his license plate number to the police, and getting everything captured on paper and film. The night of the day that I got away. That's because I'd forgotten doing it.

I remembered this part of my story when I was reading Édouard Luis' rape memoir, *The History of Violence*. Unlike me, Édouard spends half of his book describing the reporting of the assault—which he was loath to do, and his friends had to convince him to. Maybe Édouard, a homosexual man in a hetero-normative society, sensed that it would be more trouble than it was worth, which it ended up being.

He had to tell his story over and over. He was sent to different departments when he was told (always after he had been made to tell the full story again) that this was the wrong department. With each telling, notes were taken. Information was entered into computers. At one point, his entire testimony was typed up, and he asked for a copy so that he wouldn't have to be tortured by yet another telling in the next office. This strategy proved fruitless. When he handed the document to the next man and said, it's all there … you can read it … I have told the story so many times now, the man responded that he would rather hear him tell it. Again. Each time Édouard had to re-tell his story, he was re-traumatized.

I, on the other hand, really have to dig to remember making my police report. When the nice guy whose name I forget picked me up at the bus, let me stay at his place and who I fell into having clumsy sex with told me I had to go, I think I sighed and said, "Yah, okay." I remember the sad sex we had much more clearly. And how, the next morning, after I had hardly slept, I felt even dirtier.

When he told me we had to go and report it, I remember wishing we could do something else. Like go out for dinner or something. Forget about the whole thing. I was like a pouting child who felt sick at the thought of being responsible. Maybe I hung my head and scuffed my feet as I dragged myself towards the door with the hope that the adult would take pity and say, "Hey, you win. Let's do something fun."

But, when I think back on it now, my desire was not wholly frivolous. I wanted to nourish myself with not only literal food but the life-sustenance guaranteed when one cuts out a big chunk of cancer—even if it's only temporary. Even if it's bound to grow back. Go to an American tavern. You know how I like those. With the mishmash of kitsch crowded cheerfully behind the bar, the adventures to be found in an unabashed jukebox. The faces. The lives of others one can become absorbed by. Better yet, we could have some small talk. Look around the room for a topic. Any topic. Hey, what's your favourite baseball team? And, why do you like baseball? What is it about the game that intrigues you so? Why do you think baseball is the US national sport? When did you see your first baseball game? Who were you with? Blah blah blah blah. I can see these questions popping out of my recently violated mouth, pink-lipsticked lips tied neatly in a pert little bow. Even the most boring topic in the world becomes fascinating in the fight to shove aside trauma.

Of course, we didn't go out for dinner. I didn't immerse myself in the succulence and tang of chicken wings and most likely have a martini or two. We went to the Las Vegas Police Station. Before we left, though, I took a shower. I felt so dirty inside and out and, being young, self-conscious, and a bit vain, I most likely wanted to look nice for the event. But, the main thing I remember about this shower is that I wasn't supposed to have it.

Friday night in the Las Vegas Police Station was packed. With women. I don't recall seeing a single man in there—except for most of the cops. I assume now that all the women waiting had been violated in some way. Probably most of them were prostituted women. I vaguely recall short skirts, big hair, and heavy make-up; bright smears of exaggerated femininity are surfacing as I write. As I push back and through the fog of this almost-lost memory, I think I can see myself walk up to the desk. I remember now being a bit self-conscious about my appearance. I felt so plain. As though my naivety was blasting. The other women all seemed so worldly. Like they knew things I was afraid to know.

This was certainly true. I knew nothing about the lives of prostituted women in those days, the things they have no choice but to know, to act as if they enjoy, to become hardened against. And, yet, even though I felt so out of place at the time, I had had a taste of that. What they knew. These mysterious women and I actually had a lot in common: when I was trapped inside the rapist vehicle, I had been forced to do exactly the same things prostituted women have no choice but to do daily—with my experience being on a much smaller scale, minus the coercion of poverty, sexual abuse, drug addiction or the usual combination of all three and the subsequent steady stream of rapists. The women who waited were caught in a far bigger trap than I've ever been.

The nice young man whom I inadvertently snubbed was by my side. But maybe the only reason that I remember this part of walking towards the desk to report the crime is because it is the logical thing to have happened next. And maybe this gash of hyperbolized sexuality I have just described merely adds an intriguing splash of colour to an otherwise forgotten scene. Not to mention another opportunity to connect prostitution to rape.

One thing I think I remember for sure is that I didn't have to wait long. Maybe this is because I was surprised that I had jumped the queue for some reason, and I felt embarrassed and happy about that at the same time. I have no memory of looking for a seat when I don't think there were any; I don't remember sitting on the floor; I don't remember thinking, Geeeez... let's get this over with! I am pretty sure that I was attended to quickly. Maybe I was prioritized over the mass of prostituted women because I have never been forced to sell my body for a living.

One of the waiting rooms where Édouard waited to report his assault was filled with prostituted women sitting resigned, staring at their shoes. Like fossils. As though they had been stuck there for an eternity waiting for a culture that could care less about a sexually assaulted prostitute. In Édouard's report, a woman loses her patience and is crying and screaming, "Don't you give a fuck?"[21] I have no memory of this happening in my rape report story. Perhaps that is because, unlike homosexual men and prostituted women, as a heterosexual, non-prostituted rape victim, I complied more readily to cultural norms, to condoned objects of concern, and so I wasn't in the waiting room for very long.

I know now that the large number of prostituted women waiting in the Las Vegas Police Station on a Friday night is undoubtedly due to the fact that they, like the women in one of Édouard's waiting rooms, *were* being ignored. As Victor Malarek reports, this is because of the presumption that it's impossible to rape a prostitute.[22] The man pays her; the monetary transaction is proof of consent. Everything's on the up and up. Prostituted women never say 'No' if what they have 'agreed' to is not what is happening. Poverty and drug addiction are not forced consent. No need for any john-guilt. If non-prostituted women are blamed for being sexually assaulted and have their consent interrogated, those who are raped multiple times a day for a living don't have a hope in hell of getting any retribution. It appears that, in this context of the hierarchy of consent and blame, in the Las Vegas Police Station waiting room, I was a 'good' victim. Now that I write into this memory block, I do recall feeling privileged.

When, as the privileged rape victim, I was led into the spaces beyond the waiting room, everything was white. Blinding white. I may have squinted. Covered my eyes. Looked at my feet as I walked on a glaring floor. I have no idea if I was attended by a man or a woman. I have no idea where we went first. Where did this crucial memory go?

Besides being sexually assaulted and held against our wills, Édouard and I have another thing in common: we were both strangled into submission. We both experienced the shock of our lives being forced over the line of life/death. We were both made instantly aware of how acute our vulnerability is, how abruptly we can be pushed from the familiarity of the everyday onto the brink of the unknown. We were both left with the grip of the predator's hands pressed purple and black around our necks. Marks that, if inflicted a bit longer, would have become the signatures of our deaths.

When Édouard had all his wounds documented, the authorities didn't miss any. They were so thorough, he tells us how it felt like they were photographing the inside of his body.[23] Édouard was much more beaten up than I was. He had lesions, hematomas. John Linnihan hadn't broken my skin. Not literally, that is.

Édouard relates how: "they spent a long time on the purple spots around my neck; the doctor told me, 'I can confirm that he must indeed have strangled you quite hard and for quite some time.'[24] All of Édouard's wounds were documented in claustrophobic detail; everything in his testimony is hyper-real; his recollection of these events is tweaked with the sharp edges of minutiae. Why is it that I remember next to nothing? Not even whether the deep bruises, the proof of near-death that, as the beginning of trauma, as the dividing line of a never-again-before and an always-after, that I can feel closing in as I write, were photographed? Maybe it's because I wasn't really there. And that Édouard's memoir was written a year after the assaults and mine twenty-five. With so much burying in between.

Raped women and prostituted women have a lot in common. In her forty-five years plus researching the trauma inherent to violence against women in the contexts of prostitution, Melissa Farley reports how "women say they can't prostitute unless they dissociate."[25] She defines this phenomenon: "[d]issociation is a mental tuning-out to avoid unbearable and inescapable stress." I am back in Linnihan's camper/van. "A dissociative response mitigates the john's cruelty by splitting the experience off from the rest of the self."[26]

When I first read this, even though I have only ever been a rape victim and never a victim of prostitution, I knew I did this. I didn't have a term for it, but I know that I had to separate myself from my body while being sexually assaulted to, paradoxically, keep it together. I remember the first time I did it. It was probably during the fourth or fifth rape. I remember thinking: I have to get away from this. I can't really be here. I know this is going to go on for a while. I have to figure out a way to protect myself. If I can't literally escape yet, I have to escape somehow. Part of me, the most precious part of me, must not be here.

I don't recall it being that difficult to do. So strong was my will; so absolute my disgust; so powerful my desire for self-preservation. I was above, watching myself being raped. The density of my body was thin, like when there isn't enough oxygen at a high elevation or when you feel as though you are moving in slow motion through a world made of smog. Half there, half not. I watched my prone flesh on the mattress below. Legs spread. Arms flopped by my side. Blank eyes staring up. A lifeless face. From above, I felt like an angel looking down on death.

When my necessary lies gave me no choice but to act as though I liked it, not being fully present became more of a challenge. But I managed. Maybe that was because the me who was pretending wasn't me at all.

I think, as I floated above, I could look away. Or close my eyes, when the me who wasn't there wanted to get away from what she was escaping. But the problem is, you can never detach one-hundred percent. You can't be fully absent when you are being physically violated, pinned down as another body thrusts into yours. Despite all the determination in the world, a part of you is always there. And always will be.

My mission was accomplished, though. I was able to not be there enough so that I could keep my secret ruthlessness iron-clad, nary a give-away chink. Keep my cool. When my body was an object—a thing that a rapist rutted and ejaculated inside of—obviously, I didn't want to be there. Who would?

And when I think back now, twenty-five years later, about why I have next to no memory of when I reported the abduction the night of the day of my escape, I think it's because I was still dissociating. I hadn't fully come back yet. I was still hovering above the whole thing, even when it was over. I was going through the motions, a specter of my own life. Maybe that is when the trauma, the long-term effects were erected, a row of teeth between the tough, no problem me, the bravado me, and the part of me that was there all along, being hurt.

Unlike the re-traumatization that Édouard experienced when being forced to tell his tale over and over, once I got home, I liked telling my story. And maybe that's because I felt so little of it. As in the lives of prostituted women who have gotten out, the dissociation continued long past the escape. For many years after the abduction, I was an audience to my own life. And it sure was interesting: this story of psychologically over-powering a serial rapist with all the intrigue of how I got away. Like my listeners, I had never heard such a story before.

"You won't believe what happened to Karen in Arizona!" friends would say, somehow complicit in the glamour of such grit. I would never have to volunteer the telling. That was also a benefit from having such an exotic tale to tell. These moments when people crowded around a table or leaned forward from the sofa were set up for me. All I had to do was roll in in my rock star survival limo and take the stage.

"Can you tell us the story, Karen? We haven't heard it yet ... but I *do* understand if you don't want to talk about it," they would say, their desire to feed on another's suffering understanding nothing at all.

"It must be *so painful* for you," they would coax, the corners of their mouths turned down in hypocritical empathy, brows furrowed, hands reaching towards mine in false compassion while dissembling tongues dripped, "but ... please ...."

"Alright," I would acquiesce and dive into another recitation from the shallow grave.

And I would tell it again. The grand dame conducting her still bleeding story time, stuck on the same surface of sensationalism as her greedy listeners, the only difference being that she knew the whole thing intimately—and felt nothing.

Every detail was relentlessly scratched out of Édouard's recently traumatized being. He begged them not to make him tell it again; it had all been written down and it was unnecessary to do so. As I recall, all the authorities were very kind to me, sympathetic, let me leave as soon as possible like they wanted to alleviate my suffering, congratulatory towards what I had survived. I, a white, middle-class heterosexual woman; he a homosexual man, picking up men on the street, existing outside of the margins of empathy. Perhaps I, in the hierarchy of rape believability, was more normal.

I don't know if they were ever photographed. The bruises around my neck, that is. The rape kit is a different story. I remember this more clearly. This is because I had to lie again. I can feel the blare of a fluorescent-lit room that, despite the glare, was soft as cotton batten as kind, compassionate, blurry faces looked down on me. I can see my feet in the stirrups, feel the cold metal table, the routine shimmy-your-bum-down-farther, please. And the fact that I wanted it all to last a bit longer. This caring. However clinical. But I knew I would have to leave soon. There were so many others to attend to. But I wanted it to last longer. This physical contact that didn't hurt. And then there was the question:

"Have you had a shower?"

"No," I said. Without a glitch. Not considering the option to do otherwise. To tell the truth. I remember I felt that somehow, if I admitted to having had a shower, it would delegitimize my story. Take away their care. The rapist wouldn't be guilty anymore. They would all glare at me in disgust. These people who cared. I would have made the whole thing up. "Oh, she had a nice shower right away. Mustn't have been so bad," I silently fretted. Or, "she doesn't know how to play by the rules in terms of how one reports a rape." Apparently, you are supposed to run to the police station immediately, head in hands or yanking at your hair, face puffy and slick with tears, lustrous in your testament to the perfect victim: "Help! Help! I need the rape kit!" Not the feel-nothing-had-a-shower-already-complainant like I was.

I had never heard of a rape kit until I had been raped and, more importantly, until I had been raped and had someone with me who told me I had to go and get one. And until I had been raped and actually acknowledged it right after, reported the crime the night of the day I got away—unlike the rapes in Montreal that were shoved into black holes and could have resided there forever, lightless, all of their gravity crammed into a tiny space, until my body told me I was pregnant, one of the rapists' DNA locked up in an embryo.

Not knowing about not having a shower before one reports a rape could have been another checkmark against me if I had

had my own trial because none of his DNA would have been found inside of me. Which, I vaguely sense now in this writing, they told me wasn't. There was nothing there. Nary a trace of him. The he who had done his damnedest to take all of me. Nary a trace, except the bruises. I remember feeling guilty. Disappointed. Like I had made the whole thing up without a molecule remaining of all the times he had been inside of me.

As they photographed the silent howls around Édouard's neck, he told himself: *"There was no need for tears, my body was enough."*[27] I would like to think that my bruises would have been enough. That they were photographed. That there was a record made before they receded into the memory of flesh.

Hidden now. I run my fingers across them. Invisible scars that will never allow me to forget. Phantom pressure that still squeezes. War scars. And I honour their persistence. Refusing to be forgotten. Never silenced. Documented: the evidence is written in the body.

No.

"No," he said. When I'd finally gotten up the courage to ask.

"Did you ever send the information ... that advice from another man who had used prostituted women all of his life ... his one piece of advice he wants to give to all men who do that: to just look into their eyes? Did you send it to your friend?"

"No."

"Why not ...?"

"He'll get mad at me."

"Yes ... probably ... most likely ... so...?"

Silence.

"YOU do it. It was your idea!"

"You told me you would...."

"I changed my mind."

"It would be most effective coming from you. Through you and then coming from the man who stopped, through a long-time male friend, to him ... It may even make a difference."

I begged.

"Look, I'm as feminist as I can be! What do you expect from me?!"

"More," I thought. "I expect, I want, more."

———●———

Six months later, I got up the courage. I sent the advice. I hacked some holes into the PTSD wall and did it. I decided to fight against being re-traumatized by what is everywhere. I also want to live this out to some sort of end. Some sort of resolution. Good. Bad. In between. I felt like I was going to be sick. And now I am scared to open his reply.

He replied quickly. Within the same day. I didn't expect that. I actually didn't know what to expect. But, when you don't know what to expect, you are surprised by whatever happens. And, in this case, for me: jolted.

When I opened my email and saw his response, I immediately turned away and held my hand up to the screen to block it out. I saw the first phrase, though. Friendly. Familiar. Chummy: "Hey K ..."

I immediately forwarded it to a friend. Kept my hand up over the screen as I typed in her address with one finger. The proximity of the open email made me feel like I was going to puke. I asked her to read it first and then tell me what it says or just read it to me or something like that or both. Trauma is terrorizing. And I am doing my damnedest to stare it down. But I can't look his email straight on. Not yet anyway.

———●———

She reads it to me. After a segue of: "It's not good or bad. He doesn't say much. I think it's safe for you to read."

"Is that good or bad, not good or bad?" I think. "Would it be better if there were some passion one way or another?"

He wrote a few lines about Covid 19 and getting out of Costa Rica (lots of sex tourism there, I couldn't help but think).

How he's now in the mandatory two-week quarantine. Late March 2020.

"I don't actually have the same or similar lifestyle as this fellow, and those days are long gone, but thanks for your concern."

Denial? Truth? Hope? An opening?

Even though he says those days are long gone—and maybe they really are—he did have the same or similar lifestyle: the lifestyle of using young women's bodies for sex. Of absolute male entitlement. Of condoned rape. He is still an embodiment of everything I am against. But, somehow, as something I don't fully understand at this moment of writing: I don't want to fully shut him out. I want to respond. I have no idea how. But maybe someday I will write: yet.

When I first mentioned the idea:

"No ... No .... No ... " Half stammer, half statement; your opposition was far from absolute.

It was very necessary that day, though. There was a lot of snow, and it had been sticking around for a while in the cycle of melting a bit and freezing again and snowing more, building up devious sheets of ice beneath recent powder. As usual, you wanted to go for a walk, even though you barely could, and even though the car was having trouble getting out of the driveway. And, as usual, you always turned and thanked me, with the solemnity of a sacrament, when I said I would come with you.

In retrospect, how we made it up the first incline towards the winding wooded trail and then to the crest of the rain-rutted logging road was nothing short of a miracle. My body was a wedge between yours and the ground with spurts of slapstick as we slid and slipped, and I became an animated parallelogram contorting myself into any and all necessary angles to keep you up, to keep you from falling into humiliation and despair.

When we somehow arrived at the top of the steep hill next to the pond, I said,

"Let's go back now, Dad." And you said, as usual, characteristically stubborn in your delusion that you could still stride down an ice-covered logging road,

"No."

"Dad, you won't make it. There is too much snow and ice! You will fall for sure!"

"Whaddya mean?" you glared, disgusted by my lack of faith. "I don't *fall*." You stated your absolute truth from behind the scabbed gash above your left eye and the purple and yellow bruising on your right cheekbone. What is not seen is so conveniently forgotten.

"Anyway, I'm going that way. Come if you want."

There was no 'if you want' possible as I couldn't leave you lying helpless on the trail. No point in arguing. As always, you never gave up. But now, desperation accompanied your obstinate nature, desperate for your life to be what it had been and stubborn enough to be able to convince yourself that it could, even though your daughter was the brace that literally prevented you from rolling and thudding to the bottom and a rescue team having to be called in to carry you back on a stretcher. Lucky for me, I am your daughter and inherited your determination that allowed this to never happen.

Just like when you skied even after you couldn't anymore. Before your driver's licence was taken away, up you would go, regardless of Mom's upset, to fly through the white and the fresh and the snow-heavy trees and the bright blue of a mountain top like you always had, such an expert at being physically free, certain you were still the man you had always been. And you would fall. Lose your balance and fall. Not be able to get up. And the ambulance would be called. And arrangements had to be made to get your truck. Mom would be mortified again. Go on about the expense to the social system and the inconveniencing of others. But you wouldn't care. Up you would go again. And fall again. How beautifully selfish you were in your demand to still be alive.

Just like the time when you insisted on climbing onto the roof and cleaning the chimney. Like you always had. The man who cleaned the chimney and cut the wood and packed the wood and flew down mountains. You made it up the ladder and crawled onto the edge of the roof. But there you stayed. A gap of realization in your illusion as your body refused to do anything at all.

"Help! Help!" you called. And the firemen were soon on their way. They were shocked to see you up there in your tenacious lack of ability to let go of what you had been, and one of them said, "Do *not* go onto the roof ever again, Sir." I think the ladder had to be taken away so that this order could be obeyed.

Halfway down the hill, I was getting a cramp in my side from the strain of keeping you somewhat standing. We had become a single unit by now. The possibility of you being able to move at all without me was an impossibility. Halfway down the icy slope, I said again, "Dad, please, let's go back now."

"No."

Somehow, we made it to the bottom, and you wanted to go up the other side.

"Really? Okay." I was defeated at this point.

I think now, writing this, what was the length of your extent of never giving up? Even to the point of not being able to do it? How mad. Could you have stood there alone on legs that refused to move and be able to say to yourself, "Well, I can't move at all. But I am never giving up!" You most likely could have.

We didn't make it far. You finally, sadly, quietly, admitted defeat and said, "Let's go back now."

I looked at your crestfallen face and felt some mischief awaken within.

"Hey, Dad ... Do you want me to go and get the wheelbarrow?"

"No ... No .... No ... " Half stammer, half statement; your opposition was far from absolute.

The first time you said "Yes," some serious mischief started up between us. It became a shared joke, a sly game of snubbing our noses at the world, the world that had designated your life as no longer one that could go to the forest, but a life where a daughter could still give her father the magic of being a child again. "Ok, Dad, you stay here, and I'll run back and get it!!" I exclaimed, you and I both rascals and renegades. I sat you gently at the side of the trail and added as a joyful tangent to our game, "If anyone comes by and asks if you're alright, tell them your transportation is on its way!!"

And I would run back to the house, whip open the basement door, grab the key to the shop, lunge across the yard, run towards the wheelbarrow, realize I needed something soft to line it with, whiz back to the house, find a sleeping bag under the ping-pong table, bound back to the shop with sleeping bag bundled in my arms, get the wheelbarrow, line it with the sleeping bag and race back up into the forest where you sat waiting for me, enjoying the birds and the sun on your face and seemingly oblivious to the fact that you were sitting, unable to get up, at the side of a trail.

I devised a method to get you in. This was probably the first time in our lives that you had agreed wholeheartedly with all my ideas. In writing this now, through the gap of two years later, I can't remember exactly how I did it. I know that, of course, I had to get you up. I recall how I positioned the side of the wheelbarrow under your butt. I tipped it in your direction, and you basically fell in. I then levelled the wheelbarrow (yes, it is coming back to me now) and managed to spin you around so that you leaned against the sloping part in the front that was lined with the sleeping bag, and your legs could stick out between the two handles, or one could rest on either side.

And then we would fly along the trails, you in your chariot and I your devoted daughter and self-proclaimed pony as I watched you rest your head on the sleeping bag and immerse yourself in the green racing overhead and look at me with the adoration I had been waiting for all my life. And sometimes, looking at me lasted longer than gazing overhead, and I felt uncomfortable in my joy and would have to look away, or crack a joke as you gazed at me with, yes, something that then, and even more now in this act of remembering, was, indeed, holy. Your strained face softened as the innocence of old age overlapped with that of youth while you leaned back and just were, in love with the forest and the sky, and, I think, with your daughter, too.

I received a most unexpected apology from you once. But that once was enough. When you never in your most longed-for dreams expect something to happen, when it does, it has the power of all that was ever needed.

When I started fighting back, we fought. A lot. Up until then, I had just taken it; it had been absorbed by my being to the point that I was indivisible from the lack that you filled me with. The lack of feeling love (even though there was so much); the lack of being good enough (even though of course I was); the lack of self-worth (even though you should never have taken that away from me by never giving it to me). My brother told me once,

"Dad is hardest on you because he loves you the most." How can such a pathology make any sense? But it does when another has had the same thing done to them that they are now doing to their child. They pass it onto the one who resembles them most. They loathe that child because they were made to loathe themselves. You needed to try and crush my spirit because someone tried to crush yours. And, in both cases, neither you nor that other someone succeeded. Only almost.

The fact that you succeeded in overcoming the same thing that you inflicted upon me gives me strength now, Dad.

The last time we fought, I was halfway out the door.

"Why do you think I don't have any children? Why do you think I have had such terrible luck with men all my life? Always chosen ones who hurt me? Why do you think I have always only come so close to achieving my dreams?"

"You can't blame that all on me." You responded, your face made blank by the severity of my accusations and the fact that you had never imagined any of this, not to mention noticed.

"It didn't help," I stated flatly and left.

I found out later that I had made you cry.

"Good." Was all I had to say.

A week or so later, I received an email from you. You had never written me an email before. You could barely type, a tradesman long before one had to enter data into a computer. I imagined you typing this to me with two fingers, maybe only one, brow furrowed as you searched for the letters:

"I am sorry if I made your life more difficult than it should have been."

That was all. That was everything.

On one of our many wheelbarrow forays that final year of your life, you and I are sitting next to the beaver pond listening to the birds. You are leaning back regally in the scoop of the wheelbarrow lined as a nest with the sleeping bag; I am sitting on the stubble of wild grasses by your side. It must be early April as the Red-Winged Blackbirds are here with their bewitching trills, flashing winged rubies as they move from marshy perch to marshy perch.

"Let me know when you want to go back, Dad."

"It's up to you. If it's up to me, that will be a very long time."

We sit. Now that I recall it in this act of writing, I think this is one of the happiest moments of my life. The early spring sun is warm; the profound generosity of silence strung with the cadences of the bird songs I know so well consoles; the unexpected miracle that you and I are now able to be true comrades in spirit. I see a car pull up on the road above the pond. Some hikers. They notice us immersed in our sacred quietude. A woman starts to walk towards us.

"Oh, great," I mutter under my breath. "I hope it isn't another person coming to ask us if we're okay and if we need any help again." She arrives.

"We don't need any help," my words are tinged with annoyance. This had been happening semi-regularly: people thinking that we are in some sort of distress because I am pushing my dad around in a wheelbarrow. What of it? Don't we *look* alright as we race around the trails or sit and listen to the birds?

"No, no," she responds, sensing my annoyance. "I just wanted to see who the lovely daughter is who pushes her dad around in a wheelbarrow!" I smile, maybe even blush a bit, embarrassed by my presumptuous thoughts and the pleasure of feeling this acknowledgement of my gift to you.

She looks closely at you. Another person arrives on the scene. They recognize you. Two gasps of amusement. One covers her mouth in a gesture of surprise.

"Is that *you*, Richard?" she exclaims.

You have no idea who they are anymore, but your smile is as magical as the chimes of the Red-Winged Blackbirds.

"Only *you* would end up in a wheelbarrow!"

I close my eyes. Your smile is an infinite ellipsis, each point a sparkle that hangs in the air. This memory will always be in the present tense, an echo that has no end, a bell that resounds in my heart.

I forgive you everything.

December 22ⁿᵈ, 1994. Airborne.

After a while, I pulled the Whopper and milk out of the bag he had left for me at the Greyhound station. I stared out the window, smiled at the land racing past in the fast-fading light, the descent into darkness, the erasure of this place. I took a big bite. I was starving. I remember it tasted really good.

The next day, I was on the plane from Las Vegas to Vancouver. On the way to Las Vegas, I had been giddy with the excitement of a great adventure. On the way home, I was a changed person.

As I stared down at the ribs that protrude from a desert-scape when viewed from above, I felt a primal rhythm begin to rise in my body. It started slow, plodding in 4/4 time, like a wisdom being born, a power surfacing, and gradually began to speed up, the pound of each beat building as the bars accelerated. Words mysteriously began surfacing in my mind, laboured at first and growing into a life-giving pulse:

"We gaze ...
into ...
Oblivion ...
We gaze ...
Into ...
Oblivion ...
We say ya-hey-ey-hey-ey-hey-ey-he-ey-he-ey Ya!
We say ya-hey-ey-hey-ey-hey-ey-he-ey-he-ey Ya!
We say YA-HEY! Mother fucker
Give it to me, C'mon
We say YA-HEY! Mother fucker
Give it to me, C'mon!!
We gaze into Oblivion ...
We gaze into Oblivion ...
And we say:
YA HEY!!!"

This song cycled in my mind and from my lips the entire flight. I had conquered the edge. I had stood and stared fiercely into the void. I had not fallen. There is nothing more he can do to me, I thought. But there is a lot more I can do to him. I marched off the plane singing.

POSTSCRIPT: THE VISIT

have nothing planned. Except to just go. Go and sit face to face. And see what happens. Of course, there are a lot of preparations to be made. One can't just waltz into a high-security penitentiary and say, "Hey. I would like to see the man who abducted, held me hostage, and raped me a bunch of times twenty-five years ago."

The first thing I'll have to do is write a letter. To him. Hard copy, old-school style. And get his permission. For me to come and sit face to face and see what happens. Like a science experiment where a scientist puts two animals into a cage and keeps watch, I will take notes.

I am sure something will be said. Eventually. How could there not be? After so many years. Me, the bitch who caught him. Surely, he must have something to say to me.

There may be a chunk of silence at first. I mean, we didn't even know each other in the first place. It isn't as though we have anything to catch up on. "So, how's it been going with your ninety-three-year sentence?"

One can only hypothesize as to what has happened to him in there. I will let him start. I will just take a seat. I will be the artist as scientist documenting what I have instigated, the process of my own creation. There is no way of knowing exactly what will happen in the creation of art or the living of life. Isn't fiction inevitable until the story has been lived? I will look into his eyes. Mine will be slits. A sneer will most likely be rising, beginning to menace from my top lip. From loathing. From repulsion. Will I feel sick seeing him again? Will it trigger trauma? Or will it just be interesting, the artist in me taking over, always ready to gobble up every morsel of inspiration? But, if nausea, gagging, or shaking threaten, I vow here and now that I will keep them down. For the sake of pride. For the sake of art. I will hold myself together with the iron of my stare that I can feel right now. That I practice as I write.

We will be in one of those prison visiting rooms. But this time, he'll be in the cage. Up to this point in my life, prison visiting rooms are places I have only seen on TV and in movies.

No one will ever forget Hannibal Lector and the prison visits paid him by Clarice Starling. But Linnihan didn't achieve anywhere close to that level of murderous aristocracy, especially with the sinister collusion of haute couture cannibalism. And, even if he'd had the chance to start seriously killing, I am sure Linnihan's killings would have been much more of the meat and potato kind, clumsy even, no eloquent premeditation and psychological flourishes as in the psychopathic world of Lector. Not to mention the fact that Lector got out. And not only out, out in style. While John Linnihan was there for life. Twenty-three years of nothing. Not even any visitors. Until me. The one who gave him the non-life that he somehow lived out until its end. Perhaps that is some sort of sad heroism. Doing all of his time. No suicidal cop-out of what he had coming to him. No dangling from a wound-up sheet attached to a pipe that runs across the ceiling of his cell. For some reason, he endured absolutely no hope.

There won't be any of the drama of *Dead Man Walking*, either. I am far from a nun, and I have first-hand experience of the prisoner's guilt. Certainly, nowhere close to fresh-faced and tear-jerking like Paul Newman's *Cool Hand Luke*. I am not expecting any beauty in this impending visit. The exact opposite. Banal even. The horror of the environment that resides in the excess of the mundane. As I imagine it. Sterile. A life of brutality permeated by bleach with its over-determined attempt to clean away sin and only succeeding in replacing dirt with poison.

If I can predict any connection, my visit with John Linnihan will be closer to Truman Capote's with the murderer Perry Smith. Not in terms of the eventual friendship between the writer and the murderer, but rather through the cold blood of the artist doing anything for the cause of authentic research, for the sake of art, for the sake of having no choice but to live out the story to its necessary end. I, too, won't be able to resist opening the coffin, looking at the corpse of the man I pretty much killed. And opening the coffin of my own trauma as well by situating myself as both researcher and researched.

Unlike Capote, though, I will not be questioning the moral implications of this visit or care about how this serial rapist will be remembered. Perry Smith did nothing to his ruthless biographer except torture him with the terrifying beauty of the narrative he gave. But, as with all art that resists nothing, some cold blood will inevitably be spilled during my visit too.

—●—

Victims' Services in California sent me a document that traces Linnihan's life in prison: all the high-security prisons that have comprised his life after the sentencing in 1997. He has been transferred a lot. Ten times to be exact. I read that the main reason for so many transfers is that the inmate is being bullied, and their life is in danger. That makes sense based on what he is in prison for.

He has spent most of his twenty-three years in High Desert State Prison. Eight years to be exact. After being one year in a Substance Abuse Treatment Facility, he was transferred to one of the most abusive and dangerous penitentiaries in the state of California, especially for sex offenders. In the early 2000s, when he was there, High Desert State Prison was described as "a remote, isolated, lawless penal hellscape in which guards abuse some inmates and choose to allow other vulnerable groups of inmates to be abused by their fellow prisoners."[1] Sounds beyond pretty grim. It is a maximum and super-maximum security prison. What could he have done in the drug treatment facility to get himself transferred to a penitentiary with the highest level of security and one of the worst reputations in the state? I can only imagine.

I look at a photo of the prison with its rows of watchtowers along the perimeter and its double walls with the space in between as a medieval moat edged by rolls of barbed wire, and I think with an existential wow, "You're in there .... What must it be like? What must it be like to have been out here and suddenly end up in there? Did you expect this? While you were roaming around in your contraption of a camper/van, did you think: "this

272

is the risk I am taking abducting, raping, assaulting people with deadly weapons, burgling. I may be locked up forever"?

"Was it worth it?"

This has been his life since 1997. Walls painted some institutional colour of puke green or soft bile. Floors blank concrete or an overly polished hurrah of control. Steel tables as institutional flowers with utilitarian stools poking out like cold petals. American penitentiaries are proud places. Fine-tuned members of corporate capitalism. Providing jobs for entire towns. Impervious compartments. Not mashed up hell holes like in the Third World. Yet, there are still the relentless bars. Non-stop locks. Cages upon cages as labyrinths of captivity. Surrounded by everything lost in this everyday slap in the face of nothing. With no possibility of escape.

Linnihan was at the Substance Abuse Treatment Facility for a year. It's known as the largest rehabilitation facility in the world, and even such notables as Robert Downey Jr and Charles Manson attempted to kick their habits there. Especially for those with life sentences, I wonder if drug abuse is more akin to survival?

I checked it out on Google Satellite. The Substance Abuse Treatment Facility is like all the other penitentiaries Linnihan has been in. It is but another sprawling member of the Prison Industrial Complex that, from the air, resembles a world map where the earth has been splayed open like an orange peel sectioned with an Exacto knife, reminiscent of when the earth was flat, the walls being the edges that one would fall off if they could only climb over.

Before his stint in the Substance Abuse Facility, Linnihan spent three years in a prison specializing in Special Needs Yards (SNYs). In 2002, some California prisons started the Special Needs Yards, where inmates considered at high risk of prison violence were segregated for safety reasons. It's called Pleasant Valley State Prison. This was the time when Linnihan became seriously addicted to drugs. And, I suppose, when one thinks about it from a lived-reality-incarcerated point of view, a serious drug habit most likely made things a bit more pleasant.

What was your drug of choice, John Linnihan? On the outside, you certainly liked your bourbon. That's what you were drunk on the night you abducted me. Before the next day when you sobered up and started to sigh. But what did you choose in prison? What did you escape with? What did you use to live out your sentence? The up or the down? The meth or the heroin? My guess is the heroin. I think you are a heroin kind of rapist. Something that can dull what might have become agonizing guilt. Or remorse. Or resentment that escalated to the excruciating point of having to be dulled down. Or just the straight-up hell of being imprisoned. The daily suffocation of knowing you are never getting out. This is it. May as well try and enjoy yourself.

Ironically, the separate SNYs eventually became as big as the general population because any inmate could sign up to go there. I guess a lot of prisoners feel at risk. These at-risk prisoners are technically supposed to be gang dropouts, informants (or snitches), former law enforcement officers, and, to throw some perverts into the mix, sex offenders and pedophiles. The families of the informants are particularly concerned about the safety of their loved ones. This makes a lot of sense, especially if said snitches have snitched on someone in the general population. But no one seems to have any sympathy for the rapists and pedophiles. No one is out protesting for their well-being. It seems to me that part of the justice when incarcerating a sex offender is the punishment they receive on the inside.

I must say I like that rapists and pedophiles are at the bottom of the heap in the hierarchy of inmate respect. It's like an inversion of the outside where the buying and exploitation of women's and children's bodies through prostitution and pornography go so far as to being culturally condoned, and the effects that such normalization of male sexual entitlement has on violence against women and children, in general, can actually be denied. Ironically, inside the prisons, with all the inmates lumped together as dangerous offenders and threats to law and order on the outside, there is more justice when it comes to disciplining sex offenders. This version of justice has a kind of raw integrity. Sex offenders are scum because they have assaulted our wives, girlfriends, mothers, and children. On the outside, men can get away with that to various degrees. But not in prison.

According to one website I found that delineates the levels of respect in prison life, the guys on top are "successful bank robbers, or any thief who got away with a scam or a high-money robbery without actually hurting anyone. These types command a great deal of 'quiet' respect from other inmates, especially if they avoid bragging about their crimes."[2] That makes sense to me. Humble, brilliant people, fundamentally non-violent people, Robin-Hood types who are getting away with taking from those who have too much already and often achieved their level of too much through criminal means anyway. Seeing as I have told you everything else, I may as well confess that I have often fantasized about robbing a bank. That was you and I, wasn't it, Paul? Back in those reckless days of Rock & Roll when I first got back from Arizona. Paul and I had a plan that never materialized, alas, a grand plan, but how we would love to talk about it and feel the vibrations of adrenalin that maybe, somehow, someday, we could pull it off.

Paul claimed there are abandoned tunnels underneath Vancouver. We would have had to do a lot of exploring in the tunnels first and figure out if any of them went under a bank. I imagine us popping our heads out of manholes at night, scanning for possible banks we could rob. What were the odds of finding a large enough pipe that goes not only beneath a bank but also underneath the safe? Such a detail didn't matter because we never did it.

We would have needed a chemist. Who doesn't when they need to make some dynamite with the precise density of explosives to only blow a hole underneath a bank safe and not damage nearby buildings? Like the most respected inmates, we wouldn't have wanted to hurt anyone. Yes, successful bank robbers definitely deserve a lot of respect.

It could very well have been this inner deviance that helped me convince Linnihan I was as bad or worse than he was so that he fell for my lie that I would never turn him in and he let me go. I could talk the talk. This combination of ruthlessness and nonchalance is most useful in a culture that thrives on screwing other people over. I have always been a convincing storyteller. Such skills come in handy for getting away from a kidnapping rapist. Not to mention hypothesizing as to what a prison visit will be like. If Paul and I had ever followed through on our bank robbery fantasy (and had the misfortune of getting caught), we would at least have been at the top of the pecking order in prison. Unlike John Linnihan.

He was a sex offender. They are the despised inmates. In fact, they are so despised that "other inmates consider them sick bastards, not 'real' criminals. Nobody likes a rapist, not even other criminals."[3] Rapists: a whole other breed of inmate, a whole other breed of human. So different, in fact, that they are even denied any comradery in the community of criminals. Mutants. Freaks. When a rapist is incarcerated, regardless of what he did to you, he will certainly get back what he gave, and maybe, as in my case, even more.

At the High Desert State Prison, I have no doubt that he was disciplined for his sex offenses in unthinkable ways. Even the corrections staff were in on it as officers at HDSP have a reputation of pointing out sex offenders to other inmates so that they will be brutalized.[4] Perhaps it was a game for them. A gladiator-type sport of throwing the perverts to the wolves and then hanging around to watch the prison enact its eye-for-an-eye ethics, the no-messing-around belief system of violent offenders committed to protecting women and children. Some wholesome values in what is presumed a cesspool. Perhaps getting the revenge that many victims and survivors are never able to get personally. Coincidentally, this is when Linnihan started going to the hospital a lot. Ten times during his eight-year stay.

Regardless of what he did to me all those years ago, strangely enough, I feel a bit sorry for him. Nothing is ever black or white. There are always ambivalences in what one could presume would be all there is to reality. From an unlived distance, people have said to me: you must hate him, wish him dead. I don't know if I ever did. Perhaps I never cared enough. Or maybe I blocked it all out. Or maybe I have known that he got what was coming to him. To tell you the truth, there is no certainty as to how I feel at this moment. Only that I need to go. It's inexplicable. A myriad of contradictions. Through this gap of time filled up with half my life, he is so far from me, while what he inflicted has been a part of me ever since. This less than twenty-four-hour chapter has been brought back through this act of writing, and yet it sometimes feels like fiction. Did this story of abduction and escape happen to me? Did I really live it? Yes, I must have. I know all the details. I am almost finished writing a book about it. But it still seems unreal. A phantom narrative contained by my flesh.

I wonder how other people would feel if they were resurrecting a rapist from their past and are preparing to look him in the face. That is, if the rapist was already a stranger, like Linnihan was to me, and not a family member, boyfriend, or husband. Such familiarity preceding sexual violence would add a layer of trauma that I have been lucky enough to never know. A shock. A betrayal. People who have lived through childhood sexual abuse have told me about the horror that they could have loved that person, and most likely, part of them still does. A density of confusion that I can only begin to imagine.

For me, there was already the distance of not knowing the person at all, and then a barrage of violation, of rapacious intimacy, the hyper-reality of a life/death situation, and then nothing again. At this moment in writing, I feel blocked by such nothingness. Is writing this visit impeding my creativity in correspondence to how he took from me for those hours, made me think that it would be forever, a compounded chunk of time that sits as a dying tooth in the narrative of my life and I am about to jab at the root?

Last night, I thought that maybe cigarettes would help. Even though I have pretty much quit. The stereotypical tradition of the great writers of darkness and pathos all smoked, didn't they? Gitanes. Marlboros. Dunhills. Gauloises. Camus. Kafka. Hemmingway. Baudelaire. Perhaps I can stir up all the somethings that must be there through the reckless romance of a sharp inhalation followed by a luxuriously exhaled plume of the edge. Accompanied always by hard liquor. Whiskey, cognac, or absinthe as examples of the deepest commitments to the debauchery necessary to unleash the beast that courts its unsettling truth. Do we have to numb ourselves to dig deep? Like the necessity for a prostituted woman to dissociate in order to not go crazy from the violation she must daily, somehow, endure? Do we need to rough ourselves up a little to inflict the scratches in our souls so we can articulate the unsaid, the unsayable? Especially when we need to agitate our own trauma and pull out something interesting, something meaningful, for the pleasure of ourselves and the audience to our story? George Orwell said:

> Writing a book is a horrible, exhausting struggle, like a long bout with some painful illness. One would never undertake such a thing if one were not driven on by some demon whom one can neither resist nor understand.

I didn't feel this way until this part. I must admit, I have pretty much skimmed the pit. Teetered and tap-danced on its rim. Yes, I know there has been a lot of darkness, darkness that is inevitable when a person is writing and remembering violence. But there have been bursts of levity that have pulled me back up. So far, the way I see it, this narrative has been a triumph. For me, at least. On some level. I guess all we can do is see how the visit goes.

Let the game begin:
I have decided to keep the letter brief.

John,
    This is Karen Moe. I am sure you remember me. I would like to visit you. Will you give permission for me to come?

He says, Yes.

———◈———

I feel the same way that I did when I flew south to California for the trial. I watch the land descend from lush to parched; I feel the apprehension of not knowing what to expect. Unlike last time, though, when I had the quest to finally get it done and the purpose to put him away, this time, I wonder what the hell I'm doing.

"Why, you are finishing your book, my dear!" the writer-me responds, always composed and ready for more. "It is the perfect ending! You have no choice in the matter. Moreover, the fact that he has actually said 'Yes' means that much more intrigue awaits! It is your duty as an artist to explore it. Go all the way. Finish the book. As it has been predestined."

"Right," I write. "He must have something to say to me."

"Or maybe he is just as curious to see you as you are to see him. Maybe he has the same plan. To just sit there and see what happens."

"I really have nothing at all to say to him. Nothing at all."

"Don't worry. I have complete faith in you! You will find something to write about the visit. Even if nothing happens."

———◈———

This time, when I arrive at the airport, I am not greeted by an upbeat DA and a cloying pink-T-shirted teddy bear. I am not whisked away to a Holiday Inn in an unmarked police car, instructed to rest for an hour until the DA and the chief of police take me for dinner in the hotel restaurant. I don't have a couple of beers, not eat, and feign nonchalance as I shake internally. This time I don't land in LAX. I land in Reno, Nevada, the same state where Linnihan was last a free man. I have to take a two-hour bus ride to Susanville, the hometown of—a description that one would think is redundant—"one of the most dysfunctional penitentiaries in the state." A town that now exists only because of the prison. A prison town. I board the Greyhound. This time I am not getting away from the rapist: I am going back.

The bus route is through a beautiful forest. Creeks. Lakes. Snowy peaks. I let my mind float as trees blur past. I lean my head against the window and enjoy the smudges of green, blue and white, flying through a forest that I know I will never set foot in. And neither will he.

Susanville was a logging town until the last sawmill was shut down in 2002. There used to be a lot of farming as well. But now, the only industry is the prisons, with the High Desert State being the largest. A space in the fields and forest was scraped out to make room for all those lives that didn't work out but are still kept alive to live out the consequences of their bad choices. But some of those so-called free will bad choices are based on bad luck. Bad luck of being born the wrong race. Bad luck of being born into abusive families. Bad luck of being born into poverty. But can we ever excuse a rapist, or a pedophile, or, of course, a serial killer who is usually also a rapist? Can we ever commit those crimes to 'bad luck'? No.

So why do I feel even a little bit sorry for him? This feeling is making me feel ashamed at this moment of writing. Perhaps he didn't hurt me as much as one would think he did. As much as those who actually make things worse by saying they can't deal with it because it's so terrible for them. Perhaps that hurts more. Perhaps it's because I won. Perhaps it's because he had such a pathetic existence and it became even more pathetic. Perhaps it's because I always have art to reside in. Perhaps it's because I am remembering through the space of so much time. Perhaps it's because some aspects of trauma have no answers. And I am okay with that. Perhaps because it's so interesting. Perhaps it's because of my desire to write this story to the very end: the end that I have always wanted: a final confrontation. And, find out what happens when we sit face to face. And win again.

The town is relatively nondescript. There is a downtown strip with a smattering of buildings from the late nineteenth century that got in just at the tail-end of an essence of Wild West charm. The Pioneer Café, with its five-foot-tall neon martini sign, and the Sierra Theatre appear to be the hot spots. Susanville is like a washed-out version of Prescott. But maybe that's because I feel numb here, my emotions as nondescript as the town—even as I try so hard to tell you something enticing, something concrete— where, when imagining Prescott, I can still feel the glass-eyed deer stuck staring at nothing above my head; I can still hear the bartender's unruly laugh that was blanched of all frivolity when John Linnihan walked in. And my world held its breath.

In Susanville, every hotel or motel is some version of a Travel Lodge where the doors all open onto the street. I haven't stayed alone at a place like this since then. Accommodation that doesn't have the protection of a lobby and so anyone can get into your room if they really want to. I have no choice but to put my life in danger.

I am not going outside. The Pioneer looks interesting, and I would like to find out why an establishment labelled a café is advertised by a giant, flashing martini, but I am going to resist the urge to fill this particular pang of curiosity for the sake of what must be trauma. Even though he is locked up, I will stay in the safety of an uneventful Travelodge. Incarcerated or not, regardless of age and frailty, he is still near. Perhaps my "Hey, no problem! I got this covered" is beginning to be poked at. By myself.

I have dinner at the hotel restaurant. Despite the fact that this is California, a Best Western guarantees a crappy wine list. I choke down a glass of Naked Grape and instantly begin to chastise myself for my cowardice.

"You are a coward. An imposter in art," the writer accuses.

"Maybe that's because I am also a human," the human responds.

I go to the room with the flimsy door between myself and the street, lock the doorknob and attach the insubstantial chain, a feeble combination of security that could easily be kicked in. I lie on my back, stiff and ready, between inhospitable sheets. I am back in Linnihan's camper/van. This time, my mind whirling as to why I am re-traumatizing myself instead of how I am going to get away. My eyes are glued to the window with its semi-opaque, cream curtains backlit by the street lights, creating a cinema of silhouette. Headlights come and go across the screen like searchlights. People pass to and from their rooms. Doors close. Locks fasten. Locks unfasten. Snippets of relationships are uttered through sharp and soft voices. Doors open. Close. I wait for one of the silhouettes to stop and stand in front of my door. A big one, hunched, with predatory eyes that I can feel burning through this illusion of one-dimensionality. I hold my breath at each approach. This time I am prepared. On guard. Body braced to leap and grab the deadly lamp from the bedside table. I trust nothing. I don't sleep.

———◆———

I should have killed you.
  Yes, I agree. That's what I would have done.

My appointment is at 9:30 a.m. The waiting room is crowded when I arrive. I have to wait for about forty-five minutes. Another lacuna to splash around in and wait for this to be over before it's begun. Finally, my name is called. The person behind the glass asks me what my relationship is to the inmate. I want to say: victim, but the options are only family or friend. I say: friend.

Why did you destroy my life? I trusted you. You said you were my friend.
  How can you trust someone whom you violated over and over? Whom you held hostage—whose life you threatened?

*I gave it back to you, your life, as you asked me to. I kept
my promise.*

I follow a guard down an excessively polished hall that feels
like it's made of light. This insubstantiality befits my need to
detach from my body, to disassociate and rise above it now like
I did in the desert twenty-five years ago. I shade my eyes, will
myself into vapor, embody the ghost of a quarter-century ago.
And that fierce angel who floated above.

My life has been a living hell, thanks to you.
  You're welcome.

I am ushered into the high-security meeting room. I am relieved that it's the one where it is impossible to touch.

You're all a bunch of lying bitches.
  We do what we can.

I wait again for about fifteen minutes. Staring through the
Plexiglass. Trying not to exist. My stomach bunched up in
anxiety. The door opens. This time it's him. He had aged when I
last saw him at the trial twenty-three years ago, but now he is a
shell, bent and feeble, steadied by a corrections officer, shuffling
and watching the floor as he walks. Does he watch the floor to
see where he is going? Is it with loathing for himself? For me?
Is he ashamed? How could anyone be more beaten? I think. He
sits down on the other side and lifts his head.

We stare at one another through smudged, scratched plastic. A minute is filled with all that had transpired between us.
Like a video flashing fast-forward, the hyper-real of fighting for
my life, withstanding the raping, facing the fact that I could

very well be dead, cut back in, frame by frame, in this act of looking. Those eyes that had held me prisoner. Relentless. Watching. Watching. Watching. Watching. What I had to ruthlessly soften in order to escape are now watery pools that can barely maintain their sockets.

He gets up and is escorted back.

The door is shut.

The locks clank closed.

————➤◆◆◄————

I save. Lift my fingers from the keyboard and close my laptop. I look out the window from table 104. It is verging on autumn now. Soft greys have begun to infiltrate the short-lived miracle of a Canadian summer, to skim the slate of a cloud-covered sea.

The visit I researched and planned never happened. John Linnihan received his final transfer before I had the chance to write the letter. Movement type: death. Reason: death. Other Location: Unknown.[5]

I will never know if he would have accepted the visit from me, if I would have been able to live out this story to the ending I wanted. The ending that I thought I needed. But the most important thing is: I would have.

ACKNOWLEDGEMENTS

I've been preparing to write this book for many years, but it has taken many years to know how. Not only to know how to write it, how to know where to enter the story as a work of literature as well as a memoir, to know how to have the ability to be absolutely honest about how I ended up in the back of a serial rapist's vehicle fighting for my life; it has also taken me years to learn about how my story extends beyond myself and how I could situate it within the narrative of Western patriarchy, feminism, and revolution. It is also because it has taken me years to become emotionally stable enough to dive back in.

I have lost the mustard yellow suede jacket from that time. When the first line of this memoir rose to my consciousness in November 2016, *Victim: a feminist manifesto from a fierce survivor* started to pour out. The book has been my life since the revelation of this first sentence, and the people who have supported and believed in the telling of my story have helped me in so many ways to make it possible.

I would like to thank Michael Maclean who believed in this book from the beginning. I would read parts to him, and he was always excited, encouraging, and offering me valuable suggestions and recommendations and, perhaps most importantly, experiences from the male perspective. The vulnerabilities from the male gender that he had the courage to share have made the book much richer. And more honest.

I would like to thank my brother-in-law, Willard Price, for giving me the piece of police tape found at the murder site of another "Jane Doe" in 1999, the symbol that began my understanding of and commitment to what I have lived to fight against ever since.

Thank you so much to my dear friend Soressa Gardner for reading various versions of the manuscript over the years, for her interest and comments, and, most importantly, for her passion for the book and for her friendship.

I would like to thank Joe Rosenblatt, my father in art, who always believed in me and encouraged me. I would have so much liked for him to be alive so I could show him that I finally did it. I know he would have been proud of me and said, as we rapped, "You're doing very well, dear." What Joe taught me about living as an artist and keeping uncompromisingly firm to our visions has been an integral gift that feeds my life, activism, writing, and art.

In June 2019, on the advice of my friend Rena del Pieve Gobbi, a Go Fund Me campaign was started to help me finish the first draft of the book. Thank you so much to Cassandra Shaw, Cilla Lewenhaupt, Kathy Heisler, Ken Creighton, Andy Hnatyshtn, Suzy Birstein, Timothy Nicoll, Kyla Bourgh, Geoff Inverarity, Tomasz Michalak, Dennis Bolen, Soressa Gardner, Diana Day, Dwain Mayner, Janet Sadel, Brodie Davison, Rena del Pieve Gobbi and Michael Maclean for their generous donations and belief in the project.

I would like to thank Mexico and all of my friends there and for what their culture has taught me about resilience and beauty. My experiences in Mexico have deepened my understanding of not only systemic violence against women, Indigenous peoples, and the environment, but also how the injustices in Mexico extend to all cultures in a neoliberal, globalized world. However, the main thing I have learned in Mexico is the courage and resistance of those who have dedicated their lives to fighting for justice and the levity, the love of life, and the ability to smile despite all that is suffered and endured.

I would like to thank my hometown of Lantzville, BC, Table 104 at the Lantzville Pub, and all of the waitresses who patiently brought me more hot water for my tea. Thank you to the beaches, the ocean, the forests, and the mountains of where I am from for nurturing and inspiring me as I wrote the majority of this book.

Thank you to Catherine Owen, my dear friend whom I have known for decades. Our like-mindedness in both art and feminism are a life force to me. Thanks also to Catherine for her edits and insights. Her deep understanding of the subject matter (not to mention the fact that she knows almost everything about my life!) was a crucial part of the development of the manuscript. And, thank you Catherine, for always being a comrade in art, no matter what.

Thank you to Paul Kay for his friendship, for our band, and for being the only one who was absolutely there for me when I got home from Arizona. Thank you to 'Lisa' for her courage and her eyes that still sparkle.

Thank you to *Vigilance Press*. The ferocity of its vision has fortified mine.

Thank you to Emma Gougeon from Inkwell for telling me, when I started submitting the manuscript in September 2019, that *Victim* is powerful and important and for her invaluable revisions on the first draft. Thanks as well to Kelsey Levins from the Bukowski Agency for her passionate belief in the book and for the time and care she took with the second series of rigorous revisions. You both made *Victim* a better book.

Thank you to Bobbi Sue Smith for her collaboration and commitment to creating a cover that speaks to the energy of my story, voice and revolution. A special thanks to my editor Jay Christopher Gowen who, oh so gently, went for the jugular of the manuscript in the final edit. Thanks for your patience, rigor, and passion for *Victim*. Also, thank you, Jay, for giving me further insights into the male experience in a culture that is based in power abuse.

Thank you to Becky Hilliker, whom I had the pleasure of working with briefly, for her insights and commitment to this book. With a perspective very different than mine, she gave me valuable ideas I would never have thought of myself which I believe extended a complex and multi-genred book into a wider readership.

Thank you to all of the writers who are fighting the same fight. My comrades in truth. Kat Banyard, Koa Beck, Julie Bindel, Nicole Brossard, Susan Brownmiller, Lydia Cacho, Hélène Cixous, Virginie Despentes, Robyn Doolittle, Andrea Dworkin, Melissa Farley, Roxane Gay, Simon Häggström, Robert Jensen, Mikki Kendall, Gerda Lerner, Édouard Luis, Victor Malarek, Gabor Maté, Thomas Page McBee, Chanel Miller, Chimamanda Ngozi Adichie, Christine de Pizan, Lori Shenher, Sayak Valencia, Natasha Walter, McKenzie Wark, Adele Wiseman, and Emerald Fennel. Your writing, research, wisdom, and commitment to justice have inspired and enriched this book.

Thank you to my mom for her love, support, and patience as I raced around the house in the throes of creation. And, most importantly, thank you, Mom, for learning to listen to my story.

Thank you to my dad for his courage, the love that he gave me for the forest, and for the forgiveness we were able to share at the end of his life. As I hike, I still feel you leading the way, shimmering, your hiking staff in hand, all senses vital. I know all of the trails now, Dad, because you will always show them to me.

ENDNOTES

Part One

1 In 1975, Susan Brownmiller published *Against Our Will: Men, Women and Rape*—the first radical feminist analysis of what she calls the "masculine ideology of rape." (15). The ordering of her first two chapters serve to ground rape within the economic and psychological infrastructure of patriarchal culture: 'In the Beginning Was the Law' followed by 'War.' Her introduction, 'The Mass Psychology of Rape,' sets the foundation for her analysis: "[t]he earliest form of male bonding must have been the gang rape of one woman by a band of marauding men. This accomplished, rape became not only a male prerogative, but man's basic weapon of force against women, the principal agent of his will and her fear. His forcible entry into her body ... became the vehicle of his victorious conquest over her being, the ultimate test of his superior strength, the triumph of his manhood. Man's discovery that his genitalia could serve as a weapon to generate fear must rank as one of the most important discoveries of prehistoric times, along with the use of fire and the first crude stone axe. From prehistoric times to the present, I believe, rape has played a critical function. It is nothing more or less than a conscious process of intimidation by which *all men* keep *all women* in a state of fear." (14-15. Italics in the original).

2 https://www.rejectedprincesses.com/princesses/elisabeth-bathory

3 By 2018, with the escalation of the #MeToo movement, there has been *some* progress in reports of rape being acknowledged as legitimate and addressing Western culture as misogynist and driven by behavior that sexually harasses and assaults women. For example, in Canada, there has been political pressure that has resulted in the re-opening of previously discarded rape cases. Investigations and awareness of systemic sexism are no longer confined to academia and radical feminism.

Nevertheless, reactionary spokesmen like Jordan Peterson insist on selfishly instigating a sensationalist furor by taking the increased awareness of violence against women personally and creating hysteria among men with such ridiculous claims like men can't even flirt anymore without being labeled a sex predator. Perhaps his form of flirting is mimetic to his alpha-male lobsters who are entitled to jump any fertile female who happens by. Really? Certainly we are capable of aiming higher than crustaceans in terms of how we relate to one another as a species.

Regardless of these hysterical proclamations of 'woe-are-men' in the face of women and men working towards gender equality and a more egalitarian and sustainable world, journalist Robyn Doolittle points out that even when women report sexual assault, a high percentage are deemed 'unfounded.' During her 2019 study on how sexual assault cases in Canada were being handled, "Canadian law enforcement was disproportionately dismissing sexual assault complaints as 'unfounded'—a police term that means the accusation is either false or baseless ... 19.39 percent of sexual assault allegations were being discarded this way .... Canadian police claimed that 42 percent of sexual assault accusations ended with criminal charge. Once the 'unfounded' files were factored in, that number dropped to 34 percent." (Doolittle's reportage of the Canadian police calculations could be very conservative as there have been other reports that as low as 12 percent of sexual assault charges result in conviction).

Doolittle's calculations are not factoring in the percentages of unreported rapes with studies ranging from 68 to 80 to 89 percent. Doolittle reports that "[t]he false-reporting rate for sexual assault is, at most, 8 percent, which is less than the false-reporting rate of auto insurance claims." The extreme majority of men who rape are still relatively safe from taking any responsibility for their crimes. Robyn Doolittle 2019: 6-8.
https://medium.com/@jessiebrownrigg/jordan-peterson-and-the-metoo-movement-baf7e7f6da9b
https://www150.statcan.gc.ca/n1/daily-quotidien/171026/dq171026b-eng.html
https://www.usatoday.com/story/news/nation/2013/11/19/study-sexual-assaults-greatly-underreported-/3648197/
https://www.independent.co.uk/news/uk/crime/unreported-rapes-the-silent-shame-7561636.html

4   Aileen Wuornos' crossing the line between the first murder that was an act of self-defence and what became, especially with the last, an act of psychopathology can be compared to Sayak Valencia's analysis of the endriago subject in relation to the criminal class of the Third World in her book *Gore Capitalism*. The result of NAFTA and the onslaught of the neoliberal dehumanization of the majority of the Mexican people, for example, "led to defiance of the laws and efforts to seize a piece of the pie through the illegal economy. The price of

this almost instantaneous wealth was bloodshed and loss of life."
(50) Sayak defines the endriago and the premise of her analogy thus:
"The endriago is a literary character, a monster, a cross between a·
man, a hydra and a lion .... We are making an analogy between the
literary figure of the endriago ... as the new ultraviolent, destructive subjects of gore capitalism." (132). Both the very rare example
of extreme female violence as represented by Aileen Wuornos and
the much more common cartel henchmen have both been pushed
over the edge of morality: the female subject who has lived through
a lifetime of gender violence and the cartel henchmen who live in
a constant state of, what Valenica calls, economic precarity and
demasculinization who consider it an ordinary job to dissolve bodies
in acid (67) —both have become monsters.

5   Robert Jensen: 96.
6   No. We cannot leave out women sex offenders. The very few but the
existent, nonetheless. Violence against women backlash groups like
hardline anti-feminist party "Justice 4 Men and Boys" has long
rallied against women sex offenders. Apparently, there are enough
women raping men to undermine the entire feminist movement and
the fight to end violence against women by men. I would not contest
the issue that there are a comparably very *small number*—albeit
important—of men who have been forced to penetrate women and
that men (especially pre-pubescent and pubescent boys) cannot necessarily avoid getting an erection even if they are terrified of the
woman forcing them to penetrate her.

In Siobhan Weare's 2018 article "Oh you're a guy, how could
you be raped by a woman, that makes no sense: towards a case for
legally recognising 'forced to penetrate' cases as rape," Weare cites
an interview in the UK that reported that 1 in 21 men claimed to
have been forced to penetrate and that 79.2 % of the perpetrators
were reported to be female. Any person who forces another human to
have sex should be held accountable: man or woman. However, based
on Weare's study, 3.77% men claim to have been raped by women. If
one compares the statistics of 1 in 6 women in the U.S. being raped
by a man at some point in her life this means that 16.6% of women
are raped by men. That amounts to 16.6% female victims compared
to 3.77% male. A recent World Health Organization study reports
that, globally, 1 in 3 women throughout the world will experience
physical and/or sexual violence by a partner or sexual violence by a
non-partner (and in countries like Mexico where rape cannot even
be prosecuted, this involves a femicide epidemic). With such extreme
disparities, it is ridiculous that violence against women *by men* is being contested and de-validated in any way whatsoever. To accentuate
the agenda of men's rights groups in the face of their impending (or
already happened) emasculation, it has been reported that "J4MB's
approach echoes their usual style, focusing less on men's welfare
per se and focusing more on reframing women as perpetrators."

The World Health Organization "Global and Regional Estimates of Violence Against Women and the Health Effects of Intimate Partner Violence and Non-Partner Sexual Violence" (2013); Siobhan Weare "Oh you're a guy, how could you be raped by a woman, that makes no sense" International Journal of Law in Context, 14,1 pp. 110-131 (2018) © Cambridge University Press 2017.
https://www.vice.com/en_uk/article/j5n9yy/can-women-rape-men-is-a-surprisingly-controversial-question
https://www.rapereliefshelter.bc.ca/teach/learn/statistics/statistics

7   Camille Paglia *Spin Magazine* 1990 Quoted in Virginie Despentes' *King Kong Theory* New York: The Feminist Press, 2010: 38-39.

8   Roxane Gay 2018: xi.

9   In her article, "Twin Peaks and the origin of the Dead Woman Trope," Sarah Marshall points out how "there's little that interests the American public as much as a dead young woman's body." https://newrepublic.com/article/117323/twin-peaks-and-origin-dead-woman-tv-trope

10   https://shanwomen.org/tai/images/leaflets/2002-LTR-leaflet-II.pdf

11   The terms used for dichotomies of privilege are all problematic in that they re-imposed hierarchical relationships. Industrialized/industrializing is prioritizes industrialization and capitalism as the goal for those who aren't part of Western, industrialized culture; developed/underdeveloped is offensive as development is connected to culture and even intelligence and not only economies; privileged/underprivileged is more precise in that it designates access to comforts, obliviousness and the complacency that is derived by the ability to access and enjoy those those comforts and the resultant reluctance in giving any of them up; First World/Third World with its numerical ordering of the rungs of hierarchy also implies a race in terms of who came first and, therefore, is the most worthy. I think that privileged/underprivileged is the least offensive; however, I have decided to use the First and Third at this historical moment of writing because it is the most recognizable in terms of what it signifies. We cannot forget, though, that the privileged or the First World also exist in the underprivileged or Third and vice versa.

12   In the 1980s and 1990s, the Feminist 'Sex Wars' resulted in a schism between feminists. One side calls themselves 'Pro-Sex' Feminists and the other side (myself included) has been designated, 'Radical Feminists' (I always find it amusing that logic is deemed radical). The former claim individual sexual agency as the priority of women's liberation, where the latter pursue a feminist analysis of patriarchy that extends beyond not only the individual, but also women and into all relationships within a system of hierarchy and exploitation. Tragically and ironically, the Pro-Sex Feminist focus on the individual has played into the hands of neoliberalism with the short-term, greed-driven, individualist ideology that is directly responsible for all exploitation in a globalized world, be they the profits made by the

International Sex Trade or the exploitation (raping) of the natural environment. The prioritization of individual female sexual agency has also served to intensify the phenomenon of 'internalized sexism.' See: Ariel Levy *Female Chauvinist Pigs* (2005) and Natasha Walter *Living Dolls: The Return of Sexism* (2010).

13 Unbelievably, 18% of Americans believe that false accusations of rape against men are more of a crime than a woman being raped. (Doolittle: 11).

Part Two

1 https://www.businessinsider.com/r-mexicos-2016-murder-tally-exceeds-those-of-many-countries-at-war-study-2017-5/; https://time.com/5111972/mexico-murder-rate-record-2017/; https://edition.cnn.com/2019/01/22/americas/mexico-murder-rate-2018/index.html

2 https://www.azquotes.com/author/14823-Donald_Trump/tag/wall?page=2

3 On October 2nd, 1968, the Mexican army opened fire on a student protest against government violence and repression at Tlatelolco Plaza, the largest apartment housing-complex in Mexico City. The student massacre was denied by the government for decades. In 2008, the NPR reported that "Government sources originally reported that four people had been killed and 20 wounded, while eyewitnesses described the bodies of hundreds of young people being trucked away. Thousands of students were beaten and jailed, and many disappeared." There was no governmental acknowledgement of the crimes until a token official investigation in 2001 announced by the Vincente Fox government. https://www.youtube.com/watch?v=GNvV-7Ks6WA https://www.npr.org/templates/story/story.php?storyId=97546687

4 http://www.karenmoe.net/essays/INTERVIEW_Toledo_Espanol.pdf; http://www.karenmoe.net/essays/INTERVIEW_Toledo_English.pdf

5 In her essay "A Battered Wife Survives", Andrea Dworkin wrote: "The victim of encapsulating violence carries both the real and the memory of fear with her always. Together, they wash over her like an ocean, and if she does not learn to swim in that terrible sea, she goes under" (103).

6 Brownmiller:14.

7 http://www.uh.edu/socialwork/news/news-releases/2015-06-10_McPhail_FFP.pdf

8 As historian Gerda Lerner points out in her book, *The Creation of Patriarchy*, the subjugation of women as a class and as commodities for reproduction marked the beginning of private property and, quoting Susan Brownmiller, male dominance over women and male supremacy was made possible by men's ability, and propensity, to

rape (8; 24; 46; 77). In the tradition of patriarchy, women belong to men. To own and to rape. Patriarchy was founded upon rape.

9   Jordan Peterson speaks about the ambiguity of consent and says that women may accuse a man of rape when they have ostensibly consented to a one-night-stand and, as Peterson says, 'regretted it the next morning.' This is possible and would be a malicious action on the part of the woman but serves to delegitimize the literal accusations and experiences of rape. Peterson talks about 50% of rape and murder crimes being committed under the influence of alcohol and calls for a new prohibition, especially on college campuses (which is unrealistic because young people would find a way to access alcohol as happened with the speakeasies and bootlegging during the prohibition of the 'roaring' 20s). I would ask: what about the remaining 50%? And, add that alcohol or no alcohol, men need to learn empathy and how to control themselves. Period. https://www.youtube.com/watch?v=O8jgdR5k_9Q

10 See: Jordan Peterson and Camille Paglia on Sexual Assault Allegations October 6, 2017. (https://www.youtube.com/watch?v=mPQ0xsjBzeI)

11 "It is no accident that we find the most unsophisticated machismo in the working class family: the more blows the man gets at work the more his wife must be trained to absorb them, the more he is allowed to recover his ego at her expense. You beat your wife and vent your rage against her when you are frustrated or overtired by your work or when you are defeated in a struggle (to go into a factory is itself a defeat)." Federici (and what if the man has no job at all?) and/or was born in the Third World where, in countries like Mexico, it is not a coincidence that machismo is an epidemic and at least 10 women are murdered by their spouses or boyfriends every day. https://caringlabor.wordpress.com/2010/09/15/silvia-federici-wages-against-housework/

12 Sayak Valencia: 23; 55.

13 Ibid: 22.

14 See Natasha Walter *Living Dolls: the Return of Sexism* for an in depth analysis of the twenty-first century phenomenon of internalized sexism.

15 In *Reverse Cowgirl*, Mckenzie Wark relates how growing up in the 60s, there were no names, no language for those who didn't correspond to the cisgender binaries of born male and born female: "Call me …. Oh I don't know. I don't know the names. In those days there weren't any names, or weren't any sweet ones. I was a child of the sixties, teenager in the seventies, university in the eighties. Ways of being human were being born, but not always well named"(14). There is a large proportion of transwomen, of feminized homosexual men who are raped, these crimes are, once again typically committed by the cisgender male. In all cases, we are talking about the feminine, the feminized, the smaller, the physically weaker who are assaulted

and exploited to maintain his dominance in the patriarchal hierarchy, and patriarchy itself.

16 In *Feminism for Women: The Real Route to Liberation*, Julie Bindel asks: "[W]hat exactly does it feel like to be a woman? I'm a woman and I have no idea. I only know what it feels like to be treated as a woman under patriarchy." (21) Woman exists through what oppresses—and erases—her. If anything, as we roil in the throes of the twenty-first century feminist backlash, what a 'woman' is in patriarchy is more nebulous than ever.

17 "The period of the 'establishment of patriarchy' was ... a process developing over a period of nearly 2500 years, from app. 3100 to 600 B.C." (Lerner *The Creation of Patriarchy*: 8). During this time, it was the creation of private property and state formation that resulted in women being the first slaves. (See Lerner: 77).

18 Hélène Cixous "Sorties" in Hélène Cixous and Catherine Clément *The Newly Born Woman* Betsy Wing, translator. The University of Minnesota Press, 1986: 288.

19 https://www.nytimes.com/2017/04/05/us/politics/mike-cernovich-bio-who.html

20 Roxane Gay 2014: 27; 39.

21 See http://www.assaultcare.ca; Valenti, Jessica "Why we need to keep talking about 'rape culture.' *The Washington Post*. March 28, 2014 http://www.washingtonpost.com/opinions/why-we-need-to-kee p-talking-about-rape-culture/2014/03/28/58acfec4-b5bf-11e3-8cb6-284052554d74_story.html; __http://www.mujeresenred.net/spip.php?article13

Part Three

1 https://www.rainn.org/statistics/victims-sexual-violence; https://1in6.org/get-information/the-1-in-6-statistic/; https://www.rainn.org/statistics/children-and-teens

1 in 6 women have been sexually assaulted at some point in their lives. This statistic does not include sexual abuse as a child. Studies between 1996 and 2005 found that 14.2-16.4% of males and 64% of females had been sexually abused before the age of 18. In this survey, sexual abuse involved 'unwanted sexual contact involving force, threats and/ or a large age difference and power differential, not all out rape. Another survey reports that 1 in 9 girls and 1 in 53 boys are victims of sexual abuse or assault at the hands of an adult and that 82% of all victims under the age of 18 are female. Regardless of sex or gender, the motive for rape is always the domination and exploitation of another human being. Even though the percentage of young men is high, one can clearly see that females under the age of 18 are at the greatest risk of sexual exploitation.

2   Brownmiller: 49.

3   In *Amateur: A True Story About What Makes A Man*, transman, Thomas Page McBee narrates his transition from woman to man. Through his initiation into manhood as an adult, McBee has valuable insights into the mythology and the reality of 'the real man' in North American culture. As a girl, he, too, was raised to fear men. He tells us how: "[m]asculinity was ... epitomized by my stepfather, whose years of sexual abuse began when I was four." (30). During his transition, McBee states that "the central worry of all sons of bad dads [I believe the 'all' here is generous as how would rape culture be maintained if a percentage of young men were not following in their fathers' footsteps? And we are far from beyond it, yet]: How to become a man without being like our father?" (38). In rape culture, our fathers extend beyond our literal ones: they are the state, the economy, the culture, that which is historically based in keeping women in their place through intimidation, sexual abuse and assault. In rape culture, the 'real' man is one who rapes. Early on in his memoir, McBee shares his ultimate realization and core challenge: "I did not want to become a real man, I realized. I was fighting for something better." (44).

4   From Robert Service *The Cremation of Sam McGee*, my dad's favourite poem.

Part Four

1   Dr Gabor Maté: 237.

2   Historian Gerda Lerner tells us how: "*kar.kid*, the Sumerian word for female prostitute, occurs in one of the earliest lists of professions in the old Babylonian period, ca. 2400 B.C. .... On the same list we find the following female occupations: lady doctor, scribe, barber, cook. Obviously, prostitution is amongst the oldest professions although there is no evidence it is the oldest." *The Creation of Patriarchy:* 131.

3   In the introduction to *The Pimping of Prostitution: Abolishing the Sex Work Myth*, Julie Bindel points out: "There is no issue as contentious between feminists, liberals and human rights defenders as the sex trade. Radical feminists tend to argue that prostitution is both the cause and consequence of male supremacy, and that if women and men were equal, prostitution would not exist; it also means that if women and men are ever to become equal, prostitution must not exist. But for liberals who believe in an essential freedom to buy and sell sex, or for human rights campaigners who see the access to sex as a human right [regardless of the affects to the human being accessed], abolition is simply not an option" (xxx). With equality between the sexes naturally comes the end of the violence (and disciplining of women). Bindel continues to express how, "prostitution

is one way that men exert control over [women]" (xxxvii). The arguments to abolish the buying and selling of predominantly women and children's bodies make perfect sense when a rapist—and undoubtedly all rapists—is on the pro-prostitution side of the debate.

4   https://www.bitchmedia.org/article/the-wrong-kind-of-women-mal
     e-gaze

5   http://anniesprinkle.org/a-public-cervix-anouncement/

6   Ibid.

7   Koa Beck comments how: "The question of being a feminist in porn, whatever that means in a variety of interpretations, is complicated by what drives, sustains, and sires any industry: money. Women needing it, and other people trying to make it with bodies, desire, performance, consent, workplace conditions, and the ability to work again, connecting these two constraints. ... [B]eing a feminist in porn ... is a moot question. Because it's ultimately the structures that dictate women's lives, health and economic stability" (217). I agree wholeheartedly with Beck in that it's a moot point that feminism and pornography can be connected in any way. However, I think it can be stated more clearly: for the majority of women in the sex industry, their bodies are exploited and commodified and they are dependent on this exploitation and commodification to live.

8   Carol Leigh writes in her article *Inventing Sex Work*: "I had fantasies of being a prostitute, but had never considered actually doing it .... At least I could try it ... just try it .... From the very first day I was fascinated .... I was excited and intrigued to be in this environment, working with women from all over the world who were surprisingly strong and smart" *Whores and Other Feminists*, 227.

9   While perhaps there are a few women who truly enjoy selling sex, 85 to 95 per cent want to get out of the industry. Indeed, if women were "voluntarily" entering the sex industry in droves, trafficking wouldn't exist.https://www.feministcurrent.com/2016/12/09/7-bad-argument s-defense-sex-trade/; see "Prostitution and Trafficking - Quick Facts" by Melissa Farley, PhD and Emily Butler, JD Prostitution Research & Education "http://www.prostitutionresearch.com/Prostitution%20 Quick%20Facts%2012-21-12.pdf

10   http://anniesprinkle.org/the-sprinkle-story/; One of Annie Sprinkle's greatest supporters is Camille Paglia whose proclamation that women are responsible for their 'inevitable' rapes and men have nothing to do with being rapists corresponds to Sprinkle's belief that victimization is the responsibility of the victimized.

11   D.A. Clarke "Resisting the Sexual New World Order" in *Not For Sale*: 156.

12   See note 2, Part Four.

13   Cosi Fabian "The Holy Whore—a Woman's a Gateway to Power." *Whores and other Feminists*, 52. At the end of the article, Fabian explains how she has a basket that the men can put money in on the way out. Is this really 'sex work' or prostitution when money appears

to be more of a donation rather than a means of bare survival like it is for the majority of prostituted people? And should it be framed as such? No.

14 http://anniesprinkle.org/a-public-cervix-anouncement/

15 In countries like New Zealand, Germany, and Australia, where prostitution is either legalized or decriminalized (it is argued that legalization and decriminalization are different; however, fundamentally, they both result in the same things: the normalization of exploitating women and children's bodies), it is argued that prostituted people are safer because their 'jobs' have been legitimized as jobs like all others. Statistics of increased violence against women where prostitution is legal show how this couldn't be farther from the case. The only difference is: pimps are now businessmen, johns are clients and exploited women and children are now consenting employees. Sex Trade Abolitionist Julie Bindel argues how: "[t]he ... abolitionist position – favoured by feminists including myself, and every sex trade survivor I have interviewed – is: prostitution is inherently abusive, and a cause and a consequence of women's inequality. There is no way to make it safe, and it should be possible to eradicate it. Abolitionists reject the sanitising description of 'sex worker', and regard prostitution as a form of violence in a neoliberal world in which human flesh has come to be viewed as a commodity, like a burger." https://www.theguardian.com/commentisfree/2017/oct/11/prostitution-legalised-sex-trade-pimps-women. For a detailed analysis of the impossibility of 'safe' prostitution see Julie Bindel *The Pimping of Prostitution: Abolishing the Sex Work Myth* and Kat Banyard *Pimp State: Sex, Money and the Future of Equality.*

16 Juno Mac and Molly Smith compare sex work to massage therapy: "As with other jobs that women do, sexist devaluation of 'women's work' erases the emotional labour and hustle that constitutes the bulk of sex workers' actual efforts, reducing our job to simply being available for penetration at all times.... [O]ne of the key issues used to treat prostitution as 'not-work' is the idea that we are simply holes: that we are offering up *purchased consent*.... A massage therapist who—like a sex worker—sells time and services rather than physical product is not doing so 'on the premise the he can do what he likes with her body in the time that he has purchased it', and to make this statement about a massage therapist would be obviously horrifying. That it can be claimed about sex workers shows how deep the belief goes that women who sell sex give up their own boundaries: it is a belief shared—and mutually reinforced—by those who assault us and those who imagine themselves our defenders." *Revolting Prostitute: The Fight for Sex Workers' Rights:* (43-44).

How is massage therapy and being used by entitled men for their sexual release comparable? Yes, there are most likely situations where a relationship between a prostituted person and a john develops beyond sexual services, but can this really be used as a way to generalize that sex work and massage therapy are virtually the same thing when Mac and Smith claim that the prostituted person sells time and services rather than a physical product. How common is it that a prostituted person isn't used for sex when their bodies are being bought for precisely that? This very rare occasion is used to undermine the reality of the majority of people who are trapped in the sex trade because of poverty, racism, transphobia, sexual abuse, mental illness and (very often) drug addiction. As one of many examples of the illogic of this statement: there are men who say they would rape if there were not prostitutes. Can one imagine men admitting they would rape if there were no massage therapists?

The women Mac and Smith are referring to, who have the privilege to maintain boundaries when selling sex, are the minority. For the majority of women and children in the sex industry, any choice is the choice of not having one.

17 https://www.feministcurrent.com/2013/08/02/interview-meghan-murphy-on-the-sex-industry-individualism-online-feminism-and-the-third-wave/

18 Malarek: 228; Lauren Hersh, the Director of World Without Exploitation, states that "women involved in street prostitution are 60 to 100 times more likely to be murdered than are non-prostituted females." https://www.huffpost.com/entry/prostitution-is-not-just-b_9557032; https://www.worldwithoutexploitation.org/co-chairs/lauren-hersh.

19 In her memoir, *Infamy*, Lydia Cacho tells the story of how child pornographer and pedophile Jean Succar Kuri "enjoys seeing 5-year-old girls bleed while he penetrates them" (175) and how children lose their value when they have been 'used' once.

20 https://www.feministcurrent.com/2013/08/02/interview-meghan-murphy-on-the-sex-industry-individualism-online-feminism-and-the-third-wave/

21 Simon Häggström: 72-73. In 1999, Sweden criminalized prostitution and legislated 'The Nordic Model' which criminalizes the buyers of sex and protects and offers exiting resources to the prostituted people. When the sex purchasers became criminalized in 1999, 70% of the Swedish population were initially against it. However, as Simon Häggström reported in 2016: "What we've seen in 17 years is a huge change in the mindset of the Swedish population ... I would definitely say it's working." When visiting Sweden, Trisha Bapti, prostitution survivor and founder of EVE (Exploited Voices Now Educating), told me how, through public education (like billboards, public service announcements, transit signage and education in schools), Swedish youth no longer accept the buying and selling of sex in their culture: the commodification and abuse of human bodies is no longer a prevalent part of the cultural value system and psyche. As one of many statistics comparing countries with legalized and decriminalized prostitution with the Nordic Model, "[n]o prostitutes were murdered

in Sweden [in 2016]; in Germany, ... 70 were killed by pimps or buy-ers," and, like all cases of femicide, those were only the reported mur-ders. https://www.feministcurrent.com/2016/12/09/7-bad-argument s-defense-sex-trade/; https://educating-voices.com/new/ https://vancouversun.com/opinion/columnists/outlawing-the-pur-chase-of-sex-has-been-key-to-swedens-success-in-reducing-prostitu-tion.

22 The Australian Scarlet Alliance Handbook quoted in Victor Malarek *The Johns: Sex for Sale and the Men who Buy It:* 209, 210.

23 Mikki Kendall: 3; 9.

24 https://www.theguardian.com/world/2012/sep/01/lydia-cacho-mexica n-journalist-interview

25 See Natasha Walter, *Living Dolls: The Return of Sexism* for a discus-sion of so-called sexual liberation as internalized sexism.

26 Kat Banyard: 66.

27 Although I don't support reducing cultures to 'black' and 'white,' I am using the term 'white' here to designate descendants of a colo-nizing culture who may or may not continue to colonize, not in the traditional, overt sense of European Imperialism, but by continuing to exploit and benefit from the global infrastructure of cultures that exploit and cultures that are exploited.

28 China was never colonized (the European colonizers weren't able to get beyond the opium dens). Chinese men are also notorious for the exploitation and sexual abuse of women and children. Japanese men are not excluded and Turkish and Israeli men are particularly fond of young women from Eastern Europe who are called the Natashas. White skin is not a prerequisite for committing sexual acts of vio-lence against other human beings. See Lydia Cacho, *The Demons of Eden: the Power that Protects Child Pornography*; Lydia Cacho, *Slavery Inc.: The Untold Story of International Sex Trafficking*; Victor Malarek *The Natashas: Inside the New Global Sex Trade.*

29 Annie Sprinkle "13 Tips to Cure Sex Worker's Burn Out Syndrome" in *Whores and Other Feminists* Jill Nagle ed.: 67.

30 "In 9 countries on 5 continents, 89% of more than 850 women in prostitution told us that they wanted to get out." Melissa Farley: 29.

31 https://www.theguardian.com/society/2009/nov/15/diary-londo n-callgirl-phd-student-brooke-magnanti

32 Lydia Cacho: https://www.frontlineclub.com/insight_with_lydia_ cacho_slavery_inc-2/

33 We cannot forget about Amsterdam's 'famous' red-light district that prostitution defenders (usually men) always bring up as an example of 'good' prostitution, which has been a right-of-passage destina-tion for you men and a tourist attraction for decades. However, like in the legal brothels in Germany, the majority of the prostituted women in the Amsterdam's idealized red-light district are ostensi-bly sex-trafficked women from Eastern Europe and Africa. Dutch

nationals have much better things to do. See Kat Banyard, *Pimp State: Sex, Money and the Future of Equality.*

34 https://anniesprinkle.org/ppm-bobsart/script.html

35 Banyard: 44.

36 https://fightthenewdrug.org/10-porn-stats-that-will-blow-your-mind/

37 "The medical term for Rosebudding — anal prolapse —... [where] one's rectum collapses and slides its way out of the anus.... In general, an individual is immediately rushed to the emergency room when such an event happens. ...[T]he cameras keep turning as the prolapse is looked at, touched, licked, and prodded until the director believes that the viewer will have enough to satiate them. Sometimes honey is poured all over it." https://jezebel.com/heres-the-dangerous-and-grotesque-anal-sex-trend-you-ve-1593038946

38 Quoted in Malarek: 198.

39 Farley: 21; 29.

40 https://www.frontlineclub.com/insight_with_lydia_cacho_slavery_inc-2/

41 Regardless of the fact that the likes as George Bataille (known as a philosopher of pornography) mistakenly—and perhaps insidiously—calls pornography 'eroticism,' making a distinction between pornography and eroticism is important here, one that Sprinkle does not make by describing her personal pornography *as* pornography. Pornography without exploitation is no longer pornography. Pornographic acts are based on taking from and exploiting another human being. As Andrea Dworkin told us in 1978: "'[t]he psychic violence in pornography is unbearable in itself." As a response to women who proclaim themselves pro-sex (which translates into pro-pornography) and conflate the exploitation of predominantly female bodies as liberation and sexual freedom, Dworkin posits pornography as a central tenant to the maintenance of male supremacy: "pornography functions to perpetuate male supremacy and cries of violence against women because it conditions, trains, educates, and inspires men to despise women, to use women, to hurt women. Pornography exists because men despise women, and men despise women in part because pornography exists." (Dworkin "Pornography and Grief" in *Letters from a War Zone*: 19; 23. Any mutuality and spirituality that Sprinkle demonstrates in her so-called pornographic performances places these expressions of intimate human interaction into the realm of the erotic. It is dangerous to attempt to re-define pornography as personally empowering. Any legitimization of pornography, whatever the form, plays into rape culture. Is it not more useful in terms of *not* contributing in any way to condoning violence to use the term eroticism—especially as pornography re-enforces a culture that functions through hierarchical exploitation, individualism, and greed?

42 Like feminist militant Andrea Dworkin proclaimed decades ago: "I'm a radical feminist, not the fun kind."

43 Jensen: 16.

44 In 1983, Andrea Dworkin spoke to a men's group at the Midwest Conference of the National Organization for Changing Men. Her speech was called "I Want A Twenty-Four-Hour Truce During Which There Is No Rape." She addressed the men who claimed to be a part of the cause of equality between women and men: "I want to talk about equality, what equality is and what it means. It isn't just an idea. It's not an insipid word that ends up being bullshit .... [Equality] cannot coexist with rape.... And it cannot coexist with pornography or with prostitution ... I want to see the men's movement make a commitment to ending rape because that is the only meaningful commitment to equality.... I want to see you use those legendary bodies and that legendary strength and that legendary courage and the tenderness that you say you have on behalf of women; and that means against the rapists, against the pimps, and against the pornographers. [Equality] ... means something more than a personal renunciation. It means a systematic, political, active, public attack. And there has been very little of that." And, I would add, even 38 years later. *Letters from a War Zone*: 168-169.

45 https://avoiceformen.com/featured/feminism-gynocentrism-and-th e-future-matriarchal-gynocracy-the-different-types-of-societies -and-the-feminist-zero-sum-game-part-one/

46 "All cases (N = 136) of sexual assault reported to a major Northeastern university over a 10-year period are analyzed to determine the percentage of false allegations. Of the 136 cases of sexual assault reported over the 10-year period, 8 (5.9%) are coded as false allegations. These results, taken in the context of an examination of previous research, indicate that the prevalence of false allegations is between 2% and 10% ... Some of the misclassification of rape cases stems from biases and stereotypes that are still quite prevalent among law enforcement personnel. Researchers who have studied the content of police reports and/or examined police attitudes through interviews or questionnaires have found evidence of long-standing rape myths and stereotypes that influence how rape victims are perceived and how cases are classified ....Among the seven studies that attempted some degree of scrutiny of police classifications and/ or applied a definition of false reporting at least similar to that of the IACP, the rate of false reporting, given the many sources of potential variation in findings, is relatively consistent: • 2.1% (Heenan & Murray, 2006) • 2.5% (Kelly et al., 2005) • 3.0% (McCahill et al., 1979) • 5.9% (the present study) • 6.8% (Lonsway & Archambault, 2008) • 8.3% (Grace et al., 1992) • 10.3% (Clark & Lewis, 1977) • 10.9% (Harris & Grace, 1999) .... It is notable that in general the greater the scrutiny applied to police classifications, the lower the rate of false reporting detected. Cumulatively, these findings

contradict the still widely promulgated stereotype that false rape allegations are a common occurrence …. In the emotionally charged public discourse about sexual violence, it is often the case that assertions are made without reference to research data. Such assertions not only undermine rational discourse, but also damage individual victims of sexual violence. The stereotype that false rape allegations are a common occurrence, a widely held misconception, including among police officers, has very direct and concrete consequences. It contributes to the enormous problem of underreporting by victims of rape and sexual abuse. It is estimated that between 64% and 96% of victims do not report the crimes committed against them (Fisher et al., 2000; Perkins & Klaus, 1996), and a major reason for this is victims' belief that his or her report will be met with suspicion or outright disbelief (Jordan, 2004)." David Lisak, Lori Gardinier, Sarah C. Nicksa, and Ashley M. Cote. "False Allegations of Sexual Assault: An Analysis of Ten Years of Reported Cases." https://cdn.atixa.org/website-media/atixa.org/wp-content/uploads/2016/03/12193336/Lisak-False-Allegations-16-VAW-1318-2010.pdf Thank you to Canadian journalist and author of *Had it Coming: What's Fair in the Age of #MeToo?* Robyn Doolittle for sharing this article with me.

47 Here is one of many articles testifying to the urgency of violence against women on a global scale. In 2011, 48 women were raped every hour (and these are, as always, only the reported rapes). https://www.theguardian.com/world/2011/may/12/48-women-raped-hour-congo

48 https://www.washingtonpost.com/news/made-by-history/wp/2018/07/24/before-jordan-peterson-there-were-mens-rights-activists/

49 Harriet Marsden of the Independent on International Women's Day 2018: "These days, the word matriarchy carries misinterpretations. And it's important to clarify that in feminist thought, the ideal of the harmonious, nature-worshipping matriarchy is not the mirror image of patriarchy." Heide Göttner-Abendroth, founder of The International Academy Hagia for Modern Matriarchal Studies:

"In matriarchies, mothers are at the centre of culture without ruling over other members of society." The aim "is not to have power over others and over nature, but to follow maternal values, i.e. to nurture the natural, social and cultural life based on mutual respect."

Harriet Marsden: "So, patriarchy: power over others. Matriarchy: power from within." https://www.independent.co.uk/news/long_reads/international-womens-day-matriarchy-matriarchal-society-women-feminism-culture-matrilineal-elephant-bonobo-a8243046.html

"Men's assertion in patriarchy of a right to control women's sexuality and reproduction, backed by violence, was central to a process that created a world rigidly defined by 'power-over'—power defined as the ability to impose your will on others, contrasted with the collaborative conception of 'power-with.' The pathology of patriarchy, the idea that one group of people should control another—even own them, own even life itself—is at the core of today's crisis." (Jensen: 11).

Anthropologist Peggy Reeves Sanday: "The ethnographic context of matriarchy does not reflect female power *over subjects* or female power *to subjugate*, but female power (in their roles as mothers and senior women) *to conjugate*-to knit and regenerate social ties in the here-and-now and in the hereafter. Because this approach stresses the connection between the archetypal (or cosmological) and the social, rather than between power and politics it cannot be interpreted as the female equivalent of patriarchy." "Matriarchy as a Sociocultural Form: An Old Debate in a New Light" https://web.sas.upenn.edu/psanday/articles/selected-articles/matriarchy-as-a-sociocultural-form-an-old-debate-in-a-new-light/

Environmental journalist Gaia Vince: "Unlike other animals, we are cultural beings – for our species, culture is our nature, and key to understanding our behaviours and motivations. If we persist in the idea that there is a natural – a best – way to be a human, then we blind ourselves to the great diversity of potential ways of being, thinking and feeling, and impose social limitations on those whose life choices are no less legitimate than ours. It's worth noting, though, that many norms that were once believed to be set in biological stone or ordained by gods have been changed by societies – sometimes remarkably quickly. If we invented it, we can alter it." https://www.theguardian.com/books/2019/nov/02/smashing-the-patriarchy-why-theres-nothing-natural-about-male-supremacy

Gerda Lerner: "Yet the debate over matriarchy rages on .... Those who define matriarchy as a society where women dominate over men, a sort of inversion of patriarchy, cannot cite anthropological, ethnological, or historical evidence. They rest their case on evidence from myth and religion ... I am defining matriarchy as the mirror image of patriarchy. Using this definition, ... no matriarchal society has ever existed." (Lerner: 31). The mirror image of patriarchy: what male pro-patriarchy activists are so afraid of.

50 https://www.nbcnews.com/business/business-news/female-ceos-gained-ground-2018-still-trail-their-male-peers-n962641; In *White Feminism: From the Suffragettes to the Influencers and who they Leave Behind*, Koa Beck discusses women in positions of power in patriarchy as white feminists who view feminism as the ability to make as much money as men and succeed in his system. She argues that the female CEOs would be the storytellers of a self-serving 'feminism' that is based on success in business, corporate labour, and money. (Beck 144). I would argue that the privileged white feminists Beck describes are not feminists at all or, rather, to quote her title of Chapter Fourteen "Performing Feminism at a Desk," feminist *performances.* These power-house women in patriarchy are represented as feminist role-models because they have achieved individual success through the accumulation of money within the patriarchal capitalist

system. Ironically, Miki Agrawal of Thinx Underwear confides: "I only started relating to being a feminist, literally, right when I started my company" (Beck 145). Such corporate-realized feminism is more about the marketing plan than anything else and, rather than being a threat to male supremacy, plays into and maintains his system. Even though women in positions of power are seen as a threat to the men who think women are taking away their power, the smattering of women CEOs are maintaining the male system and this can be said for many women politicians as well.

51 https://vancouversun.com/news/national/record-98-women-were-elected-in-canadas-43rd-parliament/; https://www.cnbc.com/2019/03/04/the-us-ranks-75th-in-womens-representation-in-government.html; https://www.unwomen.org/en/what-we-do/leadership-and-political-participation/facts-and-figures

52 Lerner: 77.

53 Jensen: 17.

54 As I did with my friend Paul, I took advantage of his caring by using my trauma and what I had survived to my advantage. Unwittingly, I participated in Victim Culture where victims use what they have suffered to exploit others for personal gain and exist beyond account-ability. Victims must not become what hurt them.

55 Many abusers were also abused. At the end of Thomas Page McBee's memoir, he confronts his step-father who abused him as a child. During the visit, the step-father discloses the fact that he, too, had been abused as a child. As far as I know, the only sexual assault my dad experienced was the one he told me about, but one can never be absolutely certain of the physical and emotional abuse that is passed on through generations. The key is to break the cycle: the best way to end an abusive society is to not pass it on until the constructed behaviour becomes extinct.

56 Jensen: 71.

57 https://www.newscientist.com/article/mg23831740-900-why-the-patriarchy-isnt-good-for-men-and-how-to-fix-it/

58 Melissa Farley is a feminist psychologist, who founded Prostitution Research & Education, a non-profit research institute, in 1996. She has authored 40 peer-reviewed articles on the sex trade, and has concluded that based on the evidence, the sensible approach is to abolish the institution of prostitution and offer those in it sustainable alternatives.

59 Farley: 8-9.

60 During the writing of *Slavery Inc: The Untold Story of International Sex Trafficking*, Lydia Cacho visited "Hagar", a Christian NGO in Cambodia "specializing in the rescue and reintegration of girls who have been victims of trafficking and commercial exploitation." She learns how: "victims become 'favourites' by adopting hypersexual, se-ductive, and submissive personalities and by accepting exploitation. The girls are so young that this emotional conditioning becomes part

of their personalities .... Their whole lives have consisted of being slaves ... They are perfectly aware that they were born to be prostitutes ... [and] they believe this is what they were born to do" (61-63).

61 In her book *Sex Slaves and Discourse Masters*, academic Jo Doezema argues how contemporary sex-trafficking is a hysterical and sensationalist myth like that of the white slave trade of the 19th Century. She states that "a myth is a collective belief that simplifies reality." (31). She then arrives at not only a questioning of sex-trafficking as a whole, but of questioning the very existence of "trafficking itself" (39).

White skinned people were traded as sex slaves and labour slaves at many times during European history. Nell Irvin Painter's in-depth study, *The History of White People*, surfaces statistics that have been overlooked in order to maintain the mythology of white supremacy. One of many examples is that: "between one-half and two-thirds of early white immigrants to the British colonies and the Western Hemisphere were unfree laborers, some 300,000 to 400,000 people." (Painter 42). To address Doezema and other sex-trafficking deniers' accusations of hysteria amongst Abolitionist feminists in comparison with the hysteria of the White Slavery in the 19th Century of young white women is, indeed, not some sort of reductionist myth. The idealized young white female sex-slave—called 'odalisques' a term derived from the Turkish *odalk* meaning 'harem room'—were taken especially from Eastern Europe." (Painter 43; 48). Ironically, Eastern European women continue to make up a large portion of the sex-trafficking to the Western European brothels today. Doezema and other sex-trafficking deniers compare the dramatic writing style of 19th Century to the contemporary discourses on sex-trafficking as bent upon creating 'moral panic.' The Victorian writing style was fundamentally more ornamental and sentimental than the 21st; regardless, is not slavery, especially for sexual use, something to get upset about? Is it not a good idea to try to sway the public's emotions so that they care about another's very serious suffering, maybe become involved and do something to stop it?

Humorously, ex-call girl Brooke Magnanti does not deny sex trafficking globally, but does deny it exists in the UK based on the fact that: "In an age of cheap international flights ... and ample numbers of (prostituted women) women at home who go into work willingly, it makes no financial sense for traffickers to bring women here for sex when they could operate more easily, and with a more steady supply of customers, in mainland Europe or the developing world." (Magnanti: 160). Okay then! Even though there *are* trafficked women in the UK (all one needs to do is Google Search 'sex-trafficking in the UK' and come upon a stream of articles), according to Magnanti, it's fine for British punters to go to the brothels in Germany (that are filled with trafficked young women from especially Eastern Europe),

Eastern Europe itself, or pop over to Asia or down to Latin America where you can buy a young woman for $3.

Feminists and other NGOs that rescue trafficked girls and women have solid evidence that trafficking exists and are proclaimed 'moralists' and instigators of 'moral panic.' That is not much of an insult. What's wrong with having morals? And don't you think sex-trafficking of young women and children is something to panic about? Especially when it's being denied. Kat Banyard reported that in 2004, the prostitution industry made 6 billion Euros and was estimated to double that by 2016 (Banyard 58). In 2014, Lydia Cacho reported that "each year, 1.39 million peoples around the world—mostly women and girls—are subjected to sexual slavery." (Cacho 2014: 3).

62 Interview with Trisha Baptie, Vancouver, BC Canada July 23rd, 2019. https://www.facebook.com/abolitionEVE/; https://twitter.com/ abolitioneve?lang=en

63 During our interview in 2019, when ex-prostituted person Trisha Bapti was in the hospital after having been beaten up by her pimp, the police came to the hospital to get a report. One of the (male) police officers responded: "You must have done something to make him so mad."

64 https://www.vice.com/en_us/article/mvpk94/el-fotgrafo-de-chern

65 https://www.theguardian.com/world/2018/apr/03/mexico-indigenou s-town-banned-politicians-cheran.

Tragically, on January 23, 2018 María Guadalupe Campanur Tapia, a social activist who was primarily defender of the forest, and who participated in the creation of the security bodies for the Indigenous community of Cherán, was found dead with a knife wound to the neck on the road Carapan-Uruapan outside of the town and forests she had committed her life to protecting. Unfortunately, despite the victory of the people of Cherán in 2011, the fight is not over. The need for vigilance always remains. https://beforeits-news.com/immigration/2018/01/cheran-activist-found-strangled-to-death-2456632.html

66 Robert Jensen in "Blow Bangs and Cluster Bombs: The Cruelty of Men and Americans" in *Not for Sale: Feminists Resisting Prostitution and Pornography*: 28.

67 A summary from Cacho 2014: 63.

68 Malarek: 97.

69 Chimamanda Ngozi Adichie: 21.

70 One in five women will be raped or subjected to an attempted rape during their lifetime. This statistic does not include sexual harassment. Kat Banyard *Pimp State.*

71 https://www.youtube.com/watch?v=mPQ0xsjBzeI. Paglia's proclamation of having the right to risk assault in order to be free overlooks the fact that women do not have to go outside for such brutalities to not only be risked, but also to be realized. UN Women

reports that: some national studies show that up to 70 per cent of women have experienced physical and/or sexual violence from an intimate partner in their lifetime ... [and it] is estimated that of the 87,000 women who were intentionally killed in 2017 globally, more than half (50,000- 58 per cent) were killed by intimate partners or family members, meaning that 137 women across the world are killed by a member of their own family every day. More than a third (30,000) of the women intentionally killed in 2017 were killed by their current or former intimate partner. In the epidemic of violence against women in Mexico, "femicides are frequently carried out by domestic partners and often involve grotesque or degrading violence." Paglia's glib, oversimplification of women having the right to risk danger by choosing to go outside is bourgeois when one takes into consideration the complexity of violence against women in patriarchy from a global perspective. https://www.unwomen.org/en/what-we-do/ending-violence-against-women/facts-and-figures; https://www.reuters.com/article/us-women-antiviolence-mexico/id-never-felt-so-vulnerable-mexican-survivors-recount-attempted-femicides-idUSKBN20R2YI

72   In her 1979 article, 'The Night and Danger,' Andrea Dworkin quotes Hannah Arendt: "Being able to depart for where we will is the prototypical gesture of being free, as limitation of freedom of movement has from time immemorial been the precondition for enslavement. Freedom of movement is also the indispensable condition for action, and it is in action that men primarily experience freedom in the world." Dworkin continues: "The truth is that men do experience freedom of movement and women do not. We must recognize that freedom of movement is a precondition for freedom of anything else. It comes before freedom of speech in importance because without it freedom of speech cannot exist. So when we women struggle for freedom, we must begin at the beginning and fight for freedom of movement, which we have not had and do not now have." And still don't. Even 40 years later. Unless we risk being assaulted and disciplined. Dworkin connects the deprivation of a woman's right to move freely in the world without being threatened by rape and murder to pornography and its proliferation and normalization of "images of women tied and bound and humiliated and used." *Letters from a War Zone* (16-17).

73   Susan Brownmiller quoted in Doolittle: 218.

74   *Lethe* is dedicated to the Murdered and Missing Women of Vancouver, Canada. See Detective Lori Shenher's *That Lonely Section of Hell: The Botched Investigation of a Serial Killer Who Almost Got Away* for a comprehensive report on this particular story of the neglect of disenfranchised and undervalued women. See also two of numerous online resources: http://rabble.ca/columnists/2012/11/honouring-truth-vancouvers-missing-and-murdered-women; https://www.ctvnews.ca/tapes-offer-a-glimpse-into-the-mind-of-a-killer-1.539887; https://

www.theglobeandmail.com/news/british-columbia/pickton-legal-sag
a-ends-as-remaining-charges-stayed/article1377540/

75 During one of my performances of *Lethe* in Vancouver's Downtown Eastside, as I lay in the middle of the gallery wrapped in police tape, two First Nations men stood next to me for a few minutes chatting. They didn't seem to notice me. When they turned to walk away, one of them looked down and said to his friend, casually, "That looks like me last week." For the marginalized and oppressed peoples of the world, violence and trauma is a part of their everyday life, a reality that is always there—be it last night, yesterday, last week.

76 Thank you to my brother-in-law Willard Price for sharing this story with me.

77 This piece of police tape was found next to the Fraser River, Richmond, BC, Canada in the late 1990s. Thanks to my brother-in-law, Willard Price, for having the instinct and inclination to bring me this life-altering gift.

78 Chimamanda Ngozi Adichie states: "We should all be angry. Anger has a great history of bringing about positive change" (21); Andrea Dworkin talks about "useful rage." (*Letters from a War Zone* 19). I agree wholeheartedly, but this justified and motivational anger must not become toxic, destructive anger or it loses its ability to motivate and empower.

79 Robyn Doolittle comments on how "the threat of the lying woman looms large in our culture." This cultural prejudice is unmoved by the fact that social scientists estimate only 2-8% of sexual assault allegations are false. She writes how "while it's no longer politically correct to be outwardly skeptical of rape complainants, the suspicion isn't gone." Those who deny the credibility of rape reports are typically relying only on the police service's internal statistics that routinely misclassify sexual assault cases. These limited studies arrive at statistics of 20, 30 and even 40% of rape allegations being false. In one particular study that reached a 41% statistic, each of the cases that comprise that extremist percentage were recanted. However, the researchers investigated no details as to what happened during the actual interviews. In her in depth research, Doolittle learned that "the police force in question was threatening alleged victims with lie detector tests, which could intimidate someone into false recantation." (Doolittle:122-123; 128-129).

80 Doolittle: 6-7.

81 It ends up that *Unbelievable* is revolutionary and what I had wanted from the first episode happened: in the end, justice is achieved. After my very visceral response, I haven't been able (or willing) to watch the full series yet. Maybe I need to skip ahead to when it begins to shift towards justice and away from the blaming and shaming of the rape victim that has infuriated and re-victimized me most of my adult life. The fact that *Unbelievable* brings this crucial reality to the fore-front of popular culture is another sign, like with Emerald

Fennell's *A Promising Young Woman* and Chanel Miller's *Know My Name*, of change because not only are we now talking about it, ending the shaming and blaming of victims of sexual violence has entered our cultural narrative—for good.

82 "By co-opting the language of choice and empowerment, this culture creates smoke and mirrors that prevent many people from seeing just how limiting such so-called choices can be. Many young women now seem to believe that sexual confidence is the only confidence worth having, and that sexual confidence can only be gained if a young woman is ready to conform to the soft-porn image of a tanned, waxed girl with large breasts ready to strip and pole-dance. Whether sexual confidence can be found in other ways, and whether other kinds of confidence are worth seeking, are themes that this hypersexual culture cannot address." (Walter: 37).

83 Johns have commented that if men didn't have access to prostitutes, they would rape more. In an interview with 700 men in the UK who buy prostituted women, Julie Bindel reported: "One of the most interesting findings was that many believed men would "need" to rape if they could not pay for sex on demand. One told me, "Sometimes you might rape someone: you can go to a prostitute instead." Another put it like this: 'A desperate man who wants sex so bad, he needs sex to be relieved. He might rape.' I concluded from this that it's not feminists such as Andrea Dworkin and myself who are responsible for the idea that all men are potential rapists – it's sometimes men themselves." https://www.theguardian.com/society/2010/jan/15/why-men-use-prostitutes.

In Victor Malarek's study of john culture, an ex-john remarks how: "To me, I was buying a product. They didn't exist as people" (114). They are reducing women's bodies to commodities to be bought, sold and used. Women who buy into the argument of women's liberation being all about individual sexual agency and the freedom to 'choose' to sell their bodies are inadvertently not only doing patriarchy's, but neoliberalism's job for them, by supporting the legitimization and the obscene profitability of the international sex trade. Women who self-objectify are at the service of their own, and all other women's, exploitation.

84 An interview by Julie Bindel with 700 men in the UK who buy prostituted women: https://www.theguardian.com/society/2010/jan/15/why-men-use-prostitutes

85 Gail Dines in Malarek: 198.

86 Studies show that the average age of the first online exposure to porn is eleven. Ninety percent of eight to sixteen-year-olds in Canada, the U.S., Britain, Europe, Japan, and Australia have viewed porn online while doing homework. Eighty percent of fifteen to seventeen-year-olds have had multiple hard-core exposures. One study of thirteen and fourteen-year-olds by the University of Alberta

found that one-third of boys viewing porn did so 'too many times to count.' (Malarek: 205).

87 Dines in Malarek: 201.

88 First World women go to such locales as the Dominican Republic and Jamaica with the intentions of having sex with young, exoticized, locals; however, the percentage is very small in comparison to the millions of men who travel abroad for sex with young women and any abuse involved—like between the women (or girls) and the men—is non-existent. The title of Tanika Gupta's 2006 play 'Sugar Mummies' is telling in that the women have taken on the behaviour of 'sugar daddies,' not rapists; nevertheless, using one's economic privilege to access another human's body upholds a culture of domination and violence that is inherent to masculine supremacy.

Julie Bindel points out in her 2013 article, the women who travel south "are looking for attention and excitement but end up, often without realising it, being one half of a prostitution deal." Of course, as with the male sex tourist trade, poverty is the key component due to the economic disparity between the First and Third Worlds and the young men would most likely not have sex with the middle-aged women from the north if they did not have, and give them, money. The trend of women buying sex in tourist destinations like Jamaica can also be connected to female 'raunch culture' where fun feminists of the US, Canada and Northern Europe are all about sexual prowess and have, out of proclamations of sexual liberation, adapted patriarchal behavior. See Julie Bindel:
https://www.dailymail.co.uk/femail/article-2401788/Sex-tourism-Meet-middle-aged-middle-class-women-Britains-female-sex-tourists.html
https://www.theguardian.com/commentisfree/2006/aug/09/comment.gender

89 "Because no human activity takes place in an ideological vacuum — the ideas in our heads affect the way we behave—it's hard to make sense of the amount of sexual violence without the concepts of patriarchy and rape culture." Banyard: 84.

90 Cacho 2014: 134.

91 https://www.brit.co/what-ptsd-looks-like-for-sexual-assault-survivors/

92 https://www.brit.co/what-ptsd-looks-like-for-sexual-assault-survivors/

93 "Soldiers on R & R … and sailors on shore leave are notorious for paying for sex. For them, it is a rite of passage, usually the last course after a wild night of chugging copious amounts of beer. This is the classic example of 'boys will be boys,' as high-ranking officials wink and nudge at the antics and chaplains sit conspicuously silent. This tacit approval by military brass worldwide has created a sense of entitlement among young men in uniform. The bodies of girls and young women are just a few dollars away wherever they are stationed." (Malarek: 24).

94 Cacho 2014: 158, 159, 161.

95 Banyard: 26.

96 'Diehard,' a john chat forum quoted in Malarek: 98.
97 Brownmiller: 111; 107. Italics mine.
98 Lest we forget peace keeping forces who are also known to use the bodies of women in war torn countries.
    A testimony from 17-year-old Olenka in the northern Bosnia town of Tuzla:
    "I went with between eight and fifteen men a night. I did not want to have sex with any of them. If I did not do what I was told, my owner said I would be beaten to death." In the months she was held captive, Olenka figures she was raped more than 1,800 times. The men each paid the owner fifty dollars. She never saw a penny. On one particularly harrowing evening she was passed around to a dozen soldiers. The men were rambunctious, celebrating a birthday party in a bar .... She was the birthday present for the entire platoon. Whatever the UN peacekeepers wanted, she was forced to give ....[S]he remembers the uniforms ... —American, Canadian, British, Russian, German, French. Many were soldiers. Some were police officers with the UN .... When Olenka was finally rescued in a raid on the bar, she recognized eight of her 'clients' among the UN and local police who carried out the bust." (Malarek 27-28). Also see Cacho 2014: 163.
99 Like the fact that not all men are rapists or johns, not all soldiers participate in the rapes and gang-rapes and those who don't are often bullied. One Vietnam veteran quoted in Susan Brownmiller explains how: "I made friends with people in my company who I considered basically nice people .... I just couldn't figure out what was going on to make the people like this do it."(111). Soldiers who have consciences often return home with PTSD as a result of the atrocities they have witnessed—many of them being the violence waged against the local women by fellow soldiers. A Vietnam vet quoted in Cacho explains how: "The army dehumanizes you.... They train you to do something absolutely unnatural: hate a whole village that you don't know anything about; hate the village's inhabitants so much that you are unable to recognize them as human." (158).
100 Malarek: 93.
101 Brownmiller: 104-105.
102 Malarek: 46.
103 https://www.frontlineclub.com/insight_with_lydia_cacho_slavery_inc-2/
104 Malarek: 4; 10.
105 Cacho 2014: 3.
106 Malarek: xiii.
107 Cacho 2014: 4.
108 Malarek adds how "the highest rates of [sex tourism are] in Southeast Asia, with Thailand, Cambodia and Japan leading the pack at more than 70%. Thailand receives an estimated 5.1 million sex tourists a year ... [T]he difficulty with such statistics is that no one knows for

certain what the actual numbers are, because most men will never admit to paying for sex." (12-13).

109 Banyard: 61.

110 Malarek: 114.

Part Five

1 Gay 2017: 20-21.

2 Kendall: 59; 57.

3 I choose to use 'a worst' because hierarchy is implicit in 'the worst.' Everyone has their version of 'the worst' and one shouldn't be prioritized over another.

4 Miller: 282.

5 Ibid: 53.

6 At the end of her chapter "The First Pillar of Change: Stop Acknowledging Privilege; Fight for Visibility Instead,' Koa Beck discusses how many 'white feminists' (typically white, cis, straight, middle-class women who identify as feminist) acknowledge their privilege and that is where any 'activism' stops. There is no extension of that awareness into the fight for the structural changes that are what feminism makes necessary and are the source of their privilege. The awareness of hierarchical 'rank' that one has been arbitrarily born into is *necessary* so that there is an understanding of what one is fighting against and we can more readily fight for the visibility and the transformation of the lives of the structurally invisibilized. Revolution is physical, it is composed of literal action and change in the world and lives of others, but it begins with the awareness of where the self is situated. Stating one's privilege within the system one is committed to eradicating is only the first step. As Beck advises: "[w]hen you open a statement about being white, about being cis, and about being a citizen, that should be a beginning—not an end" (200).

7 We cannot overlook the fact that the Third World exists in the First. The Downtown Eastside of Vancouver, Canada is a prime example of this along with many 'Indian' Reservations in Canada that often have no potable drinking water. Nettie Wild has made this connection throughout her career as a documentary filmmaker. Her 2002 film, *FIX: The Story of an Addicted City*, is set in Vancouver's Downtown Eastside. Ironically, of Wild's four films—with two set in the Third World and the other two in the First—it is FIX, the film that focuses on a neighbourhood in the heart of a Vancouver, Canada—a city ranked as having one of the highest qualities of life in the world—that documents people living in poverty with mental illness, drug addiction, and prostituted, drug addicted women whose lives are risked daily to get another fix and who live with the trauma

of childhood sexual abuse that shows a level of human suffering which could be described as 'fourth' world.

8   Nacidos Para Triunfar (Born to Triumph) is a Non-Profit Organization in Monterrey, Nuevo Leon, Mexico that was started in 2011 by Juan Pablo García. The mission of the organization is to prevent the vulnerable youth of the impoverished barrios from joining street gangs and becoming foot soldiers for the predatory drug cartels. García is an ex-gang member and was on the street at the age of six. He developed a heavy cocaine addiction. He got out of the gang life and has dedicated his life to helping youth who grew up like him. All of the people who work for NPT are graduates of the program. The organization makes contact with all of the at-risk youth, offers them the opportunity to get out, get an education and a job and makes peace treaties between the gangs that have often been at war for generations. Despite their enormous success, NPT had to shut down operations in 2018 due to lack of funding. When I was visiting and researching the organization in 2017, García sold his car to pay the wages. NPT don't give up. In 2021. Another truce between gangs in Queretaro Mexico was negotiated by García and his organization.
http://www.npt.org.mx/; https://www.theguardian.com/cities/2017/feb/22/gang-war-peace-treaties-monterrey-mexico; https://www.vigilancemagazine.com/post/justice-begins-with-the-one-beside-you-the-quiet-revolution-of-nacidos-para-triunfar; https://www.americamagazine.org/politics-society/2021/03/24/mexico-gang-violence-peace-truce-queretaro-catholic-240300

9   Liz Misterio, editor of the Mexico City feminist magazine Hysteria, told me how young girls are abducted from impoverished cities like the Ecatepec and sold to clients as a 'package deal' where the men can rape, torture and then murder the girls. The girls are always the same type: young, pretty and with dark skin. www.hysteria.mx.

10   https://www.ncbi.nlm.nih.gov/pubmed/8765248

11   Walter: 33.

12   Lerner: 17-18.

13   https://news.gallup.com/poll/245618/abortion-trends-gender.aspx

14   Lerner: 24-25; 77.

15   Referencing Casanova and his statement: "when the lamp is taken away, all women are alike," Andrea Dworkin responds: "[t]he annihilation of a woman's personality, individuality, will, character, is prerequisite to male sexuality." *Letters from a War Zone* (14). Even if all men do not view women as objects through which to achieve individual sexual satisfaction, it cannot be ignored that such an observation and statement is a part of the foundation of patriarchal gender relations.

16   Thank you to Michael Maclean for having the courage to remember this story and share it with me.

Part Six

1   Maté: 34.

2   A year and a half after writing this section and just before the publication of this book, I kept my promise to my dad and to myself and found Lisa. She is worse. She is currently in the psych ward and having constant schizophrenic delusions that she is being raped every night as she tries to sleep. Her self-medication with street drugs continues and the doctors still, after 29 years, cannot find a psychotropic medication that works.

3   Dr. Gabor Maté "Understanding Addiction: Our Compulsive Society." https://www.youtube.com/watch?v=_-APGWvYupU

4   In her essay "Pornography and Grief," Andrea Dworkin expresses how: "[w]e all expected the world to be different than it is, didn't we? ... Not one of us could have imagined or would have believed the simple facts of life as we have come to know them; the rapacity of male greed for dominance; the malignancy of male supremacy; the virulent contempt for women that is the very foundation of the culture in which we live." In terms of my inability to imagine two men raping and 'enjoying' my unconscious body, such an act had never existed to me. And, correspondingly, as an acceleration of the same violence, Dworkin writes: "[o]ne can know everything and still not imagine snuff films." (20-21).

5   In the mid 90s, a couple of years after the abduction, I read Nicole Brossard's book, *Mauve Desert*. It is in this text that I found the wisdom: "Keep to beauty. Have no fear. Learn to bear the unbearable. The raw of all things." These words have helped me to survive. They gave me the courage to not only continue living for myself, but also to find a purpose for what I had lived through and the strength I had found within to dedicate my life to exposing injustice. Her words helped me learn how to make something terrible, not so, maybe even beautiful. Ironically, *Mauve Desert* is set in Arizona. Thanks, Nicole.

6   This story is based on the Ewanchuk sexual assault case that happened in Edmonton, Alberta Canada in 1994. Doolittle: 47-49.

7   Doolittle: 47.

8   Ibid.

9   Upon deeper investigation—and one can only speculate as to why this wasn't done at the time—it was discovered that Ewanchuk had been convicted of three counts of sexual assault ranging from the years 1969 and 1986. With all three convictions, he had spent time in jail (Doolittle 50).

10 In 2019, Canada has some of the most progressive laws in the world in prosecuting sexual assault cases; however, Robyn Doolittle reports how, "the laws aren't the problem. It's the willingness to enforce them." (29).

11 Melanie Randall "Sexual Assault Law, Credibility, and 'Ideal' Victims: Consent, Resistance and Victim Blaming." *Canadian Journal of Women and the Law*. Volume 22, p. 397, 2010. Electronic copy available at: http://ssrn.com/abstract=1742077

12 In *Caliban and the Witch: Women, the Body and Primitive Accumulation* (2004) and *Witches, Witch-Hunting and Women* (2018), Silvia Federici connects the rise of capitalism and the intensification of patriarchal relations of 16th and 17th Century Europe to the three century long witch hunt and the genocidal attack on women. She shows how destroying the power of women as healers and midwives and taking away their customary rights along with the land enclosures of the 16th Century go hand in hand with taking away people's ability to produce their own food and their subsequent reliance on, and vulnerability to, capitalist wage labor. Any resistance was persecuted as a sign of a diabolical pact and it was especially the older widowed or unmarried women who were most affected and who made their anger known. Those labeled 'witches' "were not only victims. They were women who resisted their impoverishment and social exclusion." (2018: 12; 19). So-called witches were the first unruly women.

Federici sees the same pattern occurring today with the spread of global capitalism and the enclosures of the Third World by corporations. She writes, "[i]t is not surprising ... if large-scale violence and enslavement have been on the agenda, as they were in the period of 'transition' [from feudalism to capitalism in 16th Century Europe], with the only difference that today the conquistadors are the officers of the World Bank and the International Monetary Fund." (2004: 17). She points out how: "[a] return of the most violent aspects ... has accompanied every phase of capitalist globalization, including the present one, demonstrating that the continuous expulsion of farmers from land, war, and plunder on a world scale, and the degradation of women are necessary conditions for the existence of capitalism at all times." (2004: 12-13). Federici exposes "the intensification of violence against women, including, in some countries (e.g., South Africa and Brazil), the return of witch-hunting." (2004:11).

13 Susan Brownmiller quoted in Doolittle: 221-222.

14 As recently as 2004, during the questioning of the complainant, former justice Robin Camp stated that the raped woman should have "just kept [her] knees together." Doolittle: 192.

15 Lydia Cacho tells the story of May, a rescued child sex-slave in Cambodia. "The ... girl yells out in perfect English: 'That's it, baby girl .... Good job." Her American accent is perfect .... [T]his is the phrase the traffickers used when [she] ... behaved well while she did *yum-yum* (performed oral sex) or when a client raped her. *She had to smile and kiss him, so the rape would end sooner.*" (Cacho 2014: 61; 63; 64 Italics mine). As in child sex slavery where the children are forced to deal with being raped numerous times a day, so in all

cases of rape where there is no escape; rather than pointlessly putting up a vigorous fight that will serve to prove their lack of consent in a misogynist court of law, it should be obvious that the victim's survival instinct will click over into strategies to be hurt as little as possible. It is amazing how quickly this happened for me when I realized it would potentially make things more dangerous if I tried to get the gun.

16　In Mexico City in July 2019, two young women were raped by police officers, one being a gang rape by four policemen in a police car. On August 16th, 2019, the women of Mexico City rose up en masse against not only these recent rapes by the police, but also the conservative estimate of 2175 feminicidios (femicides) in Mexico in 2019. (María Salguero tracks feminicidios in Mexico and she estimates that, in 2019, there were over 3000 in Mexico City alone). To add to these unbelievable statistics, it is estimated that only 10% of feminicidios are reported resulting in numbers that could be described as a virtual genocide. https://www.vigilancemagazine.com/post/life-of-a-woman. In 2020, during the COVID 19 lockdowns, the statistic of 8 women a day being murdered by their male partners rose to 12.

17　Randall: 409.

18　Law Professor Janine Benedet quoted in Doolittle: 133.

19　Doolittle: 133.

20　In her Epilogue, Robyn Doolittle tells the story of a young woman whose rape had been dismissed as unfounded when it first occurred. One in five sexual assault cases are discarded as unfounded by the Canadian police. Recently, there has been political pressure on the legal system to re-open these files and give the victims another chance for justice. In 2018, the sexual assault of the woman Doolittle tells us about was one of those files. Her case was deemed unfounded, again. During a phone call with Doolittle after the verdict, the woman said all was well and that she felt her complaint had been taken seriously this time; however, a few weeks later, she took her own life (250-251).

21　Luis: 186.

22　As one example, Malarek reports: "A study released in April 2008 that delved into the minds of 110 Scottish johns found that 10 percent believed that rape of prostituted women is not possible. Twelve percent believed that the concept of rape in the context of prostitution simply does not apply. Twenty-two percent said that, once they pay for sex, customers are entitled to whatever they want. More disturbingly, 10 percent admitted they would rape a woman—any woman—if they thought they wouldn't get caught." (87).

23　Luis: 190.

24　Luis: 188.

25　Farley: 35.

26　Farley: 4.

27　Luis: 188.

Postscript: The Visit.

1   https://gawker.com/california-prison-is-a-racist-violent-nightmare-1748724528

2   https://www.quora.com/What-crimes-earn-you-the-most-respect-in-prison

3   Ibid.

4   https://gawker.com/california-prison-is-a-racist-violent-nightmare-1748724528
https://globalnews.ca/news/2405244/state-report-finds-culture-of-racism-alarming-abuses-at-california-prison

5   In 2017, when I began to write this book, I started to look into the possibility of visiting John Linnihan in prison. I discovered that he had died three months before. I was able to obtain the prison documents that listed all the penitentiaries he had been in during the 31 years of the life sentence that he had served. I was able to create a fictional account that is based on the reality of his life there and the possibility of the visit I was never able to have. Thank you to Victim & Survivor Rights & Services of the California Department of Corrections and Rehabilitation for providing me with this invaluable information through which I was able to achieve the visit and closure, if not in person, but through writing.

BIBLIOGRAPHY

Adichie, Chimamanda Ngozi. *We Should All Be Feminists.* New York: Harper Collins, 2014.

Banyard, Kat. *Pimp State: Sex, Money and the Future of Equality.* London: Faber & Faber, 2016.

Beck, Koa. *White Feminism: From the Suffragettes to Influencers and Who They Leave Behind.* New York: Atria Books, 2021.

Bindel, Julie. *Feminism for Women: The Real Route to Liberation.* London: Constable (an imprint of Little, Brown Book Group), 2021.

Bindel, Julie. *The Pimping of Prostitution: Abolishing the Sex Work Myth.* London: Palgrave Macmillan, 2017.

Brossard, Nicole. *Mauve Desert.* Susanne de Lotbiniére-Harwood, trans. Toronto: Coach House Press, 1987; 2002.

Brownmiller, Susan. *Against Our Will: Men, Women and Rape.* New York: Random House, 1975.

Cacho, Lydia. *Infamy: How One Woman Brought an International Sex Trafficking Ring to Justice.* Ceclia Ross, trans. New York: Soft Skull/Catapult Press, 2016.

Cacho, Lydia. *Slavery Inc: The Untold Story of International Sex Trafficking.* New York: Soft Skull/Catapult Press, 2014.

Cixous, Hélène and Catherine Clément. *The Newly Born Woman.* Betsy Wing, trans. The University of Minnesota Press, 1986.

Despentes, Virginie. *King Kong Theory.* Frank Wynne, trans. New York: The Feminist Press, 2010.

Doezema, Jo. *Sex Slaves and Discourse Masters.* New York: Palgrave Macmillan, 2010.

Doolittle, Robyn. *Had it Coming: What's Fair in the Age of #MeToo.* Allen Lane: Penguin Random House, 2019.

Dworkin, Andrea *Letters from a War Zone: Writings 1976-1989.* New York: E.P. Dutton, 1989.

Farley, Melissa. *Prostitution and Trafficking in Nevada: Making the Connections.* Prostitution Research & Education, 2007.

Foster, Judy and Marlene Derlet. *Invisible Women of Prehistory: Three million years of peace, six thousand years of war.* North Melbourne: Spinifex Press, 2013.

Gay, Roxane. *Bad Feminist.* New York: Harper Perennial, 2014.

Gay, Roxane. *Hunger: A Memoir of (My) Body.* New York: Harper Collins, 2017.

Gay, Roxane Ed. *Not That Bad: Dispatches from Rape Culture.* New York: Harper Perennial, 2018.

Häggström, Simon *Shadow's Law: The True Story of a Swedish Detective Inspector Fighting Prostitution.* Selina Öberg, trans. Bullet Point Publishing: 2016.

Jensen, Robert. *The End of Patriarchy: Radical Feminism for Men.* Melbourne: Spinifex Press, 2017.

Kendall, Mikki. *Hood Feminism: Notes from the Women that a Movement Forgot*. New York: Penguin Books, 2020.

Lerner, Gerda. *The Creation of Patriarchy*. New York/ Oxford: Oxford University Press, 1986.

Luis, Édouard. *The History of Violence*. Lorin Stein, trans. London: Harvill Secker, 2018.

Mac, Juno and Molly Smith. *Revolting Prostitute: The Fight for Sex Workers' Rights*. Verso: London/ New York: 2018.

Magnanti, Brooke. *The Sex Myth: Why Everything We're Told is Wrong*. London: Weidenfeld & Nicolson, 2012.

Malarek, Victor. *The Natashas: the New Global Sex Trade*. Toronto: Penguin Random House, 2004.

Malarek, Victor. *The Johns: Sex for Sale and the Men Who Buy It*. New York: Arcade Publishers, 2011.

Maté, Gabor. *In the Realm of Hungry Ghosts: Close Encounters with Addiction*. Toronto: Penguin Random House Canada, 2008; 2018.

Matthews, Roger, Helen Easton, Lisa Young and Julie Bindel. *Exiting Prostitution: a Study in Female Desistance*. London: Palgrave Macmillan, 2014.

McBee, Thomas Page. *Amateur: A True Story about What Makes a Man*. New York: Scribner, 2018.

Miller, Chanel *Know My Name*. New York: Penguin Random House, 2019; 2020.

Nagle, Jill ed. *Whores and Other Feminists*. New York; London: Routledge, 1997.

Painter, Nell Irvin. *The History of White People*. New York: W.W. Norton & Company, 2010.

Pizan, Christine de. *The Book of the City of Ladies*. Translated and with Introduction and Notes by Rosalind Brown-Grant. London: Penguin, 1999.

Randall, Melanie. "Sexual Assault Law, Credibility, and 'Ideal' Victims: Consent, Resistance and Victim Blaming." Canadian Journal of Women and the Law. Volume 22, p. 397, 2010.

Shenher, Lori. *That Lonely Section of Hell: The Botched Investigation of a Serial Killer Who Almost Got Away*. Vancouver/ Berkeley: Greystone Books, 2015.

Sprinkle, Annie. "We've Come A Long Way—And We're Exhausted." *Whores and Other Feminists*. Jill Nagle, ed. New York/ London: Routledge, 1997.

Valencia, Sayak. *Gore Capitalism*. South Pasadena, CA: semiotext(e) intervention series 24, 2018.

Walter, Natasha. *Living Dolls: The Return of Sexism*. London: Virago, 2010.

Wark, McKenzie. *Reverse Cowgirl*. South Pasadena, CA: semiotext(e), 2020.

Weare, Siobhan "Oh you're a guy, how could you be raped by a woman, that makes no sense." Cambridge University Press: International Journal of Law in Context, 2017.

Whisnant, Rebecca and Christine Stark, eds. *Not for Sale: Feminists Resisting Prostitution and Pornography*. Melbourne, Australia: Spinifex, 2010.

Wiseman, Adele. *Crackpot*. First published: 1974. Toronto: McClelland and Stewart, 2008.

ABOUT THE AUTHOR

Karen Moe is a writer, art critic, visual and performance artist and a feminist activist. She has a degree in English Literature and Feminist Theory. Her work focuses on gender, systemic violence, justice and the unacknowledged. Karen has exhibited and performed across Canada, in the US and in Mexico. Her photography has been shown at Toronto's Contact Photography Festival and Nuit Blanche, Vancouver's Capture Photography Festival and Mexico City's Zona Maco. Her performance and photograhy project *Lethe: a mock metaphysics* has been performed and exhibited in New York, Toronto, Mexico City, Vancouver and Victoria BC. Her photography has also been featured in art magazines, literary journals and in books of poetry in collaboration with poets Catherine Owen and Joe Rosenblatt.

Karen's critical writing has been published in magazines and anthologies in Canada, the US, Mexico and Cuba. She is a reporter for International Art Fairs like Zona Maco, the Material Art Fair and Salon ACME. She is the editor and founder of the magazine *Vigilance: Fierce Feminisms* and Vigilance Press, venues that connect art, literature, journalism and activism internationally.

Recently, Karen has been researching and writing about the femincide epidemic and the exploitation of boys and teenagers who are recruited by drug cartels in Mexico. In Canada, she has been writing about the eco-emergency and the logging of some of the last remaining old-growth forests in the world. Karen lives in British Columbia, Canada and in Mexico City.

www.karenmoeauthor.com
@karenmoeart

Me and my Dad. Mt Cokely. Early 2000s.

9 781647 044701